A FIELD GUIDE TO
BUTTERFLIES
OF TEXAS

Texas Monthly Field Guides:

Birds of the Big Bend
Fossils of Texas
Reptiles and Amphibians of Texas
Shells of the Texas Coast
Stone Artifacts of Texas Indians
Texas Trees
Texas Snakes
Wildflowers, Trees, and Shrubs of Texas

TexasMonthly

FIELDGUIDE
SERIES

A FIELD GUIDE TO
BUTTERFLIES
OF TEXAS

RAYMOND W. NECK
PHOTOGRAPHY BY GEYATA AJILVSGI AND OTHERS

Gulf Publishing Company
Houston, Texas

Gulf Publishing Company
Book Division
P.O. Box 2608 ☐ Houston Texas 77252-2608

10   9   8   7   6   5   4   3   2   1

Printed in the United States of America

Color section printed in Hong Kong

Photographs by Geyata Ajilvsgi, Hoe H. Chuah, Paul Opler, Harry N. Darrow, and Doug Danforth

Illustrations by Mary Eleanor Neck

Printed on Acid-Free Paper (∞).

Library of Congress Cataloging-in-Publication Data

Neck, Raymond W.
    A field guide to butterflies of Texas / Raymond W. Neck ;
photographs by Geyata Ajilvsgi and others.
        p.   cm. – (Texas Monthly field guide series)
    Includes bibliographical references (p.   ) and index.
    ISBN 0-87719-243-X (pbk. : alk. paper).
    1. Butterflies–Texas–Identification.   I. Title.   II. Series.
QL551.T4N435   1996
595.78'9'09764–dc20   95-33013
                                                        CIP

This book is dedicated to
Roy O. Kendall,
the dean of Texas lepidopterology,
who has shared the fascination of butterflies with so many of us.

Acknowledgments

Long before I began to actually write this book and during the writing, many people gave me support and information crucial to this project. They were William H. Calvert, Christopher J. Durden, H. Avery Freeman, the late Perry A. Glick, Kurt Johnson, and Roy O. Kendall. Virtually every lepidopterist interested in Texas butterflies contributed to my knowledge of Texas butterfly fauna. I wish to thank them all, without whom this book would not have been possible.

Thank you to the following people for their review of the manuscript: Geyata Ajilvsgi, Hoe H. Chuah, H. Avery Freeman, and Roy O. Kendall.

The slides were provided by Geyata Ajilvsgi, Hoe H. Chuah, Paul Opler, Harry N. Darrow, and Doug Danforth.

Geyata Ajilvsgi went beyond the original limits of her involvement to get this book to publication. My wife, Pinke, gave her support, persistence, and the drawings. I thank them both.

PHOTO CREDITS

All photographs by **Geyata Ajilvsgi,** unless otherwise credited below.

Harry N. Darrow
Photos in Adults section:
20, 24, 26, 37, 40, 44, 48, 57, 89, 108, 117, 120, 126, 127, 140, 145, 161, 162, 163, 170, 178, 193, 197, 204, 206, 209, 215, 217, 222, 227, 230, 233, 341, 396

Hoe H. Chuah
Photos in Adults section:
56, 61, 62, 119, 130, 151, 176, 191, 332, 363, 380, 388, 389, 398, 416, 419

Doug Danforth
Photos in Adults section:
27, 169, 173, 216

Paul A. Opler
Photos in Adults section:
31, 55, 65, 67, 69, 98, 128, 129, 149, 154, 179, 195, 207, 218, 225, 229, 231, 244, 254, 272, 274, 316, 317, 361, 370, 444

CONTENTS

PREFACE

Many people who love various kinds of mammals and birds have a deep distrust or even disgust of the insect world. Children in our society are taught that insects are "yucky" and not to be handled, and most insects should be killed without questioning why. If an opinion poll were conducted to determine which insect group was most liked by the average person, the certain winner would be butterflies. Butterflies do not sting or bite. They do not eat our food, our clothes, or our homes. They are aesthetically pleasing to most people. Almost everyone has seen a butterfly in their yard, and it is an animal form that they can "relate to" in a positive manner. Of all the insects, and indeed, of all of the vast world of invertebrates, butterflies have the best "press"— they are as "warm and furry" as any invertebrate can be in the mind of the average citizen.

Many children collect butterflies, and not all of them stop collecting when they reach adulthood. Many of the collectors are not entomologists—many are not even formally trained biologists. They simply find butterflies an intriguing group of animals and devote many hours to a most wonderful and satisfying hobby. Many of these avocational (a word without the unfortunate connotation of the word "amateur") butterfly collectors provide invaluable data to the vocational (often called "professional") butterfly scientists. People who study butterflies are known as lepidopterists or "those weird people with butterfly nets." Many avocational butterfly collectors have made their own scientific contributions to the science of lepidopterology. Vladimir Nabokov, most famous for writing *Lolita*, was an avocational lepidopterist who produced numerous publications in the scientific literature.

A discussion of the butterflies of Texas is necessarily a discussion of the butterflies of central North America. This statement is not just another Texas brag. Rather, this statement is a reflection of the fact that the majority of the butterflies known from North America are also known from Texas. Part of the reason for the large number of butterflies present in Texas is the sheer size of the state. However, the geographic position of Texas near the boundary zone between the tropical and temperate zones is the most important reason. Equally significant is the location of Texas across the middle of North America where the moist forests of the southeastern United States give way to the prairies of the central United States and eventually to the deserts of the southwestern United States.

Vastly differing habitats occur in these various areas of Texas and support their own communities of plant and animal life, including butterflies. Elevations varying from sea level along the Gulf Coast to over 9,000 feet above sea level in the Guadalupe Mountains of far western Texas also increase the number of habitats and, consequently, the number of species of butterflies present within the political boundaries of Texas. Widely varying geological substrates also contribute to the ecological diversity of the state. The substrates vary from hard igneous and metamorphic rocks to limestones, chalks, and sandstones and further to soft clays and loose sands. An incredible diversity of soil types have developed on these substrates, favoring different plants that are available for the suitable butterfly species to use as a food plant for its caterpillar.

A relatively small portion of my life was spent actually writing this book, yet my whole life went into it. I collected insects as a child, as did many children— but I never stopped. Particularly when I realized that people could make a living "playing with bugs," I was hooked on the idea. I wish to thank all those involved in my early life for not discouraging what was undoubtedly a strange hobby for a child in the Rio Grande Valley in the 1950s and 1960s (this was before the real '60s when anything "went"). My parents, Raymond and Joyce Neck, always encouraged me to learn whatever interested me at the time and allowed innumerable kinds of animals in their house. During my school years in South Texas, the entomologists at the USDA lab were always willing to share their knowledge and experiences. Of particular help were M. J. "Luke" Lukefahr and the late Perry Glick. My major professor in graduate school at the University of Texas at Austin, Dr. Guy L. Bush, will always be an outstanding example of what a major professor should be to a graduate student. The interest of my wife, Pinke, and my children, Kristine and Patrick, in the study of butterflies and caterpillars continues to encourage me.

When I wrote this book, I envisioned an accurate guide that would open the fascinating world of butterflies to a larger audience. I hope this goal has been met.

How To Use This Field Guide

The systematic arrangement of this book is based on *A Catalogue/Checklist of the Butterflies of America North of Mexico* by Miller and Brown and subsequent supplement by Ferris published by the Lepidopterists' Society. A major exception to systemic arrangement is the placement of the skippers (Hesperioidea) following the true butterflies (Papillionoidea), which is a common practice in modern field guides. A few updated generic placements have been adopted. The decision to place the Apaturidae in family Nymphalidae as subfamilies Charaxinae and Apaturinae is based on research by Tim Friedlander. Differences in the Hesperiidae classification from the previously cited references are based on information provided by H. Avery Freeman. Common names used in this book generally follow those names in *The Common Names of North American Butterflies* by Miller. A few species not covered in this publication have new common names created by the author of this book. Plant names are according to the *Checklist of the Vascular Plants of Texas* by Hatch, Gandi, and Brown. Additional major botanical references are the *Manual of the Vascular Plants of Texas* by Correll and Johnston and the *Manual of Cultivated Plants* by Bailey.

Other books on butterflies have used slightly or even quite different arrangements of families and subfamilies. Such variety of opinion is both the bane and salvation of systematic biology. No such system is absolutely correct, and each only approximates the true evolutionary history of the butterflies. Don't worry very much about whether the longwings are a separate family or a subfamily of the Nymphalids. Your ability to identify and study longwings is not affected by differences in systematic opinion.

Each species account is numbered in this book. The **boldface** number indicates the species is pictured in the color section. The letters following the number indicate the following:

E—pictured with eggs
L—pictured with larvae
C—pictured with chrysalids
A—pictured with adults

The accounts are divided into five topics: **Descriptions, Food Plants, Range, Life History,** and **Comments.**

The **Description** begins with an average size of the wing span of a spread specimen given in American measure (metric measure in parentheses). This spread specimen measure can be obtained from a pinned specimen in a collection or estimated from a specimen that is at rest with the wings held out flat. These measurements are only an estimate of an average size because individual specimens may be larger or smaller depending upon the quality and quantity of food available during the larval stage. In my opinion, a butterfly less than ⅝ in (16 mm) is classified as tiny, up to 1½ in (38 mm) is small, up to 2½ in (64 mm) is medium, and above that measurement is large.

The description continues with comments on the species' similarity to other species as well as the distinctive features of the body, antennae, or wing shape, if such features are significant for identification. The wing surfaces (Figure 1) are described from the upper surface (referred to as "above") to the lower surface (referred to as "below"). Within the above and below descriptions, the following abbreviations are used:

AFW—above forewing
AHW—above hindwing
BFW—below forewing
BHW—below hindwing

Comments on variation within a species may also be provided. Most commonly these differences involve sexual dimorphism, such as differences in size, shape, or color pattern of the wings of the particular species. Some species have major seasonal variations in these same characters.

Food Plants lists the larval food plants. The family name is given first, followed by the specific plant species or genera of the food plants used in Texas. If more than one family is used, the species or genera belonging to each individual family follow that family. Some descriptions also list the food plants used outside of Texas.

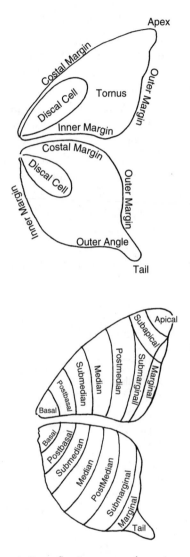

Figure 1—Butterfly wing areas and margins.

Life History provides several pieces of information. The number of generations is designated as univolite (one generation per year), bivoltine (two generations per year), or multivoltine (more than two generations per year) followed by the typical months in which they occur in parentheses. For some of the larger, more common, or more noticeable species, a description of the egg, larva, or pupa may be given. For a limited, but still disconcertingly high, number of species, the life history section is marked "unknown," because no published information is available. For many of these species, reference to related species provides a clue as to which plants or plant groups are likely to be used. However, we have very little biological information about many of the species that stray rarely into the Valley from Mexico. Although several very thorough workers have provided much information about butterfly life history in these areas, much information is not available for many of these species. Study of these species by some of you reading this book would make a very worthwhile and permanent addition to the knowledge of Texas butterflies.

Range divides the normal geographical area occupied by a particular species into two parts. The first part is the range of the entire species.

Figure 2—Geographical areas of Texas.

This area may include several states or even countries. The second part is the range of the species within the borders of Texas. These areas are given in sections of the state, illustrated by Figure 2. These areas are East, North Central, Central, Coastal Margin, South, Rio Grande Valley, Southwest, Panhandle, High Plains, Trans-Pecos, Big Bend, and Far West. An attempt is made in the descriptions of some species to provide both the normal permanent resident range as well as temporary late season ranges (usually farther north or west than the residential range). A general range map accompanies the description of each individual species for quick location of that species. The solid colored area indicates an established breeding population and a patterned area indicates a migratory, impermanent or reduced population.

The **Comments** section includes other pertinent and interesting information on these species. Often in the case of rare species, not much is known about their life history, but, if known, the months of observation will be given following the word "Recorded." This section also contains the name or names of the subspecies found in Texas. When the subspecies' common name differs from the species' common name, the subspecies' common name will be in parentheses following the subspecies' scientific name. When two or three subspecies are given for a single species, information on the visual and geographical differences between the subspecies is provided. For the few species with many more alleged subspecies, only geographical range is given. The differences in appearance of these subspecies may be very subtle, too involved to list here, or repetitive of the geographical separation provided.

In order to conserve space, the species accounts are written in a form that contains a minimum of verbs and prepositions. The style may be somewhat foreign during the initial reading of this book. However, we believe that the information provided will become clear with a little practice.

A FIELD GUIDE TO
BUTTERFLIES
OF TEXAS

THE BIOLOGY OF BUTTERFLIES

This section presents an overview of the biology of butterflies. More detailed accounts have been published, some of which are listed in the bibliography near the end of this book. The purpose of this section is to introduce the reader to the wonderful world of living butterflies. It is the author's hope that you will then invite butterflies into your world.

What Is a Butterfly?

Butterflies are insects classified in the phylum Arthropoda. This enormous phylum includes all the jointed-leg invertebrates and is the largest in both numbers of species and individuals of all of the animal and plant groups that inhabit the planet Earth.

Butterflies have the same body characteristics as all other insects (Figure 3). The body is divided into three major sections: head, thorax, and abdomen. The head contains the eyes (both simple and compound), antennae, mouthparts, and a simple brain. The simple eyes, known as ocelli, are three single-faceted sensory organs that are located on the top of the head. The antennae are paired, long, multi-segmented organs that detect chemicals in the general environment (somewhat analogous to smell in humans). The mouthparts include several paired organs that function to obtain the food necessary for life to continue. Even the long, coiled, hollow proboscis of adult butterflies is a paired organ. Immediately upon emergence, the two halves of the proboscis are carefully fitted together via a natural tongue-and-groove mechanism that evolved in butterflies millions of years before humans "discovered" this technique of tightly binding two objects together.

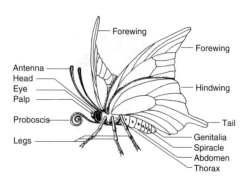

Figure 3. Body of the adult butterfly.

Butterflies and moths are a group of insects called Lepidoptera. The word "lepidoptera" is not as threatening as it might appear at first look. Taken from two Greek words that mean "scale" and "wing," the word lepidoptera simply means "scale-wing" and refers to the minute, shingle-like scales (Figure 4) that give color and pattern to the wings of butterflies and moths. These scales are attached by a narrow process on one end of the scale that attaches to a very small socket on the surface of the wing. The color of the scale may be either pigmental or structural in nature. Pigmental color is produced by the differential reflection of light from a chemical called a pigment. For example, a red pigment reflects red wavelengths of light preferentially and absorbs much of the light of all other wavelengths. No matter how complex the color pattern of the wings of a butterfly, any individual scale produces the effect of only a single color. Structural colors are produced by minute ridges and grooves on the individual scale that produce a diffraction pattern or trap all light except for the color that "escapes" and is viewed by our eyes. Beyond producing color, some scales are involved in the production of pheromones (sex attractant chemical scents).

The wildly colorful patterns of wings of butterflies did not evolve to please human eyes. These patterns existed long before there were human eyes to observe and appreciate them. Color patterns in butterflies function to attract suitable mates, provide camouflage to prevent detection by predators, or as flash coloration to confuse predators if they are detected. Butterfly fossils are known from Cretaceous

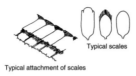

Typical scales

Typical attachment of scales

Figure 4. Scales

deposits, a time when the dinosaurs were the largest land animals (although insects were undoubtedly the most numerous life form, as they are today). The colorful patterns may have evolved subsequent to the Cretaceous period as color-visioned birds, a significant predator group for butterflies, evolved and diversified. The patterns that humans see in "visible" light may not be the most significant portion of the color pattern of butterflies. Some butterflies have light reflecting patterns in the ultraviolet spectrum that are remarkably different from the pattern that we view. These ultraviolet patterns function to signal potential mates and may help to deter predation. When two different species are similar in pattern and coloration, this is referred to as mimicry, which can be divided into two types: Müllerian or Batesian. In Müllerian mimicry, two distasteful species resemble each other to derive greater protection from predators. Batesian mimicry refers to a palatable species possessing the coloration and pattern of a distasteful species to deter predators.

In common with other insects, butterflies possess an exoskeleton, that is, the support of the internal organs and muscles comes from the outer skin of the animal as opposed to the internal skeleton of bones that occurs in humans and most other vertebrates. The skin, or integument, of insects not only protects the animal from the external environment and retains valuable fluids, it also provides the skeletal system. The various segments of an insect body are linked together by tight fitting joints or expandable membranes.

In insects, the transport of oxygen to the individual cells is not a function of the blood as it is for humans and other vertebrates. In insects, the tracheal or breathing system consists of a set of tubes, ever-decreasing in diameter, that extend from the surface of the insect to individual cells throughout the body. The slight increase and decrease in the size of the abdomen of insects (especially visible in the larger ones such as grasshoppers) is actually the breathing effort of these animals. These abdominal movements help to pump air through the tracheal system. Openings in the body wall known as spiracles (Figure 3) can be seen along the abdomen of large insects without scales. Valves may close the spiracles when moisture conservation is more important than maintenance of high oxygen levels in the body. When oxygen levels inside the body of an insect are low, insects can become temporarily inactive. Oxygen consumption of insects is much lower than the consumption of oxygen by warm-blooded animals such as birds and mammals. In very small animals, direct transport of oxygen to the cells is more efficient than the use of a blood system to carry oxygen. However, this advantage in efficiency is rapidly lost as body size increases. This loss in efficiency is a major restriction on the possibility of increasing the body size of insects. Therefore, there are no insects as large as humans or automobiles, despite what you may have seen in your favorite horror movie.

Butterflies and Moths

In the previous section I have already mentioned that moths are also members of the order Lepidoptera. Many of you may ask, "What is the difference between a moth and a butterfly?" That is a good question that deserves a good answer. However, the answer is somewhat involved. There are several differences between moths and butterflies, but, unfortunately, not one of them is totally reliable in differentiating between them. The absolute difference between moths and butterflies involves details of the pattern of the veins in the wings and other complex structures in the body of these insects.

There are a number of simple differences between most butterflies and most moths that will serve to answer the question at hand (Figure 5). Generally, most butterflies fly during the day, and many will not fly unless the sun is shining. Most moths fly at night, but there are a number of moths that fly during the day. A few of the day-flying moths are incredibly colored in a pattern of iridescent hues that rival the patterns of the most brilliantly colored butterfly. Butterflies may be considered to have narrow bodies in relation to their length, whereas many moths have rather thick bodies. Perhaps the best differentation involves the antennae. Butterfly antennae are slender with a gradually enlarging knob at the end; whereas, many

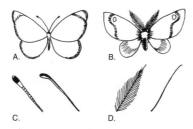

A. Typical butterfly with narrow body and clubbed antennae.
B. Typical moth with broad body and pointed feathered antennae.
C. Types of butterfly antennae.
D. Types of moth antennae.

Figure 5. Differences between butterflies and moths.

moths have a feather-type antenna (particularly males who detect chemicals released by the female). Moths that do have a thread-like antenna do not have a club on the tip; the thread becomes progressively smaller at the free end. Many moths spin a silken cover over the pupa, which is known as a cocoon. No butterfly has a true cocoon, although the amount of silk spun by the caterpillar or larva prior to formation of the pupa varies considerably.

How Many Butterflies Are There?

One of the commonly asked questions about butterflies involves the number of species of butterflies in the world. Unfortunately, there is no exact number available, because no one person keeps a complete list of all the species of butterflies. Such a feat would be monumental, because various workers may disagree on how many species occur in even a single genus or portion of a genus. Some workers, the "splitters," tend to separate all variations into separate species. Other workers, the "lumpers," tend to recognize more variation within a species and, therefore, recognize fewer species.

At least one reasonable, scientifically based estimate provides a total of between 15,000 and 17,000 species of butterflies in the world. Of these 17,000 or fewer species, about 763 are known from North America north of Mexico. The current list of butterflies known from Texas and used in this book contains 446 species. During the time between writing this book and publication, butterfly species could be added or deleted from this list.

You should not engrave the numbers provided in the previous paragraph in any kind of permanent stone, because the number is constantly changing. Species previously unknown to scientists are described continually. Some species will go extinct. Some scientists will split a single species into two or three or even more separate species. Elsewhere another scientist may combine two or more species into a single species. The splitters and lumpers never cease in their tireless efforts to correct each others "mistakes."

The number of species known from Texas will undoubtedly increase as more field collecting occurs in certain areas. Additional species are continually recorded from the Lower Rio Grande Valley as tropical species disperse northward when climatic conditions are favorable. The Guadalupe Mountains contain habitats at high elevations that occur nowhere else in Texas. Those willing to hike to these far flung areas (and possessing proper permits from the National Park Service!) will be rewarded with memorable views and experiences and possibly even a species not previously reported from Texas. Additional species also undoubtedly occur in the Davis Mountains. Many of the species in this area will have a single, time-restricted flight period during the year. The Panhandle, Far West, northern section of East, and eastern corner of the Coastal Margin will undoubtedly reveal additional species simply because their location places them closer to areas from which individuals may periodically disperse. The subtropical climate and vegetation as well as the location of the Rio Grande Valley has produced many records of species not known anywhere else in the United States.

Names of Butterflies

Many readers of this book may be unfamiliar with scientific names—those ominous-looking Latin names in italics with a seemingly endless supply of syllables. If you are not familiar with these names, do not be concerned. Common names are now available for essentially all of the butterflies of North America, although the names are not as widely recognized as are the scientific names. Besides, even readers without much experience with the italicized version of scientific names have some experience with Latin words. Commonly used words for many plants and animals are really scientific names that have become known and are used by the general public. Such names include rhododendron, hippopotamus, rhinoceros, chrysanthemum, and even the simple sounding vanilla and gorilla.

Knowing the origin of some of the Latin names of various butterflies may remove some of the trepidation felt when encountering these names. These names may be in honor of someone, for example, *edwardsi* (named for William Henry Edwards, a 19th-century lepidopterist), and *freemani* or *kendalli* (named after H. Avery Freeman or Roy O. Kendall, two of the most prominent of the twentieth-century Texas lepidopterists). Some species, such as *Thessalia chinatiensis,* are named after the location from which they were first collected: the Chinati Mountains of Presidio County in western Texas.

Scientific names are accepted all over the world. Very detailed rules, not unlike those in a law book, dictate the use and changes of scientific names. Common names may be easier to use by some people, but their application is not standardized. The butterfly known as the Mourning Cloak in North America is known as the Camberwell Beauty in Europe. However, in both continents and around the world, this same species is known as *Nymphalis antiopa.* Anyone familiar with butterflies knows exactly what species is being discussed. In other instances, the same common name may be used for different species in different localities.

Each scientific name in this book has at least two words. The first word is capitalized and is the name of the genus of which the individual species is a member. The name of the genus is analogous to the human surname in European cultures. The second word in a scientific name is the species name and is not capitalized. No two members of a genus can have the same species name. Occasionally, a species is divided into subspecies and, in that case, the individual would have three words in the scientific name. Scientific names (*Genus species subspecies*) are italicized or underlined if the option of using italics is not available. If you are unfamiliar with scientific classification, it may help to visualize classification as a pyramid. At the very bottom are all the individual species of butterflies. Closely related species are in a group called a genus (genera, pl.). Further up, the genera can be grouped into tribes and then the tribes into sub-families. Finally, all of these groups are called a family. The complete classification of *Chlosyne lacinia* (Bordered Patch) would look like this:

Chlosyne lacinia
Bordered Patch

Kingdom	Animalia
Phylum	Arthropoda
Class	Insecta
Order	Lepidoptera
Superfamily	Papilionoidea
Family	Nymphalidae
Subfamily	Melitaeinae
Genus	*Chlosyne*
Species	*lacinia*
Subspecies	*adjutrix*
Common name	Bordered Patch

The lack of a list of long-accepted common names for butterflies is a result of the traditional use of scientific names by all who study butterflies, both vocational and avocational workers. Whereas bird watchers typically use only common names in their listing efforts, essentially all people who have studied butterflies in the past have used the scientific names. The wide use of these names should allay fears of the difficulty of learning these names. However, the use of common names in this book will allow even the most Latin-phobic person to learn to identify butterflies and converse with others about the particular species that they have observed.

Life Cycle of the Butterfly

Butterflies have a life cycle that is typical of those insects with a complete metamorphosis, because there are four major stages in the life cycle of an individual (Figure 6). These four stages are the egg (or ova), caterpillar (or larva), pupa (or chrysalis), and adult (or imago). Other insect groups that undergo a complete metamorphosis similar to butterflies include moths, bees, wasps, ants, flies, fleas, and caddisflies. These four stages can be contrasted with a three-stage life cycle called simple metamorphosis. The three stages are the egg, nymph (or naiad), and adult. Occasionally, simple metamorphosis has also been

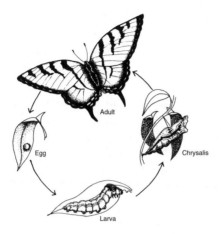

Figure 6. Life cycle of the butterfly.

called incomplete metamorphosis, which is an inappropriate term because any metamorphosis that results in a reproductive adult is obviously not incomplete! Insect groups with a simple metamorphosis include dragonflies, true bugs, aphids, cicadas, grasshoppers, and roaches.

Any individual butterfly begins its life cycle as an egg. The basic shape of butterfly eggs is spherical but may be slightly compressed into the shape of a lozenge or a bun. Further compression produces an egg that is the shape of a disc. Alternatively, the egg may be narrowed into a cylinder (either barrel- or spindle-shaped). The surface of the egg may be smooth or ornately covered with ribs or small processes. Eggs of some species become covered with scales from the abdomen of the female during the act of egg laying. The outer layer of the egg is called the chorion, a continuous covering that has a single opening called the micropyle through which the sperm enters the egg in the female reproductive tract.

Usually, the egg is laid (oviposited) by the female on a plant that is suitable for proper development of the larva (although occasional mistakes do occur). Eggs may be laid singly, in small clutches of three to five, or huge masses containing up to 500 eggs. Following laying (oviposition), the egg remains attached to the leaf or twig surface by a glue substance. However, some gossamer wing and skipper females drop their eggs at the base of grass plants (Poaceae).

Following fertilization and the laying of the egg, a tiny embryo grows and develops into a very small larva. The yolk and embryo of the newly laid egg of a butterfly resembles the yolk and embryo of a fertilized chicken egg, although the relative amount of yolk and embryo is quite different. As time passes, the embryo grows as cells grow and divide; later, tissues are detectable. Eventually, the tissues form organs and organ systems that are arranged to form a very small larva. During this period, the egg begins to darken and the form of the larva may be visible through the shell of the egg.

Hatching occurs when the larva is fully formed. The time between oviposition and hatching can be as short as several days or as long as a year. Exiting through the egg membrane and shell may be accomplished by physical pressure from inside the shell by movements of the larva. Such movements are accompanied by an increase in size of the larva by breathing in additional amounts of air following partial exiting from the egg. Some larvae will eat the remains of their egg shell in an attempt to obtain vital nutrients and minerals from the shell.

The larva can best be described as an eating machine. The function of this stage is to convert plant (or animal) tissue into butterfly tissue. Abdominal fatty deposits developed during this stage will be used by the adult butterfly for nutrition. Larvae may be solitary feeders from the day of their hatching if the eggs of their species are laid singly. In species that lay eggs in clusters or masses, the younger larvae usually feed together in gregarious groups. Eventually the larvae of gregarious feeders begin to disperse, and the final instars (the stage between molts) are usually spent as solitary feeders. The larva will feed on leaf, flower, or fruit material of the proper food plant in order to survive. An exception to this is the Harvester (*Feniseca tarquinius*), which occurs over much of eastern North America including the eastern half of Texas. The larva of this species feeds on aphids rather than plant matter.

The body of a newly hatched larva is dominated by the head (Figure 7). Particularly large are the jaws (mandibles) that tear the plant material and assist in transporting this material to the mouth of the larva. The larva also has very short antennae that are discernible only under high magnification. The only eyes present are several small ocelli, or simple eyes, that are present on the side of the head. The head also contains the silk glands. Silk is used to form walking mats

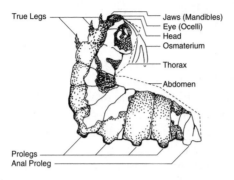

Figure 7. Body of the larva (caterpillar).

for the young larva, shedding mats used to assist in shedding of the skin, the button used for attachment of the pupa, and for entangling small parasitoid wasps.

Behind the head, the body of the larva is divided into thirteen segments (three in the thorax followed by ten in the abdomen). Attached to the thorax, the larva has three pairs of jointed (or true) legs, each having six segments. The true legs assist in manipulation of the food material more than they are used in locomotion. Also present are five pairs of prolegs on the abdomen. These prolegs are extensions of the body wall that have a circular set of crochets or hooks, a type of "sucker foot." The skin of the larva may be smooth or covered with hairs, spines, or a few fleshy projections. Some of these fleshy projections may be sufficiently long to resemble tentacles, such as the larvae of the Queen (*Danaus gilippus*).

The larval stage of butterflies (indeed all insects, spiders, crustaceans, centipedes, millipedes, and many other species classed as arthropods) must periodically shed their skin, a process called ecdysis, in order to increase in size. This is necessary as the larval skin does not stretch or grow. As the larva grows and approaches the maximum volume allowed by its current exoskeleton, a new exoskeleton is being formed underneath the old one. Some of the critical minerals and organic chemicals are removed from the old exoskeleton and used in the formation of the new one. Upon completion of a new exoskeleton, the larva breathes in extra air and splits the old skin, usually down the middle of the dorsal (upper) surface of its body.

Then the larva literally crawls out of its old skin. The act of shedding an old exoskeleton is called a molt.

The stage of the larva between any two molts is called an instar. The newly emerged larva is in the first instar. Following its first molt, it becomes a second instar caterpillar. Different species of insects, and even different species of butterflies, may have a different number of instars, but the number of instars is generally constant for a given species. The most common number of instars for butterfly larvae is five.

Although the most significant difference between successive instars is an increase in size, other features, particularly in general color pattern of the body, may change drastically. These changes are for defense from predation. Many first and second instar larvae are green so they blend with the coloration of their food plant. Very young larvae may also be a mottled, glistening gray and white to mimic bird dung so that the larva appears to be an inedible object. Larger larvae are not able to fool potential predators into thinking that they are an extra large piece of dung. In many of these larvae, the later instars may retain their gray and white coloration, but the pattern is changed so that the larva has a blotched appearance and blends with the bark of the trunk and stems of its food plant. A good example of this type of change of pattern is exhibited by the larvae of the Giant Swallowtail (*Heraclides cresphontes*).

Other swallowtail larvae may be green in both early and later instars. However, as illustrated by the Tiger Swallowtail (*Pterourus glaucus*), the older larvae also have two large dark spots of pigment that resemble the eyes of vertebrates. When these larvae are threatened by a predator, they raise up their front end (the head is turned down) and appear to enlarge their body size. These eye spots then appear even more menacing, and the would-be predator may think twice about attacking this seemingly small-but-threatening potential food item. Together with eyespots, swallowtail larvae can suddenly evert a foul smelling "y" shaped organ (osmaterium) from the area between the head and thorax (Figure 7) to deter predators. Another larval defense is the development of spines on the body in later instars that would feel uncomfortable to a predator. Although several moth larvae have spines that contain chemicals that cause burning stings, no butterflies in Texas have larvae with stinging spines.

When the final instar larva has grown to its maximum size, it prepares to molt once again. However, the changes that are about to occur are even more dramatic than the previous changes. Initially, the larva finds a safe location that offers protection from inclement weather and potential predators. There it spins some form of silken mat or "button" (but not a cocoon covering itself), and often a silken thread or girdle that acts as a safety belt. When the silk button is finished, the caterpillar grasps it with its anal prolegs and either leans back against its "safety belt" or hangs upside down. Some larvae merely spin a silken sheet on a leaf or object of protective covering. When the larva sheds its skin this time, a quite different stage is revealed. The appearance of the chrysalis of a butterfly varies from smooth to highly irregular, oval-shaped to cylindrical, and green to brown or white. These variations are an attempt to blend in with the surrounding area to avoid predation during the pupal stage.

The chrysalis is a non-mobile stage, but reference to this stage as the resting stage belies the massive reorganization of both the internal and external organs that is occurring inside. This period of reorganization may take a week or may take months. Most of the time period in these longer term species is a waiting period for the correct environmental signals to indicate the proper time for emergence of the adult.

When emergence of the adult is imminent, the appearance of the color pattern of the wings and body may be seen through the skin of the chrysalis. The chrysalis breathes in air through the tracheal system to enlarge its size, thereby breaking the skin of the chrysalis. Very feebly at first, the new adult butterfly crawls to a site, such as the underside of leaves, that is large enough to allow it to expand its wings while it is still reasonably safe from predators.

When it emerges, the adult butterfly has very small wings and an oversized body. The wings are expanded by pumping fluids from the body through the network of veins which must occur before the wings dry. Excess fluid that is present in the body at the time of emergence is released during this period, allowing the abdomen to shrink to the normal size for the adult butterfly. The adult has developed a proboscis, a long coiled suctioning tube through which the adult feeds. The prolegs of the larval stage are gone, but the six true legs are present. Emergence usually occurs in the early morning when humidity is high, temperature is relatively low, and predators are not yet active.

Even with emergence occurring in the early morning, the first flight may not occur until the afternoon.

When the adult is fully expanded and dry, the first flight of its short adult life occurs. Different species are characterized by different flight patterns, which are the characteristic manner of flight of any individual species. Variables include speed, altitude, pattern and the ability to direct their flight. Some flit here and there so fast that one never gets a really good look at the animal, while others glide without much wing movement. Some fly high in the tree tops and others fly only inches above the ground. An entire superfamily, the Hesperioidea, derives its common name, the skippers, from its rapid, skipping flight pattern.

All adult butterflies must have some food and water to continue their life processes. Most butterflies go to flowers to obtain nutrition to supplement the fatty deposits in their abdomen, which were developed during the larval stage. Butterflies visit many types of flowers and various species have their own preferences as to size, nectar type, shape, and color of flower. At one time all flower nectar was thought to be essentially the same diluted sugar solution. However, later research has revealed that nectars differ in the concentration and type of sugars present, as well as the presence of amino acids or other sources of nitrogen. Another food source produced by flowers is the pollen. A few tropical butterflies are able to collect pollen on their proboscis and actually obtain protein from these small grains.

Besides flowers, some butterflies also visit fermenting sap flows, rotting fruit, carrion, dung, and wet soil. Both fermenting sap and rotting fruit contain bacteria and yeasts that provide a protein source for adult butterflies. Carrion and dung provide minerals and protein to the adult butterfly. Visits to moist soil, known as "mud-puddling," commonly occur in large concentrations of mostly male butterflies. The purpose of mud puddling is to obtain sodium and nitrogen; similar to the use of salt licks by mammals. The relative frequency of visits to flowers, sap, fruit, carrion, dung, and moist soil varies dramatically among the various species of butterflies.

Some species are sexually and/or seasonally dimorphic in size, color or pattern. However, most species exhibit only minor differences between males and females except for obvious differences in the reproductive organs (Figure 8). Usually the body of the female is slightly larger than that of the male, because the female must produce the eggs within her body. Males of many species, such as hairstreaks and grass skippers, possess specialized scales that produce pheromones (sex attractant chemical scents) as well as providing variation to the wing pattern. Such scales may be located as a stigma or an androconial patch on either wing or as a costal fold on the forewing.

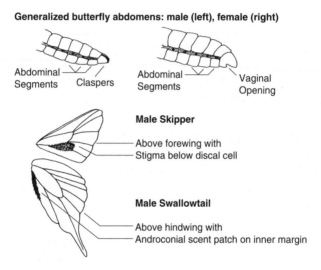

Generalized butterfly abdomens: male (left), female (right)

Abdominal Segments   Claspers

Abdominal Segments   Vaginal Opening

Male Skipper
Above forewing with Stigma below discal cell

Male Swallowtail
Above hindwing with Androconial scent patch on inner margin

Figure 8. Sexual differences in butterflies.

Females of some species, such as fritillaries and duskywings, have pheromone producing glands on the abdomen.

Courtship in butterflies often involves very complex patterns of behavior. Initial contact with an individual of the opposite sex of the correct species is usually accomplished by recognition of the wing pattern of the adult or detection of pheromones. Actual coupling occurs after both individuals are convinced they are courting an individual of the correct species. Mating may continue for several hours. If the pair is disturbed while they are mating, only one of the individuals will fly while the other hangs with closed wings. The sex of the flying partner differs between species but is consistent within most species.

Following the end of a successful mating, the female will search for the proper plant on which to lay the eggs she is carrying. While obtaining nectar at flowers, a mated female butterfly may be visited by additional males that wish to mate with her. Subsequent matings do occur, but often the female reacts by fluttering her wings in a characteristic signal that indicates to the male that she is not interested in mating. Just as the butterfly must consume plant material (as a larva) or various nutrient-filled liquids (as an adult), there are other species in the environment that attempt to feed on the various stages of the butterfly. Potential consumers of butterflies include parasites, parasitoids, and predators. Parasites include species that live inside the host (endoparasites, for example, microscopic pathogens) and species that live outside the host (ectoparasites, for example, blood-sucking mosquitoes and other flies). Normally, parasites may weaken their host but do not kill it. Although with suitable environmental conditions, many microscopic pathogens (bacteria or viruses) may cause extensive mortality in a population. One of these bacteria, *Bacillus thuringensis,* is currently being marketed as a "biologically friendly" pesticide of larvae that feed on various plants. This bacterium has no method of determining which species it is attacking, and will attack any larva, even those that you may be attempting to encourage in your butterfly garden. Parasitoids live inside their host and eventually kill that host, but not until the parasitoid is sufficiently mature. Most parasitoids of butterflies are various small wasps and flies whose larval stage lives inside the larva of the butterfly. Some very small wasp parasitoids complete their egg, larval, and pupal stages within the eggs of butterflies. Predators are larger animals that feed on a number of prey items during their life span. Major predators that consume the various stages of butterflies include birds, lizards, spiders, ambush bugs, mantids, wasps, and robber flies.

Selection of the Proper Food Plant

One of the most important pieces of information about a species of butterfly is the specific plant, or plants, that are eaten by the larva of that species because without the proper food plant, the species will die. Generally, related species of butterflies use related species of food plants. Plants have a diverse collection of chemicals in their cells. Many of these plant chemicals (phytochemicals) are essential to the primary, or everyday, function of these cells to keep the plant alive.

However, other phytochemicals appear to function mainly in the deterrence of animals that would eat the leaves of a plant. These chemicals (secondary phytochemicals) function to deter feeding by both invertebrates and vertebrates. Many of the distinct flavors of our commonly used vegetables are examples of these secondary phytochemicals. The cucurbitacins in the gourd family give cucumbers a distinctive taste and the mustard oil glycosides of the crucifer family provide a common flavor to cabbage, broccoli, cauliflower, kale, and brussel sprouts.

Although some secondary phytochemicals are actually toxic to animals that feed on the plant material, many insects, and butterflies in particular, have evolved a system of food plant location and consumption that uses these very same phytochemicals. A particular species of butterfly, such as the Cabbage Butterfly (*Pieris rapae*), has evolved chemical methods to deactivate these poisons. The same phytochemicals that are used by the adult to locate the proper food plant may even act as feeding stimulants that encourage the consumption of leaf material by the larva. An additional use of secondary phytochemicals involves defense against predation. The Black Swallowtail (*Papilio polyxenes*) uses secondary phytochemicals ingested during the larval stage to protect the adult by giving the adult a bitter taste.

These phytochemicals can be detected by the female butterfly as she flies. If she detects some of the proper chemical wafting in the air, the flight pattern will change so that she flies up the trail of increasing concentration of the phytochemical. She may land on several plants or several leaves of the same plant. In addition to detecting the phytochemical in the air, the butterfly may actually prick the leaves with very small spines that are located on the forelegs of many butterflies. If the proper phytochemical is detected, then egg laying may occur unless the female is disturbed by a predator or wind. During the act of oviposition, she is particularly vulnerable to predation.

Human Impact and Butterfly Conservation

The impact of modern civilization upon populations of butterflies has been varied and often negative. However, a number of butterfly species that use weedy plants as their larval food plants are undoubtedly more common today in Texas than they were 150 years ago. Disturbed habitats, whether due to road or building construction, vegetation clearing, or reservoir construction, are much more common now than they were during the last century. Prior to widespread human disturbance of the environment, disturbed habitats were found mainly along streams that flooded, animal trails, fire scars, and similar areas. Habitat disturbance by populations of aboriginal humans was somewhat limited due to smaller populations and lower technological levels. One particular species of butterfly, the Bordered Patch (*Chlosyne lacinia*), was restricted to such limited areas of disturbed habitat where *Helianthus* (sunflowers and related species) would grow. As more and more habitat disturbance occurred, these weedy sunflowers became more abundant, allowing the development of larger populations of insects that fed on these plants, including the Bordered Patch.

Impact on other butterflies has been complex. The native Checkered White (*Pontia protodice*) has experienced severe population declines in the eastern United States following the introduction of the Mustard White (*Pieris rapae*) from Europe. In addition to feeding on cabbage and other cultivated crucifers, the Mustard White uses the native food plants of the Checkered White and "out-competes" the native species. In the central and western United States, the introduced Mustard White is found on cultivated Brassicaceae, especially cabbage, but it is not as successful on the native, weedy crucifers. Therefore, in these areas, the Checkered White is actually now more abundant than formerly, because the native, weedy crucifers that it uses as food plants are more abundant due to the widespread habitat disturbance by man.

Many people ask, "Why aren't there as many butterflies as there used to be?" Well, the world is not the same world of 40 or 50 or, in some instances, only 20 years ago. More people live in large urban concentrations. Residential areas increasingly cover land that was formerly in natural or semi-natural stands of vegetation.

When a tract of land is developed for a housing development, much or most (sometimes all) of the native vegetation is removed. When the houses are built, streets and driveways cover even more of the land. Homeowners landscape the yard that is left between adjacent houses with a very restricted selection of plants. Usually the plants are chosen because they are aesthetically pleasing, are fast growing, need little care, and are not eaten by insects (including caterpillars!). Many yards are covered by non-native plants containing phytochemicals that the local insects have not evolved defenses against because they have had no evolutionary history during which time they could adapt to these plants. Consequently, these yards have very few butterflies.

Even those butterfly species that can feed on these non-native plants or on some selected few native plants that are allowed or encouraged to grow have other obstacles in the typical urban area. What does the average resident do when he or she finds an insect feeding on a prized plant? He or she reaches for a can or a bag of poison (or a big boot!). A yard maintenance firm may come to their yard and spray everything in sight with chemicals to stimulate the growth of plants and cause the death of anything that would have the audacity to feed upon the prized plants. And then, people wonder why there aren't as many butterflies as there used to be!

Beyond these chemicals, another powerful force in reducing the number of butterflies and other insects in urban Texas is another group of insects: fire ants. These voracious predators consume protein when and where they find it. Caterpillars are wonderful packets of food that are rich in protein. Millions of caterpillars and even some adult butterflies fall prey to fire ants every year.

Do not be discouraged because there aren't as many butterflies as there used to be. There is hope! Read on to the short discussion of butterfly gardening to discover what you can do to encourage butterflies in your yard, your neighborhood, and your community—indeed the world!

Butterfly Gardening

Butterfly gardening in North America is a relatively recent phenomenon as far as the general public is concerned. However, a few of us long-time butterfly watchers have been gardening for butterflies for many years. Butterfly gardening includes several techniques that anyone can use to increase the number of species and individuals of butterflies in any yard.

Many people begin butterfly gardening by planting flowers of different shapes, sizes, and colors to attract different kinds of butterflies.

This activity may increase the time spent by various individual butterflies in your yard/garden, but it does not increase the number of individual butterflies in your neighborhood. In addition to flowers for nectar, butterflies must have the proper food plant for the larval stage. A butterfly will not fly long distances merely for nectar. Therefore, a successful butterfly garden must provide nectar sources and food plants for the larval stage.

The typical gardener wants a deep green plant with bright flowers and no holes in the leaves. In order to properly garden for butterflies, the gardener must allow some of the plant material to be eaten by the larvae. There is almost always more plant material than there are larvae. Instead of regarding the larvae as the enemy, think of them as future butterflies. Many larvae are quite attractively colored or uniquely decorated with hair or spikes.

Several books are available that cover the subject of butterfly gardening in greater detail. In particular, *Butterfly Gardening for The South* by Geyata Ajilvsgi is an excellent resource for Texas butterfly gardeners.

Zoogeography of Texas Butterflies

Zoogeography is the study of the geographical distribution of animal species. Texas butterflies can be grouped into various geographical areas of occurrence of particular species. Butterflies, however, will complicate any such analysis because of their tendency to wander. Stray individuals may be found hundreds or even thousands of miles from their usual or "normal" range. Despite this minor complication, Texas butterflies can be discussed in relation to their geographical distribution with very definite patterns of occurrence because the establishment of range depends on proof of a breeding population.

The eastern portion of Texas contains a group of species with the majority of their geographical range in the eastern and southeastern United States. As this area is the western edge of the true southern forests and receives more rainfall than the rest of Texas, the butterfly species would have food plant and humidity requirements difficult to meet in the remainder of the state.

The immediate coastal habitats of Texas also contain a special grouping of butterflies. These species typically require food plants that grow in coastal marshes or meadows. Many times Poaceae (grasses) is used. They also require the higher humidity or relatively constant temperatures that characterize this geographical area. Combined with these requirements, the relative lack of stands of taller trees seems to be a preference of these butterfly populations.

Many of the tropical and subtropical species that are found in the United States are found no farther north than Texas. In the species accounts that follow, you will frequently encounter the phrase "Stray to Rio Grande Valley" or "Very rare stray to Rio Grande Valley" under **Range**. These species are not true breeding residents of Texas, because they are not able to establish permanent populations here. The reasons for the absence of a permanent population could include the lack of suitable larval food plants or the occurrence of severe climatic conditions, usually involving cold weather or drought. Additional species found in the Rio Grande Valley as permanent residents may not occur north of this area except as rare strays (annual strays in some cases). Another group of species may be able to live throughout South Texas, the Rio Grande Valley, and the southernmost area of the Coastal Plain until the climatic conditions become temporarily unfavorable. When the conditions return to normal, then migrant individuals will again establish breeding populations in these areas.

The Texas species found only in the western area of the state and west through the southwestern United States can be divided into two groups. One group of species is typical desert or semi-desert adapted species that have food plant, high temperature, and low humidity requirements. The other group of species in the same area are montane (mountain) species typical of portions of the Rocky Mountains. Their occurrence in the western area of Texas is the result of the milder temperatures and increased humidity found in the higher elevations of the various mountain ranges.

The butterfly fauna of the Texas Panhandle is dominated by species that have very wide geographical ranges. Many of these species use grasses and other prairie plants as larval food plants. However, a few butterfly species occurring in this region are found nowhere else in the state. These Rocky Mountain or western Great Plains species are found associated with wetland habitats in the Panhandle area.

The above analysis necessarily involved the indigenous butterflies of Texas—those species that occur naturally without the interference of man. Such interference could involve land clearance, introduction of non-native plants, regulation of naturally occurring fires, or the restraint and control of natural waterways. Other non-native butterfly species have established populations in modern Texas due to the growing of non-native plant species that are suitable larval food plants. The previously mentioned Cabbage Butterfly is a common pest of backyard gardens. The Guava Skipper (*Phocides palemon*) has been able to establish permanent breeding populations in the Lower Rio Grande Valley following the planting of at least two species of commercial guava (*Psidium guajava, P. cattleianum*). However, an unusually severe freeze, which may occur only once in 20 years, could destroy either the required food plant or the butterfly itself.

Palamedes Swallowtail (*Pteroumus palamedes*)

The Butterflies and Skippers of Texas

About 534 species of the easily recognizable swallowtail butterflies are known in the world. Of this total, 31 are known from North America and 18 of these are from Texas.

Eggs are nearly spherical and are deposited singly or in small clusters of generally less than ten eggs. The majority of the larvae are smooth with no horns, spikes, or hairs. They possess a Y-shaped organ, the osmaterium, located immediately behind the head on the thorax, which can be dramatically everted (turned inside out). This organ produces substances that are repellant to predators by smell and taste.

Larval food plants of the Texas swallowtails represent several plant families with the Aristolochiaceae (birthwort family), Annonaceae (custard-apple family), Lauraceae (laurel family), Rutaceae (citrus family), and Apiaceae (carrot family) being the most frequently used. These plant species in these families typically contain volatile oils, phenolics, or alkaloids. These secondary phytochemicals are foul tasting and often poisonous. They are often retained by the larvae and may produce distastefulness, even in the adult stage. This situation has allowed the evolution of extensive mimicry complexes involving swallowtail and other butterflies.

Swallowtail chrysalids are attached to a branch or tree trunk by a cremaster and a silken girdle around the middle of the body. They often have two projections from the head end in order to further camouflage their appearance on branches. The color varies, often even within a species, in order to better match the background.

The adults are large, have six fully developed walking legs, and many species have a characteristic projection, or "tail," from the outer angle of the hindwing. They fly slowly, but generally stay at least two meters or more above the ground surface. Adults readily visit flowers, but most swallowtails flutter above rather than resting with all of their weight on the blossom. No other butterflies hover above a flower in this manner. Males are frequently seen on wet soil as they "mud-puddle" and will patrol in search for females. The female is the flying partner when a mating pair is disturbed. Either the chrysalis or the adult may overwinter, depending upon the species and latitude. In some species both stages are capable of surviving the winter.

All Texas swallowtails belong to the subfamily Papilioninae. The other subfamily of Paplilonidae, the Parnassinae (not represented in Texas), contains the apollos, which are mostly gray, black, and white with limited amounts of red coloration. These more moth-like butterflies are found in the northern latitudes of the northern hemisphere with one species found as far south as the mountains of north central New Mexico.

Texas swallowtails are grouped into three tribes. The Troidini or birthwort swallowtails includes the genera *Parides* and *Battus* in Texas; the larvae of this group feed on Aristolochiaceae. These dark-colored butterflies with the hindwing tail reduced or lacking are related to the birdwing butterflies of Southeast Asia. The second tribe is the Leptocercini or kite swallowtails. Texas species in this group belong to the genus *Eurytides* and are black and white with long tails. The larvae of this group feed on Annonaceae. The third tribe, the Papilionini or fluted swallowtails, includes the majority of Texas swallowtails (in the genera *Papilio, Heraclides,* and *Pterourus*). Wing patterns are quite diverse in this group, but are generally black, dark brown, and yellow with red and blue spots or highlights. The larvae of this group feed on Lauraceae, Rutaceae, and Apiaceae.

1

CATTLE HEART
Parides eurimedes

Description: 2½–2¾ in (64–70 mm); above black-brown; AFW with large green median patch (male) or large cream patch (female); AHW with red median patch and pink marginal fringe.

Food Plants: Aristolochiaceae - *Aristolochia*.

Life History: Unknown; multivoltine in Mexico; red-brown eggs develop into purple-brown larvae with black patches.

Range: Venezuela to Mexico; Texas–rare stray to Rio Grande Valley.

Comments: Adult distasteful model in mimicry complexes in tropics; species has also been called *arcas*; Texas subspecies -*mylotes* (Mylotes Cattle Heart).

2 E,L,C,A

PIPEVINE SWALLOWTAIL
Battus philenor

Description: 3–4 in (75–100 mm); short tails; above velvet black; AHW with iridescent blue overscaling (heavier on male) and small yellow outer margin crescents; below dark gray-brown; BHW with white spot at base, iridescent blue band from discal cell to outer margin with seven black-capped orange submarginal spots, and white outer margin crescents.

Food Plants: Aristolochiaceae - *Aristolochia erecta* in Central through Rio Grande Valley, *A. wrightii* in Trans-Pecos, *A. coryi* in Big Bend, *A. serpentaria* in East, and *A. tomentosa* in Coastal Margin. Dutchman's Pipe; Calico Flower

Life History: Multivoltine (Jan–Oct); reddish brown eggs singly or clusters of less than 10; reddish-purple larvae with long and short fleshy projections frequently seen crawling on exposed soil, even in the heat of summer, looking for additional pipevine plants after eating the original plant to the ground.

Range: Most of southern North America, from New Jersey to Iowa and California, southward into Mexico; Texas—entire, uncommon or periodic in west Texas and upper north Texas.

Comments: Adult is the model in Batesian mimicry complex that involves several butterfly species; Texas subspecies -philenor.

3 A

POLYDAMAS SWALLOWTAIL
Battus polydamas

Description: 3–4 in (76–102 mm); orange-spotted body, scalloped wings without tails; above black-brown with row of yellow submarginal spots (larger on hindwing); AHW with yellow outer margin crescents; below more brown with yellow BFW submarginal spots; BHW with wavy red submarginal lines.

Food Plants: Aristolochiaceae - *Aristolochia pentandra.* Dutchmans Pipe, Calico Flower

Life History: Multivoltine (Mar—Dec); rough surfaced yellow-orange eggs; larvae are brown-black to red-brown.

Range: Brazil to southern U.S., rare strays northward; Texas—Rio Grande Valley and Coastal Margin, strays along coast to east Texas.

Comments: Probably distasteful to predators; involved in mimetic complexes in tropics; Texas subspecies -polydamas.

4 E,L,A

ZEBRA SWALLOWTAIL
Eurytides marcellus

Description: 2½–3¼ in (64–82 mm); rust-colored antennae, triangular forewings, and long narrow tails; above green-white with black stripes; AHW with red spot on inner angle, blue spots near tail; below white with black stripes; BFW with broad brown outer margin band; BHW with distinctive black bordered red diagonal stripe, blue spots near tail.

Food Plants: Annonaceae - *Asimina parviflora, A. triloba.*

Life History: Multivoltine (Mar–Oct); egg laid singly; green larvae with black dots and yellow rings between segments; chrysalis more compact than typical for swallowtail chrysalids; can be found in leaf litter.

Range: Eastern North America; Texas–East.

Comments: Rapid, zipping flight about three to four feet above ground; most often found along trails and sunny spots in forested areas; spring generation adults smaller, lighter in color than summer generation; short proboscis limits adults to wide-throated or short-tubed flowers.

5

DARK ZEBRA SWALLOWTAIL
Eurytides philolaus

Description: 2½–3 in (64–76 mm); similar to Zebra Swallowtail (*Eurytides marcellus*) but darker, above white, and below green-white; above brown-black with white submarginal crescents; AFW with narrow white lines along costal margin and broad dagger-shaped white median band; AHW with red spots on inner angle and broad white median band; below green-white with distinctive BHW black bordered narrow red stripe.

Food Plants: Annonaceae - *Annona, Sapranthus.*

Life History: Unknown; bivoltine (Mar–Dec) outside Texas.

Range: Costa Rica to Mexico; Texas–very rare stray to Rio Grande Valley.

Comments: Four male specimens from Cameron Co. (1958, 1974); recorded (Jul).

6   L,A

BLACK SWALLOWTAIL
Papilio polyxenes

> **Description:** 3–3½ in (76–89 mm); above black with two rows of yellow spots past median (smaller, lighter spots in female); AHW with iridescent blue spots on lower half of submargin (broad blue band on female), large red spot with black center on inner margin; below black; BFW with yellow spots; BHW with line of orange-red median and outer margin spots, small blue caps on median spots, large black centered red spot on inner margin. *Queen Anne's Lace*
> **Food Plants:** Apiaceae - *Anethum graveolens, Daucus carota, D. pusillus; Petroselinum crispum;* Rutaceae - *Ruta graveolens, Thamnosoma texana.*
> **Life History:** Multivoltine (Feb–Nov); cream-colored eggs; green larvae with yellow spots and black bands; chrysalis is light green with yellow highlights or brown, patterned like wood.
> **Range:** South America to West Indies and all but western North America; Texas—entire.
> **Comments:** Adult female is mimic of Pipevine Swallowtail (*Battus philenor*); Texas subspecies *-asterius* (Parsnip Swallowtail).

7

THOAS SWALLOWTAIL
Heraclides thoas

> **Description:** 4–4½ in (102–114 mm); similar to Giant Swallowtail (*H. cresphontes*) but more brown with paler yellow bands; long tail with yellow dash; above brown-black with broad pale yellow band crossing body from apex to apex; AFW with subapical pale yellow spots; AHW with band of small pale yellow submarginal spots and small red crescent on inner angle; below yellow with brown-black scalloped margins and veins; BHW with median

row of blue crescents, orange cell spot, and red crescent on inner angle.

Food Plants: Unknown; piperaceae - *Piper marginatum* in Vera Cruz; Texas records on Rutaceae refer to Giant Swallowtail.

Life History: Unknown; multivoltine outside of Texas; olive-brown and white mottled larvae resemble bird droppings.

Range: South America to extreme southern U.S.; Texas—occasional stray to Rio Grande Valley.

Comments: One of the three largest North American butterflies; very difficult to separate females from Giant Swallowtail, some Texas records of Thoas Swallowtail undoubtedly refer to Giant Swallowtail; Texas subspecies -*autocles.*

8   L,C,A

GIANT SWALLOWTAIL
Heraclides cresphontes

Description: 3¾–5 in (95–127 mm); very similar to Thoas Swallowtail (*H. thoas*) but darker with deeper yellow bands and spoon-shaped tail with yellow dash; above dark brown-black with two broad bands of deeper yellow spots; AFW band crosses body from apex to apex; AHW with curved submarginal band converging with forewing submarginal band, blue-capped red-orange spot on inner margin angle, thin yellow crescents on outer margin; below pale yellow with black scalloped margins and veins; BHW with black-rimmed shiny blue median crescents, orange spot at end of discal cell, orange spot on inner margin.

Food Plants: Rutaceae - *Poncirus Ptelea trifoliata, Ruta graveolens;* ~~Wild Orange~~ *Zanthoxylum clava-herculis, Z. fagara, Z. hirsutum.* Lime Prickly Ash

Life History: Multivoltine; olive-brown and white mottled larvae resemble bird droppings.

Range: Central America and eastern and southern U.S. along southern border states into California, rare in southern Canada; Texas—entire, more common in east, central, south and coastal Texas.

Comments: One of the three largest North American butterflies; citrus growers refer to larvae as "orange dogs"; adults often fly consistent routes, or "trap lines," in search of flowers several times a day.

9

ORNYTHION SWALLOWTAIL
Heraclides ornythion

Description: 4 in (102 mm); male similar to Giant Swallowtail (*H. cresphontes*) but browner, tails lack yellow dash; dimorphic females may be similar to male or almost all brown; yellow wash in AFW discal cell.
Food Plants: Rutaceae - *Poncirus.*
Life History: Multivoltine.
Range: Guatemala to extreme southern U.S.; Texas–lower Rio Grande Valley.
Comments: Adults wander with Mexican migrants flying as far as New Mexico and Arizona; can be found in commercial citrus groves.

10

LYCOPHRON SWALLOWTAIL
Heraclides astyalus

Description: 4 in (102 mm); male similar to Giant Swallowtail (*H. cresphontes*) but yellow diagonal band broader; narrow tails without dash; sexually dimorphic, female without yellow diagonal band or tail but may have short point instead; above brown-black with yellow spot at end of AFW cell; female AHW somewhat variable with three rows of spots: postmedian orange spots before blue submarginal spots and white outer margin spots.
Food Plants: Rutaceae - *Poncirus* Rutaceae - *Poncirus,* especially commercial orange *(Poncirus aurantifolia* and lime *(P. sinensis).*

Life History: Multivoltine.

Range: Argentina north to extreme southern U.S.; Texas–Rio Grande Valley.

Comments: Females stay in wooded areas, thus are rare in collections; males fly in open areas; can be found in commercial citrus groves; Texas subspecies *-pallas* (Pallas Swallowtail).

11

ANCHISIADES SWALLOWTAIL
Heraclides anchisiades

Description: 3½–4 in (89–102 mm); tailless; above black; female AFW with hazy white discal cell patch; AHW with distinct pink postmedian patch.

Food Plants: Rutaceae - *Poncirus,* especially commercial citrus; *Zanthoxylum;* also *Casimiroa edulis* in Mexico.

Life History: Multivoltine (Apr–Nov); green-brown larvae different from other swallowtail larvae with five longitudinal rows of short tubercles and light cream streaks and dots.

Range: Argentina north to southern U.S.; Texas–Rio Grande Valley.

Comments: Has been placed in genus *Priamides* by some workers; probably mimics *Parides* in tropical America; occasionally a pest in citrus groves in Mexico; rare migrants to Kansas; Texas subspecies *-idaeus* (Idaeus Swallowtail).

12

PHARNACES SWALLOWTAIL
Heraclides pharnaces

Description: 3½–3¾ in (89–95 mm); short tails or tailless; above brownish-black; AHW with two rows post median and submarginal pink spots and white outer margin crescents.

Food Plants: Rutaceae - *Poncirus.*

Life History: Unknown.

Range: Mexico and extreme southern U.S.; Texas—rare stray to Rio Grande Valley.

Comments: Single specimen record in Rio Grande Valley.

13   L,A

TIGER SWALLOWTAIL
Pterourus glaucus

Description: 3½–5 in (89–127 mm); sexually dimorphic; body is black above and yellow below; above yellow with four black lines (broad at forewing costal margin becoming narrower across wing) and broad black outer margins with small yellow dashes; AHW with blue and red outer angle spots; below similar but paler yellow with hazy black submarginal band, broader on BHW and dotted with pale blue; BHW with row of black bordered orange outer margin crescents; females dimorphic with some individuals similar to male but with broader lines and more blue on AHW; dark form with iridescent blue scales on AHW (the large size and faint black stripes on AFW will separate this form from the Pipevine Swallowtail (*Battus philenor*).

Food Plants: Oleaceae - *Fraxinus* spp; *F. velutina* preferred. Arizona Ash

Life History: Multivoltine (Feb–Nov); large green egg; mature larvae are smooth and green with two yellow-ringed black eyespots, yellow and black stripe across body between thorax and abdomen; brown chrysalis with green, black, and brown markings.

Range: Alaska to Labrador south through U.S. and into Mexico to Veracruz; Texas—East, eastern half of North Central, Central, and Coastal Margin north of Corpus Christi.

Comments: Similar to Two-Tailed Swallowtail (*P. multicaudatus*); dark form females mimic the Pipevine Swallowtail (*B. philenor*); in Central Texas, almost all females are dark, but the percentage of yellow females increases eastward and northward in Texas; in northeastern U.S., where Pipevine Swallowtail is absent, all Tiger Swallowtail females are yellow; Texas subspecies *glaucus*.

14 A

TWO-TAILED SWALLOWTAIL
Pterourus multicaudatus

Description: 4–4½ in (102–114 mm); two tails (shorter tail below long tail); above yellow with black lines much narrower than Tiger Swallowtail (*P. glaucus*) but black outer margins are broader and dotted with orange spots; AHW with blue submarginal spots in lower halves of wing; female more orange than yellow with more blue on AHW.

Food Plants: Rutaceae - *Ptelea trifoliata;* rarely Oleaceae - *Fraxinus velutina, Ligustrum quihoui.*

Life History: Multivoltine (Feb–Nov); light green larvae become red-brown when mature.

Range: Western North America south to Michoacan, Mexico; Texas–western halves of Central, High Plains, Trans-Pecos, Southwest, Big Bend, and Far West; disjunct records on coast.

Comments: Can tolerate drier, hotter habitats but prefers moist canyon bottoms.

15

THREE-TAILED SWALLOWTAIL
Pterourus pilumnus

Description: 3¾–4 in (95–102 mm); three tails; similar to yellow form of Tiger Swallowtail (*P. glaucus*) but with three black lines on AFW instead of four like *P. glaucus* and *P. multicaudatus.*

Food Plants: Unknown; Lauraceae - *Litsea* outside of U.S.

Life History: Green larvae with brown heads.

Range: Guatemala and Mexico; Texas–very rare stray to Rio Grande Valley.

Comments: Single record of male, Cameron Co. (1932).

16   E,LC,A

SPICEBUSH SWALLOWTAIL
Pterourus troilus

Description: 3½–4 in (89–102 mm); similar to Pipevine Swallowtail (*Battus philenor*) but AFW with cream outer margin spots, orange spot on AHW inner angle, and BHW with two rows of orange spots; above dark black-brown; AFW with cream outer margin spots; AHW with blue-green (male) to blue-gray (female) outer margin spots and orange spot on inner angle; male AHW with iridescent blue-green wash from discal cell to spots; below more brown; BFW with a few cream spots; BHW with two rows of orange spots (postmedian and outer margin) with a hazy blue band between.

Food Plants: Lauraceae - *Lindera benzoin, Sassafras albidum.*

Life History: Bivoltine (Apr–Oct); light green eggs; larvae have two pairs of black-ringed eyespots, first pair is black and yellow while second pair is solid yellow; larvae make leaf nests; chrysalis can be yellow, green, dull red, or brown.

Range: Eastern North America; Texas–East, eastern half of Coastal Margin, and southeastern Central.

Comments: Texas subspecies -*ilioneus* (Coastal Spicebush Swallowtail).

17   L,A

PALAMEDES SWALLOWTAIL
Pterourus palamedes

Description: 3½–5 in (89–127 mm); rounded forewing costal margin and short hindwing tail; above brown-black with broad yellow post median band (broken into spots on AFW, solid on AHW) and thin yellow outer margin crescents; AHW with row of blue submarginal spots; below brown; BFW with two rows of cream spots; BHW with straight orange line parallel to abdomen across inner third, two rows of curved orange spots enclosing a row of blue postmedian spots.

Food Plants: Lauraceae - *Persea borbonia*, *Sassafras albidum*.

Life History: Bivoltine (Mar–Dec); single green eggs; green larvae with yellow line along sides and numerous small blue spots.

Range: Coastal area of U.S. from New Jersey to Texas; Texas—East and eastern half of Coastal Margin.

Comments: Slow flying adults easily seen from observation tower at Aransas National Wildlife Refuge; prefers evergreen swamps and damp woodlands; Texas subspecies *-palamedes*; *-leontis*, a very rare stray to Rockport area, Aransas Co., with smaller spots.

18

VICTORINE SWALLOWTAIL
Pterourus victorinus

Description: 4–4½ in (102–114 mm); tailless;
above brown-black with two rows of light yellow postmedian and marginal spots; BHW of male with two rows of postmedian and marginal red spots; dimorphic female, one form similar to male, second form has AHW with green band instead of yellow spots.

Food Plants: Unknown; Lauraceae - *Persea americana* in Central America.

Life History: Unknown; multivoltine (Jan–Nov) in Mexico.

Range: Central America to extreme southern Texas; Texas—South, Webb Co.

Comments: Flies in open areas but near wooded habitat; one record (Aug 1974).

WHITES AND SULPHURS—FAMILY PIERIDAE

This family contains about 1,100 species worldwide with 60 in North America and 36 of these in Texas. The Pieridae is divided into five subfamilies, four of which are represented in the Texas fauna. The subfamily Pseudopontiinae contains only a single African species and therefore is not found in Texas. Most of the Texas species belong to either the Pierinae (whites) or the Coliadinae (sulphurs), both of which are found worldwide. Several members of the Anthocharinae (marbles and orangetips) and a single representative of the largely neotropical Dismorphiinae are known from Texas.

Eggs are spindle-shaped (like a narrow vase) and are usually white, yellow, or orange. Most pierids lay eggs singly, but a few species produce clusters containing a few neatly spaced eggs. The larvae are generally cylindrical with short hairs. A few tropical species have short spines. Larvae generally feed upon Brassicaceae (mustard family) or Fabaceae (legume family).

The chrysalis is similar to that of the swallowtails, being upright (at about a 45° angle) with attachment by cremaster and a silk girdle. The head usually has a single projection that is often quite elongated. The wing pads are extended ventrally over the middle portion of the body. Chrysalids of some species may occur in aggregations of many individuals in particularly favorable microhabitats.

Most species are medium-sized, although a few small and a few large species are known. Adults possess six fully developed walking legs of equal length with forked claws. The wings are generally white, yellow, or orange with black markings commonly present. Colors of pierids are due to a class of pigments called pterins, which are formed from the waste product, uric acid. Many pierids have seasonal forms with the spring form usually having more red or black color below.

Adults of all species visit flowers and many are habitual mud-puddlers, especially the males. The flight pattern varies somewhat, but the typical pattern is fluttering in a straight line at a steady pace. Long dispersal flights are common with true migration present in many species. The male is the active flying partner during mating. The subfamilies, Pierinae and Anthocharinae, overwinter as pupae; the subfamily Coliadinae overwinters as adults.

WHITES—SUBFAMILY PIERINAE

Containing about 700 species, the Pierinae is the largest subfamily of the Pieridae, although only 13 species are known from North America, and eight occur in Texas. Species are common in all temperate regions, but many species are also known from tropical regions of the world. Adults are recognized by their well-developed palps and long antennae. Wings are usually white and black with orange or red patches present in a few species. Larvae of most species are found on Brassicaceae (mustard family), Capparidaceae (caper family), or Tropaeolaceae (nasturtium family), but a few species feed on the unrelated Pinaceae (pine family), Viscaceae (mistletoe family), and Euphorbiaceae (spurge family). The Texas Pierines include one non-native species that has been transported worldwide wherever cabbage and related cultivated crucifers are grown.

19

MISTLETOE WHITE
Catasticta nimbice

> **Description:** 2 in (51 mm); above white with black borders and veins; below similar but more black.
> **Food Plants:** Viscacaea - *Phoradendron*.
> **Life History:** Unknown; multivoltine in Mexico; gregarious larvae regurgitate green fluid when disturbed.
> **Range:** Panama to extreme southern U.S.; Texas—Big Bend.
> **Comments:** Older, worn adults known from middle and lower elevations of Chisos Mountains, breeding not yet documented in Texas; Texas subspecies -*nimbice*.

20 A

TROPICAL WHITE
Appias drusilla

> **Description:** 2½ in (64 mm); forewing pointed with slight concave outer margin; above white with gray AFW costal margin (male);

AFW may have narrow black outer margin; AHW with variable yellow to orange wash (female).

Food Plants: Capparidaceae; Brassicaceae.

Life History: Unknown; multivoltine outside Texas; white eggs turn yellow; larvae can be cannibalistic.

Range: Brazil to West Indies, Mexico, and extreme southern U.S.; Texas–Rio Grande Valley, strays north through remainder of state.

Comments: Migratory adults may disperse as far as Nebraska and New York; Texas subspecies -*neumoegeni* (Florida White).

21

CALIFORNIA WHITE
Pontia sisymbrii

Description: 1½ in (38 mm); above white (male) or cream (female); AFW with charcoal spot at end of cell and charcoal spots on apex and outer margin; below with grainy brown vein lines; BHW with band of submarginal V-shaped spots.

Food Plants: Brassicaceae - *Arabis, Caulanthus, Descaurania, Sisymbrium, Streptanthus.*

Life History: Univoltine (Mar); blue-green eggs turn orange; younger larvae feed on leaves but more mature larvae seem to prefer flowers.

Range: Western Canada and western U.S.; Texas–Far West.

Comments: Texas subspecies -*sisymbrii.*

22   A

CHECKERED WHITE
Pontia protodice

Description: 1½–2 in (38–51 mm); sexually dimorphic; above white; AFW with several median and postmedian black spots (male); above more spotted (female); below both sexes with dark brown or olive markings; below can have yellow wash (female).

Food Plants: Brassicaceae - *Arabis, Brassica, Caulanthus, Capsella, Descaurania, Lepidium, Thelypodium.*

Life History: Multivoltine; larvae prefer flower buds, flowers, and fruits.

Range: Southern Mexico and Cuba north to southern U.S., strays throughout U.S. and southern Canada; Texas—entire.

Comments: Wide dispersion, common in urban areas.

23

MUSTARD WHITE
Pieris napi

Description: 1½ in (38 mm); rounded costal margins; above white; AFW with small charcoal postmedian spot and apical dashes; below white with variable dark vein lines.

Food Plants: Brassicaceae - *Arabis, Brassica, Cardamine, Dentaria, Draba, Lepidium, Rorippa, Sisymbrium.*

Life History: Bivoltine (Apr–Aug).

Range: Europe, Asia, Canada, Alaska, and higher latitudes and elevations of U.S.; Texas—Panhandle.

Comments: Texas subspecies *mcdunnoughi* (McDunnough's White).

24 A

CABBAGE BUTTERFLY
Pieris rapae

Description: 1½–2 in (38–51 mm); above white or cream with black submarginal spots (one in male, two in female); AFW with dark apical patch (both sexes); BFW with black spot and pale to bright yellow apex patch; BHW pale to bright yellow.

Food Plants: Brassicaceae - *Brassica oleracea; Arabis, Caulanthus, Descaurania, Lepidium;* Tropaeolaceae.

Life History: Multivoltine.

Range: Native to northern Africa and Eurasia; Texas—entire, uncommon in Rio Grande Valley.

Comments: Only introduced butterfly in Texas; first North America record in Quebec in 1859, New York by 1868; may have reached Texas as early as 1881.

25 C,A

GREAT SOUTHERN WHITE
Ascia monuste

Description: 2–2½ in (51–64 mm); rounded forewing costal edge; above white; AFW outer margin with triangular black marks (more extensive but diffuse in female) giving wings a scalloped appearance; below similar to Cabbage Butterfly (*Pieris rapae*) without black spot; dimorphic female has dark form (usually migratory) with both wing surfaces suffused with gray-brown haze.

FoodPlants: Brassicaceae - *Armoracia, Brassica, Lepidium, Raphanus;* Tropaeolaceae; Capparidaceae.

Life History: Multivoltine; color polymorphic larvae.

Range: Argentina to West Indies and southern U.S.; Texas–Rio Grande Valley, Coastal Margin; disjunct records in Central.

Comments: Strongly migratory, often moving in South Texas with Lyside (*Kricogonia lyside*); Texas subspecies *-monuste.*

26 A

GIANT WHITE
Ganyra josephina

Description: 2½ in (64 mm); above white; AFW with small black spot at end of cell and vague dark smudges on outer angle; below similar.

Food Plants: Unknown; Capparidaceae - *Capparis, Forchammeria* in Mexico.

Life History: Unknown; multivoltine in Mexico.

Range: Central America and West Indies to U.S.; Texas–periodic resident in Rio Grande Valley, straying northward.

Comments: Occurrence in Texas may be as dispersing populations; Texas subspecies -josepha.

MARBLES AND ORANGETIPS—SUBFAMILY ANTHOCHARINAE

This small subfamily is restricted to the middle and northern latitudes of the northern hemisphere. Of the ten species known from North America, five are known from Texas. Eggs are laid singly on Brassicaceae (mustard family). Species tend to be small and are commonly white and black in basic wing pattern with mottling of the underside of the hindwing prevalent. The mottling or marbling is often seen faintly from above. The Orangetips have orange or red pigment on the forewing apex, which is restricted to males in some species. The head and thorax are often covered with short, fine hairs giving the butterfly's body a fuzzy appearance. Many species are univoltine with bivoltine species also present. Overwintering is accomplished by the pupal stage, but some species pass the summer period as pupae.

27 A

PEARLY MARBLE
Euchloe hyantis

Description: 1½–1¾ in (38–44 mm); white antennae and narrow extended forewing; above clear white; AFW with black bar on middle of costal margin at end of cell and charcoal checkered apex; BFW similar but with olive-green checkered apex; BHW with olive-green marbling that may be faintly seen from above.
Food Plants: Brassicaceae - *Arabis, Caulanthus, Descaurania, Lepidium, Streptanthus, Thelypodium.*
Life History: Univoltine (Mar–May); larvae prefer flowers and fruits.
Range: Western North America, Canada to Mexico; Texas–Far West.
Comments: Texas subspecies -lotta (Southern Marble).

28

OLYMPIA MARBLE
Euchloe olympia

Description: 1½–1¾ in (38–44 mm); very similar to Pearly Marble (*E. hyantis*) but apical checkering reduced to smudged subapical line; below with paler marbling.

Food Plants: Brassicaceae - *Arabis, Descaurania, Sisymbrium.*

Life History: Univoltine (May); bright green larvae with gray and yellow lengthwise stripes.

Range: Central North America from southern Canada to central Texas, also Appalachian Mountains; Texas–eastern half of North Central and northern half of East.

Comments: Found in open habitats, including prairies.

29

PIMA ORANGE TIP
Anthocharis pima

Description: 1¼–1½ in (32–38 mm); above yellow; AFW with black bar at end of cell and large orange apical patch bordered by yellow and black outer margin; below similar but BFW apical patch paler orange; BHW with olive marbling.

Food Plants: Brassicaceae - *Caulanthus, Thelypodium, Descaurania, Streptanthus.*

Life History: Univoltine (Feb–Mar).

Range: Southwestern deserts of U.S. and Mexico; Texas–desert areas of Far West.

Comments: Prefers dry habitats.

30

SARA ORANGE TIP
Anthocharis sara

Description: 1½ in (38 mm); above white with black checkered wing fringes; AFW with prominent red-orange apical patch with black border from costal margin to tornus; BFW similar but lighter; BHW with open grainy olive marbling.

Food Plants: Brassicaceae - *Arabis, Sisymbrium.*

Life History: Univoltine (Mar–Apr); a different subspecies in coastal California has a partial second brood.

Range: Alaskan peninsula south through western U.S. to northwestern Mexico; Texas–foothill and montane areas of Far West.

Comments: Texas subspecies -*inghami* (Ingham's Orange Tip).

31   A

FALCATE ORANGE TIP
Paramidea midea

Description: 1¼–1½ in (32–38 mm); extended forewing with rounded, curved apex (falcate); above white; AFW with black cell spot and black spotted outer margins giving a ruffled appearance; AFW with orange apex patch (male) or without orange patch (female); BHW with olive marbling (more open in male, darker in female).

Food Plants: Brassicaceae - *Arabis, Lepidium, Cardamine.*

Life History: Univoltine (Mar–May); larvae varying between olive to blue-green with white side stripes, dull orange dorsal stripe; chrysalis may live two to three years during drought periods.

Range: Eastern U.S., Connecticut to Nebraska south to Georgia and central Texas; Texas–East, Coastal Margin, Rio Grande Valley, southeastern halves of Central, North Central, and South.

Comments: Texas subspecies -*midea.*

SULPHURS—SUBFAMILY COLIADINAE

The Coliadinae has its greatest species diversity in the tropical regions of the world, but is worldwide in distribution with about 300 species. Substantial numbers of species occur in the temperate regions, but only 36 species occur in North America. This subfamily is represented by 22 species in Texas and North America, which is more than the Pierinae, although the Coliadinae contains fewer species than the Pierinae worldwide. Adults may be recognized by their short antennae and generally square wing shape. Most species are yellow or orange with white or black markings. Many species exhibit sexual dimorphism with the male being orange or yellow and the female being lighter versions of these colors or white. Seasonal variation within a species is common with the amount of dark pigment (relative to yellow and orange pigment) and even the wing shape being variable. Larvae of most species are found on Fabaceae (legume family) with the related Zygophyllaceae (caltrop family) as well as the unrelated Simaroubaceae (quassia family) and Asteraceae (sunflower family) also being used. A large number of the Texas Coliadines are periodic strays from the tropics of Mexico.

32 A

CLOUDED SULPHUR
Colias philodice

Description: 1¾–2 in (44–51 mm); above lemon yellow; female dimorphic with a yellow form or a white form more green than white; AFW with round black spot at end of cell and broad black (male) or blotchy black (female) outer margin band; AHW with black band tapering before outer angle; below yellow (more green in spring and fall); BFW with a row of small dark submarginal spots; BHW with red-rimmed silver spot at end of cell and a row of dark submarginal spots.

Food Plants: Fabaceae - *Astragalus, Baptisia, Lupinus, Medicago, Vicia, Trifolium.*

Life History: Multivoltine (Mar-Dec); larvae may be common in alfalfa (*Medicago sativa*) fields.

Range: Alaska and Canada south through U.S. into northern Mexico; Texas—entire, except Coastal Plain and Rio Grande Valley; strays through remainder of state.

Comments: Males do not reflect in ultraviolet (see next species); occasionally hybridizes with Alfalfa Butterfly (*C. eurytheme*); Texas subspecies *-philodice*.

33   C,A

ALFALFA BUTTERFLY
Colias eurytheme

Description: 1¾–2½ in (44–64 mm); similar to Clouded Sulphur (*C. philodice*); above variable between orange, yellow-orange, or in some females, white; AFW with black spot at end of cell and broad black outer margin band with row of oblong yellow spots on band; AHW with red-orange cell spot, black outer margin band tapering, not reaching outer angle; below variable between orange, yellow, or green-yellow; BHW has red rimmed silver spot at end of discal cell and small faint brown submarginal spots.

Food Plants: Fabaceae - *Astragalus, Baptisia, Melilotus, Phaseolus, Senna, Trifolium*; can be abundant in alfalfa (*Medicago sativa*) fields.

Life History: Multivoltine (Mar–Dec); dark green larvae with pink side stripes below white side stripes, covered with short fine white hair.

Range: Southern Canada through U.S. to southern Mexico; Texas—entire.

Comments: Common in urban areas; spring adults have reduced orange areas (yellow instead) due to winter chilling of pupae; males reflect ultraviolet in non-black areas of wing; occasionally hybridizes with Clouded Sulphur (*C. philodice*).

34   L,C,A

DOG FACE
Zerene cesonia

Description: 2–2¾ in (51–70 mm); forewing pointed at apex; above yellow; AFW with extensive black outer margin scalloped to form a profile of a dog head, black cell spot suggests dog's eye; AHW with small orange cell spot and narrow black scalloped submarginal band; below yellow; winter form *rosa* has heavy pink BHW suffusion.

Food Plants: Fabaceae - *Dalea pogonothera, D. frutescens;* also *Amorpha, Medicago, Trifolium.*

Life History: Multivoltine; polymorphic black-dotted green larva may be plain, striped, or with bands of yellow and black.

Range: Argentina to southern U.S., migrates northward in summer; Texas–entire.

Comments: In late summer and fall of some years, a rare female form *immaculsecunda*, without the dog face marking, is normally resident in Mexico but occasionally appears in Texas; Texas subspecies -*cesonia*.

35

WHITE ANGLED SULPHUR
Anteos chlorinde

Description: 2¾–3 in (70–76 mm); pointed, curved forewing and short hindwing bump on middle of outer margin; above white; AFW with orange-ringed black spot at end of cell adjacent to yellow median patch (males and some females); AHW with orange-ringed black spot at end of cell; below pale gray.

Food Plants: Fabaceae - *Senna, Pithecellobium.*

Life History: Multivoltine in tropics.

Range: Argentina north to West Indies, Mexico, and southern U.S.; Texas–Rio Grande Valley, strays northward.

Comments: Orange spot of males reflects ultraviolet; periodically migrates in a strong flight pattern, rarely to Colorado; recorded (May–Dec); Texas subspecies *-nivifera* (Chlorinde).

36 A

YELLOW BRIMSTONE
Anteos maerula

Description: 3 in (76 mm); extended forewing with rounded apex (falcate); above solid yellow or green-yellow; AFW with small black spot at end of cell; below variable between yellow and jade green.

Food Plants: Fabaceae - *Senna.*

Life History: Unknown; multivoltine in tropics.

Range: Peru northward to West Indies and southern U.S.; Texas–periodic migration to Rio Grande Valley, rare strays northward.

Comments: Unlike White Angled Sulphur (*A. chlorinde*), males do not reflect ultraviolet; recorded (Aug–Dec).

37 L,C,A

CLOUDLESS SULPHUR
Phoebis sennae

Description: 2½–2¾ in (64–76 mm); above yellow; female may be white or yellow; AFW (female) with small black spot at end of cell and black outer margin spots; below yellow (or white in white female form).

Food Plants: Fabaceae - *Senna bicapsularis.*

Life History: Multivoltine; yellow-green larvae with rows of black dots make tents of silk and leaves of host plant.

Range: Paraguay north to West Indies and southern U.S.; Texas–East, Coastal Margin, South, Rio Grande Valley and eastern half of Central; strays through remainder of state.

Comments: Strong flier, common in urban areas; Texas subspecies -eubele in east and upper coastal area; -marcellina in south.

38 A

ORANGE-BARRED SULPHUR
Phoebis philea

Description: 2½–3 in (64–76 mm); sexually dimorphic; above yellow (male) with broad orange AFW bar crossing discal cell and AHW with broad orange outer margin; above variable between gold, yellow or white (female), AFW with black cell spot, black apex, and black spotted outer margin and AHW with widely spaced black outer margin spots; below (both sexes) mottled with lavender, orange and pink and black cell spot on both wings.

Food Plants: Fabaceae - *Caesalpinia, Senna, Pithecellobium.*

Life History: Multivoltine (Aug–Dec); larvae prefer flowers rather than leaves but will eat leaves.

Range: Argentina northward to West Indies and southern U.S.; Texas–Rio Grande Valley; periodic migration north.

Comments: Occasionally migrating to southern Canada; largest species in genus *Phoebis;* Texas subspecies -*philea.*

39 A

ARGANTE GIANT SULPHUR
Phoebis argante

Description: 2½ in (64 mm); very similar to Large Orange Sulphur (*P. agarithe*) except for offset in dark line below; sexually dimorphic; above orange (male) or yellow-orange to white with dark markings on AFW margin (female); below (both sexes) yellow speckled with pink, lavender, and orange and dark jagged offset postmedian line; BFW with rust spot at end of cell.

Food Plants: Fabaceae - *Caesalpinia, Inga, Senna, Pithecellobium.*
Life History: Unknown; multivoltine in Mexico.
Range: Paraguay to West Indies and southern U.S.; Texas–periodic migrant to Rio Grande Valley.
Comments: Texas subspecies -*argante.*

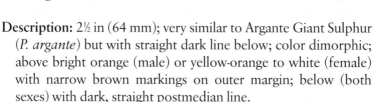

40   A

LARGE ORANGE SULPHUR
Phoebis agarithe

Description: 2½ in (64 mm); very similar to Argante Giant Sulphur (*P. argante*) but with straight dark line below; color dimorphic; above bright orange (male) or yellow-orange to white (female) with narrow brown markings on outer margin; below (both sexes) with dark, straight postmedian line.
Food Plants: Fabaceae - *Pithecellobium flexicaule; Senna;* also *Inga* in Latin America.
Life History: Multivoltine; green larvae with narrow yellow side stripes lined with darker green.
Range: Brazil to West Indies and southern U.S.; Texas–South and Rio Grande Valley, periodic migrant northward.
Comments: Strong migrant to northern U.S.; Texas subspecies - *agarithe.*

41

YELLOW LONG-TAILED SULPHUR
Phoebis neocypris

Description: 3½ in (89 mm); sexually dimorphic; short broad tail on hindwing; above yellow-orange (male) or variable between yellow to white (female); AFW (male) with orange patch from base through cell; AHW (male) with orange outer margin.
Food Plants: Fabaceae - *Senna.*
Life History: Unknown.

Range: Central America to southern U.S.; Texas–rare stray to Rio Grande Valley.

Comments: Some workers believe records of this species in the U.S. to be records of the Tailed Sulphur (*Phoebis intermedia*).

42

STATIRA
Aphrissa statira

Description: 2¼–2½ in (57–64 mm); above yellow fading into broad creamy outer margin bands (male) or pale yellow with AFW black cell spot, apex and outer margin (female); below yellow with cream BFW band.

Food Plants: Fabaceae - *Calliandra, Entada, Senna.*

Life History: Bivoltine (Jun–Sep, Nov–Feb).

Range: Argentina to West Indies, southern U.S.; Texas–regular migrant to Rio Grande Valley.

Comments: Texas and Florida with separate populations; very rare stray to Nebraska and Massachusetts; Texas subspecies -*jada* (Cramer's Embossed-Wing Sulphur).

43 A

LYSIDE
Kricogonia lyside

Description: 1½–1¾ in (38–44 mm); many seasonal forms; short antennae, square forewing with pointed apex, and round hindwing; above variable between white and yellow; AFW with gold patch at base; often AHW (male) with black dash on outer end of costal margin; below yellow-green with yellow BFW patch at base.

Food Plants: Zygophyllaceae - *Guaiacum angustifolia.*

Life History: Multivoltine; dull green larvae with bright gray dorsal stripes.

Range: Northern South America to West Indies and southern U.S.; Texas–Rio Grande Valley, South and Central, strays north and west.

Comments: Sexual and seasonal dimorphism with many named forms; migrations of thousands of individuals common in southern Texas in summer and early fall.

44 A

BARRED YELLOW
Eurema daira

Description: 1–1¼ in (25–32 mm); seasonal and sexual dimorphism; above yellow or white (female) with black outer margins and apex; AFW (male) with black bar on inner margin; below red-brown or tan with dull orange margin fringe (winter) or white with yellow margin fringe (summer).

Food Plants: Fabaceae - *Desmodium, Medicago, Mimosa, Senna, Trifolium.*

Life History: Multivoltine.

Range: Brazil northward to West Indies and southern U.S.; Texas–Extreme eastern fourth of Coastal Margin, periodic stray to Rio Grande Valley.

Comments: Prefers open habitats, somewhat migratory; Texas subspecies *-daira* in eastern Coastal Margin; *-lydia*, stray to Rio Grande Valley.

45

BOISDUVAL'S YELLOW
Eurema boisduvalianum

Description: 1½–1¾ in (38–44 mm); similar to Dog Face (*Zerene cesonia*) but without black cell spot; sexually dimorphic; short, pointed tail on hindwing; above (male) orange-yellow with jagged black AFW outer margin band forming vague dog head or (female) yellow with black AFW apex; AHW (male) with jagged black border not found on female; below yellow with red-pink marbling (more in winter, less in summer).

Food Plants: Unknown; Fabaceae - *Senna pendula*; *S. occidentalis* in Veracruz, Mexico.

Life History: Unknown.

Range: Central America and Mexico, straying northward to southern Texas, Arizona, and Florida; Texas—stray to Rio Grande Valley.

Comments: Typical of arid or semi-arid hot habitats, also known as Poodle Face Sulphur.

46 A

MEXICAN YELLOW
Eurema mexicanum

Description: 1¾–2 in (44–51 mm); similar to Boisduval's Yellow (*E. boisduvalianum*) but paler, hindwing projection more prominent; above pale yellow to cream with irregular black AFW outer margin band forming long-nosed dog head silhouette; broad yellow costal margin bar on male AFW.

Food Plants: Fabaceae - *Acacia, Robinia, Senna*.

Life History: Univoltine (Jul–Sep); multivoltine outside the U.S.

Range: Northern South America to southern U.S.; Texas—most common South, Southwest, and Rio Grande Valley, Big Bend, southern Trans-Pecos; strays through remainder of state.

Comments: Strong migrant northward, rarely to south central Canada; males fly all day, patrolling; also known as Wolf Face Sulphur.

47

SALOME YELLOW
Eurema salome

Description: 1½–2 in (38–51 mm); similar to Boisduval's Yellow (*E. boisduvalianum*), but slightly larger, deeper yellow, reduced marginal markings, and hindwing projection more angled.

Food Plants: Unknown; Fabaceae - *Diphysa* in Costa Rica.

Life History: Univoltine (Aug–Sep); multivoltine in Latin America.

Range: Peru northward to Mexico; Texas–rare stray to Rio Grande Valley.

Comments: Also known as Monkey Face Sulphur; Texas subspecies *-limoneum* (Salome Sulphur).

48 A

TAILED ORANGE
Eurema proterpia

Description: 1½–1¾ in (38–51 mm); sexually dimorphic and seasonal variation; winter form with short angled hindwing tail; summer form without tail and with black veins; above orange with black AFW costal margin (male) or black costal margin, apex, and outer margin (female); below yellow (male) or orange (female) with red-brown mottling.

Food Plants: Fabaceae - *Chamaecrista flexuosa, Prosopis reptans,* and *Desmodium.*

Life History: Bivoltine (Aug–Nov); multivoltine in Latin America.

Range: Peru northward to West Indies and southwestern U.S.; Texas–Rio Grande Valley, periodic northward migrant.

Comments: Winter form with tail was previously considered a separate species *E. gundlachia*, now considered only a seasonal form.

49 C,A

LITTLE YELLOW
Eurema lisa

Description: 1–1½ in (25–38 mm); sexually dimorphic; above yellow with black outer margin markings; occasionally females cream-white with small black spots on outer margins; below yellow or cream-white speckled with rust in varying degrees, narrow vague mauve outer margin bands; BHW with apical rust spot (sometimes with pink center).

Food Plants: Fabaceae - *Chamaecrista fasciculata; Amphicarpa, Desmanthus, Senna, Trifolium.*

Life History: Multivoltine; very small green larvae with fine hair, white side stripes.

Range: Central America and Mexico northward to southern U.S., mainly coastal eastward from Texas to North Carolina; Texas—entire, abundant in South, Rio Grande Valley, and Coastal Margin.

Comments: Common in urban areas, prefers open habitats; flies close to the ground, often within 15 cm (6 in); strong migrant recolonizes northeast U.S. each season but cannot overwinter in any form; Texas subspecies *-lisa.*

50

JAMAICAN SULPHUR
Eurema nise

Description: 1–1¼ in (25–32 mm); similar to Little Yellow (*E. lisa*) but without AHW dark outer margin; sexually dimorphic but without white female form; above yellow-orange with dark markings on AFW apex; AHW (female) with dark spot on outer margin; below yellow with or without small scattered rust smudges.

Food Plants: Fabaceae - *Mimosa pudica; Desmanthus.*

Life History: Multivoltine; green larvae with light and dark lengthwise lines.

Range: Argentina northward to West Indies and southern U.S.; Texas—Rio Grande Valley, rare stray northward to Central.

Comments: Commonly found near woods and will dash into wooded areas when alarmed; Texas subspecies *-nelpha* (Nise Sulphur).

51

DINA YELLOW
Eurema dina

Description: 1¼–2 in (32–51 mm); sexually dimorphic; above orange with narrow dark AFW outer margin markings; AFW (female) with black apex; below deep yellow with three black BHW spots.

Food Plants: Unknown; Simaroubaceae outside the U.S.

Life History: Unknown; multivoltine in Mexico.

Range: Central America, West Indies, and southern U.S.; Texas–stray to Rio Grande Valley.

Comments: Texas subspecies -*westwoodi* (Westwood's Yellow).

52 A

SLEEPY ORANGE
Eurema nicippe

Description: 2–2¼ in (51–57 mm); sexually and seasonally dimorphic; females smaller and less intensely colored; above bright orange with irregular dark brown margin markings; AHW margin (female) becomes vague towards outer angle; BFW orange; BHW dark orange (summer form) or darker red-orange or tan (winter form).

Food Plants: Fabaceae - *Senna*, *S. roemeriana* preferred, *Trifolium*.

Life History: Multivoltine; slender, green larvae with short hair and side stripes of white, yellow, and black.

Range: Brazil northward to West Indies and southern U.S.; Texas–entire.

Comments: Many explanations for common name, but flight pattern is rapid, not "sleepy"; this butterfly cannot tolerate cold weather and often "sleeps" or rests under cover on cooler days; also known as Rambling Orange.

53   A

DAINTY SULPHUR
Nathalis iole

Description: ¾–1 in (19–25 mm); sexually and seasonally dimorphic; elongated forewing; above yellow with extensive diffuse black bars along AFW costal and inner margins; AHW yellow with dark narrow outer margin dashes; below yellow with olive speckles; BFW with broad basal orange or yellow patch and small black spots on outer margin; BHW yellow (summer) or dull green (winter), both forms with vague dark areas.

Food Plants: Asteraceae - *Bidens, Dyssodia, Helenium, Palafoxia, Thelesperma.*

Life History: Multivoltine; chrysalids lack projection on head section which is common on most other pierid chrysalids.

Range: Colombia to West Indies and U.S.; Texas–entire, more common in southern half of state.

Comments: Smallest U.S. pierid; migrates far northward every year, being known even from southern Canada.

Cloudless Sulphur (*Phoebis sennae*)

MIMIC SULPHURS—SUBFAMILY DISMORPHIINAE

This subfamily contains only about 100 species that are restricted to the American tropics except for one genus found in the Old World. A single species has been reported on rare occasion from deep southern Texas. Adults are readily recognizable due to the long narrow antennae, the long narrow forewing (especially in the male), and the oval shaped hindwing that is often substantially larger than the forewing. Wing colors include yellow, white, cream, black, and red. Many adults are in mimetic complexes with various species of longwing butterflies.

54

TROPICAL MIMIC WHITE
Enantia albania

Description: 2¼ in (57 mm); sexually dimorphic; hindwing is larger than forewing (more narrow in male); above (male) yellow with reduced dark markings; forewing with squared apex (female), above (female) white with extensive dark markings on AFW apex.
Food Plants: Unknown; Fabaceae - *Inga* in Central America.
Life History: Unknown.
Range: Central America north through Mexico; Texas—rare stray to Rio Grande Valley.
Comments: Common species in parts of Mexico; flight slow, fluttering; some tropical species of genus mimic Longwings; two Texas records.

GOSSAMER WINGS—FAMILY LYCAENIDAE

Numerous species belong to this family with over 3,200 species worldwide, 127 of these in North America, and 65 of these occurring in Texas. The greatest species diversity in this family is in southeastern Asia.

Lycaenid eggs are rather short and broad, resembling small buns or discs. The larvae often produce honeydew and are tended by ants. Ants feed on the sweet honeydew and protect the larvae from predators. In some parts of the world, larvae of a few species are actually carried down into the nests where the caterpillar feeds on larvae of the host ant, but no North American lycaenid species has this type of parasitic life cycle. Larvae feed on a variety of dicotyledonous plants and usually feed on the flowers and immature fruits of these plants. Older larvae are slug-like in shape and are typically covered with tiny hairs. The head of the typical lycaenid larva is tiny and can be retracted into the body for protection or extended to bore into the tissues of green fruit of the food plant. Lycaenid chrysalids are rounded and may be found on leaves, in leaf litter, or under rocks or bark.

Adults have six walking legs, although males have fewer segments in the foot than females. The antennae are dark with conspicuous white rings. Flight is usually close to the ground and often jerky in appearance but rather rapid in actual speed. Adults usually rest with the wings held above the body. Often the hindwings move forward and backward out of synchrony so that the wings move in opposite directions. This movement and the hindwings' hair-like tails, which resemble antennae, function to draw a predator's attack to the non-vital outer wing area and away from the head.

The family Lycaenidae in the Texas fauna contains species that represent four subfamilies: Miletinae (harvesters), Lycaeninae (coppers), Theclinae (hairstreaks), and Polyommatinae (blues). The names of the latter three are rather descriptive, but some coppers are blue and others have tails similar to the hairstreaks. Some hairstreaks are blue, some are copper-colored and some lack tails. There are copper colored blues and even blues with tails. Apparently the butterflies don't read the biology books.

HARVESTERS—SUBFAMILY MILETINAE

The harvester subfamily contains only about 50 species worldwide, most of which inhabit tropical areas of Asia and Africa. A few species are known from the northern latitudes of Eurasia, and a single species is known from North America, including eastern Texas. The most unusual characteristic of the species in this subfamily is the carnivorous food habit of the larva, which feeds on aphids. Scale insects and tree hoppers are sometimes used. Larvae of harvesters have no direct relationship with ants other than avoiding predation and often hide in silken webs covered with aphid carcasses. The chrysalis has several bumps that give the impression of the face of a monkey. Adults do not feed at flowers, but do visit the honeydew secretions of aphids. The overwintering stage is believed to be the older larva.

55   A

HARVESTER
Feniseca tarquinius

Description: 1¼ in (32 mm); lacks tails above brown with orange to yellow-orange lobed patch in center of AFW; AHW brown with large orange to yellow-orange area from median to outer angle, brown spots in submarginal orange area; below orange-brown; BFW with brown oblong spots; BHW darker with small dark dots and pattern of gray irregular circles.

Food Plants: *Schizoneura, Pemphigus.* (wooly aphids).

Life History: Multivoltine.

Range: Eastern North America from southern Canada to the Gulf Coast; Texas—East, eastern half of Coastal Margin, and eastern half of Central.

Comments: Larvae are only carnivorous butterfly larvae in U.S.; unfortunately for butterfly gardeners, the harvester does not feed on all aphids; prefers shaded areas, such as swamps or riverbanks; Texas subspecies -*tarquinius*.

COPPERS—SUBFAMILY LYCAENINAE

The coppers are a small subfamily with about 50 species world-wide, most of which occur in Eurasia and North America. Of the 14 species in North America, only one has been reported from Texas. A few species of coppers occur in New Zealand, New Guinea, and tropical areas of Asia, Africa, and the Americas. Adults of most species are at least partially copper in color, although yellow, brown, blue, and gray colors also occur. Larvae of most species feed on plants in the family Polygonaceae (knotweed family). Sexual dimorphism in wing patterns is common, but only moderate differences occur between the sexes with the female being colorful but not as brightly colored as the male. Larvae of the Lycaeninae have no relationships with ants. The overwintering stage for most of the North American species is the egg (larval stage overwinters in many Old World species including two species introduced into North America). If a mating pair is disturbed, either the male or female may be the actively flying partner.

56 A

GREAT COPPER
Gaeides xanthoides

Description: 1½–1¾ in (38–44 mm,); sexually dimorphic, lacks tails; above gray-brown with very narrow dark outer margins; AFW (female) with small black spots and orange spots at tornus; AHW (male) with short row of orange-capped black outer margin spots; or AHW (female) with wavy orange marginal band surrounding black outer margin spots; below (both sexes) light gray with many small black spots; BHW with narrow orange outer margin band.

Food Plants: Polygonaceae - *Polygonum, Rumex.*

Life History: Univoltine (May–Aug); polymorphic larvae green, lime green, or magenta with orange stripes.

Range: Central and western North America; Texas—uncommon in Panhandle.

Comments: Largest of the American coppers; associated with wetland areas in prairies; Texas subspecies *dione* (Diane Copper).

HAIRSTREAKS—SUBFAMILY THECLINAE

The hairstreaks include about 2,000 species in all portions of the world with the greatest species diversity occurring in the New World tropics where about 1,000 species live. About 80 species occur in North America with 50 known from Texas. Sexual dimorphism in wing patterns is weakly expressed in these species, and the females are the more colorful sex in some species. Temperate zone hairstreaks tend to be subtly colored with gray or brown being the basic color with small red or orange spots. Tropical zone species may be brilliantly iridescent. Larvae feed on plants in a variety of families of dicotyledons. When at rest, the adults frequently move the hindwings back and forth alternately to draw attention to the fake head and antennae produced by the eyespot and hair-like tails on the hindwing.

57 A

CYCAD BUTTERFLY
Eumaeus toxea

Description: 1¾–2 in (44–51 mm); abdomen below is orange-red; above black with three rows of iridescent pale green spots along AHW margin; below black; BHW with three rows of iridescent pale green outer margin spots, large orange-red spot on outer angle.

Food Plants: Unknown; Cycadaceae - *Zamia loddingsii* in Mexico.

Life History: Unknown.

Range: South America north to northeastern Mexico; Texas—very rare stray to Rio Grande Valley.

Comments: Previously referred to as *Eumaeus minijas;* recorded Hidalgo Co. (1915).

58 A

GREAT BLUE HAIRSTREAK
Atlides halesus

> **Description:** 1½–1¾ (38–44 mm); sexually dimorphic (female noticeably larger and less iridescent than male); one long and one short tail (short tail usually absent in Texas subspecies); above iridescent blue over brown-black background; AFW (male) with oval stigma at end of cell; below purple-brown with red spots at base of wings; BHW with iridescent bands and spots of blue and light green at outer angle.
>
> **Food Plants:** Viscaceae - *Phoradendron.*
>
> **Life History:** Bivoltine (Feb–Apr, Jul–Oct); green larva with dark dorsal stripe, yellow side stripes, lightly covered with short orange hair.
>
> **Range:** Southern Mexico north to southern U.S.; Texas–East, North Central, Central, Coastal Margin, South, Southwest, Rio Grande Valley, and Big Bend.
>
> **Comments:** Long known as the "Great Purple Hairstreak," this beautiful butterfly is blue and the common name should reflect this fact; adults commonly found on white flowers; Texas subspecies *-estesi.*

59

TELEA HAIRSTREAK
Chlorostrymon telea

> **Description:** ¾ in (19 mm); above light brown with bluish highlights; below chocolate; BHW with blue, red, and white "w" shaped bands.
>
> **Food Plants:** Unknown; Meliaceae - *Swietenia* in Florida.
>
> **Life History:** Unknown.

Range: Bolivia northward to southern U.S.; Texas–stray to Rio Grande Valley.

Comments: Captive larvae known to feed on flower buds of *Albizzia*.

60

SIMAETHIS HAIRSTREAK
Chlorostrymon simaethis

Description: ¾–⅞ in (19–22 mm); above iridescent purple-brown with dark outer margins (female duller); below green with distinctive broad silver median band crossing both wings; BHW silver band forms "v" near outer angle; broad brown speckled outer margin band with narrow white wing edges.

Food Plants: Sapindaceae - *Cardiospermum halicacabum* , *C. corindum.*

Life History: Bivoltine (Apr–May, Aug–Sep); larvae varies between pale green to pale brown with short black hairs, wavy black side stripes, green-black dorsal stripe.

Range: Argentina northward through Mexico to southern U.S.; Texas–Rio Grande Valley.

Comments: May stray to Central occasionally; Texas subspecies - *sarita* (Sarita Hairstreak).

61   A

SOAPBERRY HAIRSTREAK
Phaeostrymon alcestis

Description: 1 in (25 mm); two tails of unequal length; above unmarked gray-brown except for dark spot on AHW outer angle near tails; below gray-brown with white dash at end of cell, black and white median line; BFW with narrow black submarginal line; BHW with wavy coral submarginal band, two black spots separated by a blue-gray patch at outer angle.

Food Plants: Sapindaceae - *Sapindus saponaria* var. *drummondii.*

Life History: Univoltine (Apr–Jul).

Range: South central and southwestern U.S. and adjacent Mexico; Texas–entire, except East, Rio Grande Valley, lower elevations of Trans-Pecos, or Far West.

Comments: Two subspecies in Texas -*oslari* in Davis Mountains and westward; -*alcestis* in remainder of range.

62   A

CORAL HAIRSTREAK
Harkenclenus titus

Description: 1–1¼ in (25–32 mm); sexually dimorphic; tailless; above (male) almost solid brown with pointed forewing; or above (female) paler brown with rounded forewing and yellow-orange AFW highlights and AHW outer margin spots; below gray-brown with open wavy row of small black postmedian spots; BHW with submargin row of black-tipped coral-red spots (more prominent in female).

Food Plants: Rosaceae - *Amelanchier, Prunus*.

Life History: Univoltine (Jun–Aug); hairy yellow-green larvae with pink dorsal stripe feed at night, tended by ants.

Range: Southern Canada and much of U.S., southward to Nevada and Georgia; Texas–Panhandle; northern halves of East, North Central, and High Plains; isolated population in Hill Country area of Central.

Comments: Texas subspecies -*mopsus* in northern Texas, -*watsoni* in Central.

63

BEHR'S HAIRSTREAK
Satyrium behrii

Description: 1 in (25 mm); tailless; above pale orange; AFW with broad dark gray-brown costal margin band curving along outer margin; AHW with narrow dark gray-brown inner margin and outer margin; below gray-brown with gray haze (heavier on BHW), wavy band of narrow white-edged black postmedian dashes, open band of white-capped black submarginal spots, and brown outer margin edged with fine white line; BHW with one orange-capped black spot above outer angle.

Food Plants: Rosaceae - *Cercocarpus montanus.*

Life History: Univoltine (Jul); green larvae with pale yellow or darker green stripes and marks, covered with short yellow hair.

Range: British Columbia south through higher elevation areas of western U.S.; Texas—Palo Duro Canyon in Randall Co. and Armstrong Co. in Panhandle.

Comments: Texas subspecies *-crossi* (Cross's Hairstreak).

64

EDWARDS' HAIRSTREAK
Satyrium edwardsii

Description: 1–1¼ in (25–32 mm); one tail; above gray-brown; AHW with subtle dark spot surrounded by orange-yellow; below pale gray-brown with white-ringed oblong brown dash at end of cell on both wings, uneven row of white-ringed dark brown postmedian spots and line of white-edged dark brown submarginal dashes; BHW with two large red-orange spots separated by blue patch at outer angle.

Food Plants: Fagaceae - *Quercus.*

Life History: Univoltine (Jun–Jul); young larvae eat buds and later eat young leaves; larvae tended by ants.

Range: Southern Canada, southward to Georgia and Texas; Texas—East, occasionally straying into Central.

65 A

BANDED HAIRSTREAK
Satyrium calanus

> **Description:** 1–1¼ in (25–32 mm); similar to Edward's Hairstreak (*S. edwardsii*) but less white below and less orange flanking BHW blue patch; above dark gray-brown; below lighter with dark basal areas; two rows of dark dashes with single white edge; BHW with two orange-red spots separated by large blue patch at outer angle.
>
> **Food Plants:** Fagaceae - *Castanea, Quercus;* Rosaceae - *Malus, Prunus;* Juglandaceae - *Juglans microcarpa, J. cinerea, Carya* spp.; and Aceraceae - *Acer.*
>
> **Life History:** Univoltine (May–Jun); dull yellow larvae with yellow-brown stripes on sides, broad brown dorsal stripe.
>
> **Range:** Eastern North America to Manitoba, Colorado, and Texas; Texas–East, North Central, Central, and eastern half of Coastal Margin.
>
> **Comments:** Aggressively Territorial; Texas subspecies -*falacer* (Falacer Hairstreak).

66

KING'S HAIRSTREAK
Satyrium kingi

> **Description:** 1–1¼ in (25–32 mm); two tails of unequal length; above dark gray-brown with narrow blue band; AHW (female) with two dark spots near tails; below brown with broken bands of thin white and black dashes in postmedian and submarginal areas on both wings; BHW with blue spot at outer angle flanked by black-capped orange spots.
>
> **Food Plants:** Symplocaceae - *Symplocos tinctoria.*
>
> **Life History:** Univoltine (May–Jun).

Range: Southeastern U.S.; Texas–eastern half of East and extreme eastern section of Coastal Margin.

67   A

STRIPED HAIRSTREAK
Satyrium liparops

Description: 1–1¼ in (25–32 mm); very similar to King's Hairstreak (*S. kingi*) but more extensive banding below; above gray-brown; below with more numerous broken broader bands; BHW with small black-capped orange spots flanking blue patch at outer angle near tail.

Food Plants: Juglandaceae - *Carya*; Betulaceae - *Betula, Carpinus*; Fagaceae - *Castanea, Quercus*; Rosaceae - *Crataegus, Malus, Prunus, Rubus*; Oleaceae - *Fraxinus*.

Life History: Univoltine (Jul–Aug); grass-green larvae with yellow stripes.

Range: Eastern North America, Canada to Gulf Coast; Texas– East, eastern half of Coastal Margin.

Comments: Found in various habitats including deciduous forest, wooded areas around prairie stream, and foothill canyons; despite the wide variety of acceptable food plants and habitats, this butterfly is not common; Texas subspecies -*strigosum*.

68

BLACK HAIRSTREAK
Ocaria ocrisia

Description: 1 in (25 mm); sexually dimorphic; above (male) black and dark iridescent blue; or above (female) brown or brown with blue patch; below mottled brown with lines of darker dashes.

Food Plants: Unknown.

Life History: Unknown.

Range: South America northward to central Mexico; Texas–very rare stray to Rio Grande Valley.
Comments: Single specimen from Texas in 1968 following Hurricane Beulah.

69 A

CLYTIE HAIRSTREAK
Ministrymon clytie

Description: ¾–⅞ in (19–22 mm); one tail; above pale blue and brown; AFW brown with large pale blue patch on inner margin (female darker blue with dark AHW margin); below pale gray with red dashes and broken red postmedian band; BHW with two orange-capped black spots separated by blue patch at outer angle.
Food Plants: Fabaceae - *Prosopis reptans*.
Life History: Multivoltine.
Range: Southern Mexico northward to Texas and Arizona; Texas– Rio Grande Valley, strays northward to Central.
Comments: Spring brood darker than summer.

70

LEDA HAIRSTREAK
Ministrymon leda

Description: ¾–⅞ in (19–22 mm); similar to Clytie Hairstreak (*M. clytie*) but darker with more brown above than blue and below with less red-orange; two tails of unequal length; seasonally dimorphic: darker fall (sometimes spring) form with gray abdomen without red-orange below, summer form with red-orange abdomen and red-orange lines below; above gray-brown with large blue area on lower half of AHW and small black spots at outer angle; below gray speckled with brown, fine black-edged red-orange postmedian lines, and fine black-edged outer margin;

BHW with two orange-capped black spots near outer angle (may have blue patch between).

Food Plants: Fabaceae - *Prosopis glandulosa* var. *torreyana*.

Life History: Bivoltine (May–Jul, Sep–Oct); light green larvae with pale yellow marks, short brown hair.

Range: Southwestern U.S. south into Mexico; Texas–Trans-Pecos, isolated records in Rio Grande Valley.

Comments: Some workers recognize several forms but do not consider them seasonal variations as they occasionally appear together.

71

AZIA HAIRSTREAK
Ministrymon azia

Description: ½–¾ in (13–19 mm); above solid brown (male) or brown with extensive white AHW patch (female); below gray with red-orange dashes almost continuous postmedian band; BHW with black-capped orange spots at outer angle.

Food Plants: Fabaceae - *Mimosa malacophylla*.

Life History: Unknown; multivoltine in tropics; larvae feed on flower buds and do not make nest.

Range: South America to extreme southern U.S.; Texas–Rio Grande Valley, occasional stray northward.

Comments: Formerly named *Tmolus azia*, was considered related to Echion Hairstreak (*T. echion*), recorded (Mar–Sep).

72

ECHION HAIRSTREAK
Tmolus echion

Description: 1–1¼ in (25–32 mm); similar to Clytie Hairstreak (*Ministrymon clytie*) but larger and deeper colored; two tails of unequal length; above brown with extensive AFW iridescent blue basal area; AHW with iridescent blue in center; below gray with broken lines of red-orange dashes enlarged into spots (one line on BFW, two lines on BHW); BHW with two orange-capped black spots at outer angle.

Food Plants: Verbenaceae - *Lantana camara;* also Acanthaceae - *Aphelandra;* Anacardiaceae - *Mangifera,* Malpighiaceae - *Stigmaphyllon* in tropics.

Life History: Multivoltine in tropics.

Range: South America to southern U.S., Hawaii; Texas—rare stray to Rio Grande Valley.

Comments: Introduced into Hawaii in 1902 to control *Lantana,* larvae now also feed on solanaceae (potato, eggplant, peppers); Texas subspecies *-echiolus* (Larger Lantana Butterfly).

73

TEPHRAEUS HAIRSTREAK
Siderus tephraeus

Description: 1 in (25 mm); above iridescent blue (male) or dull blue (female), AFW with black apex; below pale gray with lighter colored streaks.

Food Plants: Unknown.

Life History: Unknown; multivoltine in Mexico.

Range: Brazil to extreme southern U.S.; Texas—rare stray to Rio Grande Valley.

Comments: Recorded (Nov).

74

AQUAMARINE HAIRSTREAK
Oenomaus ortygnus

Description: 1¼ in (32 mm); two tails of unequal length; above intense iridescent green-blue (male) or duller blue (female); below pale gray-rose with few scattered black marks; BHW with iridescent blue-gray area and small black patches near tails.

Food Plants: Unknown; Annonaceae - *Annona globifolia* in Mexico.
Life History: Unknown; larvae bore into fruits.
Range: South America northward to West Indies and extreme southern U.S.; Texas–very rare stray to Rio Grande Valley.
Comments: Two specimens, Brownsville, Cameron Co., (Dec. 1962).

75

MARIUS HAIRSTREAK
Rekoa marius

Description: 1–1½ in (25–32 mm); one tail and short projection; above gray and intense blue (male) or whitish (female); below gray with single continuous dashed line; BHW with orange and blue-black spots at outer angle.
Food Plants: Unknown; Fabaceae - *Andira* in Panama.
Life History: Unknown.
Range: Northern South America to extreme southern U.S.; Texas– very rare stray to Rio Grande Valley.
Comments: Formerly referred to as *Thereus zebina*; two females collected in Rio Grande Valley (1950).

76

PALEGON HAIRSTREAK
Rekoa palegon

Description: 1–1¼ in (25–32 mm); one tail; above gray-blue and bright blue (male) or light brown and gray-blue (female); below gray with yellow-brown dashes, spots, and marginal band on both wings.
Food Plants: Unknown; Asteraceae, Solanaceae, Verbenaceae in tropics.
Life History: Unknown.

Range: South America to extreme southern U.S.; Texas–very rare
stray to Rio Grande Valley.

Comments: Formerly placed in genus *Thereus*; single specimen
from Rio Grande Valley in 1968 after Hurricane Beulah.

77

BLUE-METAL HAIRSTREAK
Allosmaitia pion

Description: 1 in (25 mm); one tail; above gray-brown and iridescent blue (male) or blue-gray (female); male scent patch on AFW;
below gray-brown with smudged postmedian dark brown line
on both wings; BHW with orange spot, blue spot, and black spot
at outer angle.

Food Plants: Unknown.

Life History: Unknown.

Range: Central America to extreme southern U.S.; Texas–very rare
stray to Rio Grande Valley.

Comments: Single worn specimen from Rio Grande Valley (1968)
after Hurricane Beulah; called *Allosmaitia strophius* by some
workers.

78   A

RED-BANDED HAIRSTREAK
Calycopis cecrops

Description: 1 in (25 mm); two tails of unequal length; above dark
gray-brown with iridescent blue-gray AHW patches (more extensive in female); below gray-brown with thin red costal margin
and bright red band edged with black and white becoming
jagged on bottom half of BHW; smudged black spots flanking
one gray spot at outer angle.

Food Plants: Anacardiaceae - *Rhus copallina, R. aromatica*; Myri-
caceae - *Myrica cerifera*; Euphorbiaceae - *Crotonopsis linearis*.

Life History: Multivoltine; eggs laid among leaf litter; dull yellow larvae covered with brown hair, dark green dorsal stripe.

Range: Southeastern U.S.; Texas–East, eastern half of Coastal Margin.

Comments: Closely related to Dusky-Blue Hairstreak (*C. isobeon*).

79 A

DUSKY-BLUE HAIRSTREAK
Calycopis isobeon

Description: ¾–⅞ in (19–22 mm); similar to Red-Banded Hairstreak (*C. cecrops*) but more red below; two tails of unequal length; above dark gray-brown with blue AHW patches (more extensive in female); below gray-brown with thin red BFW costal margin and bright red band edged with black and white (red bleeds past line on BHW); BHW with red spots flanking gray spot at outer angle.

Food Plants: Unknown; larvae will eat detritus (dead leaves and insects), even bread crumbs in lab.

Life History: Multivoltine (Mar–Nov).

Range: Panama to southern U.S.; Texas–Rio Grande Valley, southern half of South; migrant northward.

Comments: Occasionally migrates to Kansas; closely related to Red-banded Hairstreak (*C. cecrops*).

80

MISERABILIS HAIRSTREAK
Cyanophrys miserabilis

Description: ¾–1 in (19–25 mm); sexually dimorphic; one tail; above (male) iridescent blue with brown AHW costal and inner margins; or above (female) brown with blue-gray basal areas; below light green speckled with rust and thin rust outer margin; BFW with gray inner margin and dark rust apical spot; BHW with open band of white postmedian dashes and dark rust spots at outer angle.

Food Plants: Fabaceae - *Parkinsonia aculeata.*

Life History: Multivoltine (May–Dec).

Range: Costa Rica to southern Texas; Texas–Rio Grande Valley, strays northward.

Comments: Previously called *Strymon pastor*; common in Rio Grande Valley.

81

GOODSON'S HAIRSTREAK
Cyanophrys goodsoni

Description: ¾–1 in (19–25 mm); similar to Miserabilis Hairstreak (*C. miserabilis*) but lacks tails, more brown above, and more yellow than green below; sexually dimorphic; above (male) dark gray-brown with silver-blue highlights; or above (female) mostly dark gray-brown with lavender basal areas; below yellow-green speckled with rust and fine rust outer margins; BFW with gray inner margin; BHW with small rust-capped white postmedian spots and one dark rust spot at outer angle.

Food Plants: Phytolaccaceae - *Rivina humilis.*

Life History: Multivoltine (Jun–Nov).

Range: Costa Rica to extreme southern U.S.; Texas–Rio Grande Valley.

Comments: Previously called *Strymon facuna.*

82

TROPICAL GREEN HAIRSTREAK
Cyanophrys herodotus

Description: 1 in (25 mm); similar to Miserabilis Hairstreak (*C. miserabilis*) but deeper colored with one spot at BHW outer angle and one short tail; above (male) iridescent blue; or above (female) gray-blue; below dull green with brown-gray background.

Food Plants: Unknown; Verbenaceae - *Clerodendron, Lantana;* Anacardiaceae - *Lithraea, Schinus, Mangifera;* Asteraceae - *Mikania* in tropics.

Life History: Unknown; multivoltine in Mexico.

Range: Mexico and extreme southern U.S.; Texas–very rare stray to Rio Grande Valley.

Comments: Three Texas specimens, Hidalgo Co. (1972, 1975), possible resident; recently recorded from Big Bend National Park area, Brewster Co.

83 A

JUNIPER HAIRSTREAK
Mitoura siva

Description: 1–1⅛ in (25–28 mm); two tails of unequal length; above dark gray-brown with varying number of rust spots; AHW with rust spots at outer angle; below bright olive-green with orange haze on outer half of BFW and white postmedian line becomes irregular and rust-edged on BHW; BHW with small black submarginal spots at outer angle.

Food Plants: Cupressaceae - *Cupressus, Juniperus.*

Life History: Bivoltine (Jun–Jul); bumpy green larva with irregular yellow marks.

Range: Higher elevation areas of western central North America from Alberta to northern Mexico; Texas–Far West, restricted to montane areas.

Comments: Texas subspecies *-siva.*

84 A

OLIVE HAIRSTREAK
Mitoura grynea

Description: 1 in (25 mm); similar to Juniper Hairstreak (*M. siva*) but more white below; one tail and short projection; above dark brown with variable amounts of yellow-orange from postbasal to submarginal area; below bright olive-green speckled with rust, postmedian white band edged with rust; BFW with thin rust costal margin and thin rust-capped white outer margin dashes; BHW with scattered white median marks, postmedian band more irregular than band on BFW, and small submarginal black spots on blue-gray area near tails.

Food Plants: Cupressaceae - *Juniperus virginiana, J. ashei.*

Life History: Multivoltine (Mar–Sep).

Range: Eastern U.S.; Texas—entire except Panhandle, High Plains, Far West, South, and Rio Grande Valley.

Comments: Texas subspecies *-grynea* in area east of Balcones Escarpment is darker; *-smilacis* in west Texas is paler; some consider these subspecies as full species, still others combine these two forms and Juniper Hairstreak (*M. siva*) as a single species.

85

XAMI HAIRSTREAK
Xamia xami

Description: ¾–1 in (19–25 mm); similar to Juniper Hairstreak (*Mitoura siva*) but BHW postmedian band forms "W" near tails; one tail and short projection; above pale yellow-brown with brown costal and outer margins (female darker); male with brown stigma at end of AFW cell; below pale olive-brown with white postmedian band forming "W" near tails; small black dots on gray area between "W" mark and tails.

Food Plants: Crassulaceae - *Echeveria, Sedum.*

Life History: Multivoltine (Jun–Dec); light green larvae with red-brown marks burrow into succulent leaves of food plant.

Range: Southern Mexico to southwestern U.S.; Texas—Rio Grande Valley, South, Southern Coastal Margin, and Big Bend; strays to Central.

Comments: Texas subspecies *-texami.*

86

SANDIA HAIRSTREAK
Sandia mcfarlandi

Description: 1–1¼ in (25–32 mm); similar to Xami Hairstreak (*Xamia xami*) but without tails, deeper colored with reduced darker outer margins above, and BHW postmedian line not a distinct "W"; above dull yellow with brown margins (female may be more red-brown); male with oblong stigma on AFW; below pale green with thin black-edged white postmedian line; BHW with white outer margin and a few hazy black spots near outer angle.

Food Plants: Liliaceae - *Nolina texana*.

Life History: Univoltine (Apr–May); polymorphic larvae varying between pink, maroon, or green feed on flower heads and immature fruit.

Range: Mexico north through New Mexico and western Texas; Texas–Far West, Trans-Pecos, and Big Bend.

Comments: Texas subspecies *-mcfarlandi*.

87 A

FROSTED ELFIN
Incisalia irus

Description: ⅞–1 in (22–25 mm); several short hindwing projections; above (male) gray-brown; or above (female) orange-brown; below similar but speckled with gray, irregular fine brown-edged white postmedian band (darker edged on BHW), and checkered outer margins.

Food Plants: Fabaceae - *Baptisia, Crotalaria, Lupinus*.

Life History: Univoltine (Apr–May); lime-green larvae feeds on flowers and fruits.

Range: Eastern U.S.; Texas–East and eastern third of Coastal Margin.

Comments: Texas subspecies *-hadra* (Hadros Elfin) found only in Arkansas, Louisiana, and Texas.

88 A

HENRY'S ELFIN
Incisalia henrici

> **Description:** 1 in (25 mm); one tail and short projection; above gray-brown with orange-brown highlights (more extensive in female); below brown base paler lighter brown and gray; BFW with thin white postmedian band; BHW with irregular white postmedian band between distinct pale and dark areas.
>
> **Food Plants:** Ebenaceae - *Disopyros texana*; Rosaceae - *Prunus*; Fabaceae - *Cercis, Sophora*; Ericaceae - *Vaccinium*; Caprifoliaceae - *Viburnum*.
>
> **Life History:** Univoltine (Mar–Apr); red to olive-green larvae with light dashes on sides.
>
> **Range:** Eastern North America; Texas–East, eastern half of North Central, Central, eastern half of Coastal Margin, montane areas of Far West and Big Bend.
>
> **Comments:** Texas subspecies -*solata* in central and western Texas; -*turneri* in eastern areas.

89 A

EASTERN PINE ELFIN
Incisalia niphon

> **Description:** 1–1¼ in (25–32 mm); without tails; above (male) gray-brown; or above (female) yellow-brown; below brown speckled with gray on basal area, white-edged dark brown bands and bars, dark brown submarginal band of chevrons, and slightly scalloped dark brown checkered outer margins.
>
> **Food Plants:** Pinaceae - *Pinus taeda*; Cupressaceae - *Juniperus virginiana*.
>
> **Life History:** Univoltine (Mar–Apr).

Range: Southern Canada and eastern U.S.; Texas—East, eastern third of Coastal Margin.

Comments: Texas subspecies -*niphon.*

90

JADA HAIRSTREAK
Arawacus jada

Description: 1–1¼ in (25–32 mm); one tail and enlarged hindwing outer angle; above shiny blue with brown costal margins, broad brown apical patch, and brown outer margins; below cream with mustard-brown striping; BHW with orange on tail and enlarged outer angle.

Food Plants: Unknown; Solanaceae - *Solanum umbellatum* in Mexico.

Life History: Unknown; multivoltine in Mexico.

Range: Central America to extreme southern U.S.; Texas—rare stray to Rio Grande Valley.

Comments: Only hairstreak in Texas that is cream colored below.

91 A

NORTHERN HAIRSTREAK
Fixsenia ontario

Description: 1–1¼ in (25–32 mm); two tails of unequal length; above dark gray-brown with yellow patches; below lavender-brown with thin wavy white and brown postmedian band forming "W" near BHW outer angle; BHW with black submarginal band before orange-capped black spots flanking a blue outer angle patch.

Food Plants: Fagaceae - *Quercus virginiana, Q. fusiformis, Q. laurifolia.*

Life History: Univoltine (Apr–May).

Range: Eastern North America; Texas—East, Central, Southwest, eastern half of Coastal Margin, and northern area in Trans-Pecos.

Comments: Some workers include this butterfly as part of the Southern Hairstreak (*Fixsenia favonius*); Texas subspecies - *autolycus* (Autolycus Hairstreak) in eastern, central, and southern Texas, -*ilavia* (Ilavia Hairstreak) in west Texas.

92

POLING'S HAIRSTREAK
Fixsenia polingi

Description: 1 in (25 mm); one tail; above brown with subtle hindwing outer marginal spots; below lighter brown with white-edged black postmedian line forming small "W" on hindwing near tail; BHW with two small orange-capped black spots flanking a blue patch.

Food Plants: Fagaceae - *Quercus grisea, Q. emoryi*.

Life History: Bivoltine (May–Jun, Aug–Sep).

Range: Texas–Davis Mountains in Trans-Pecos, Chisos Mountains in Big Bend, and Franklin Mountains in Far West.

Comments: Texas subspecies -*polingi*.

93   A

WHITE-M HAIRSTREAK
Parrhasius m-album

Description: 1¼–1½ in (32–38 mm); two tails of unequal length; above deep iridescent blue with wide dark brown margins; below light brown with thin white dashes and postmedian line forming a black edged "M" near outer angle; BHW with thin hazy white submarginal line, prominent red spot at shorter tail, and black patch near enlarged outer angle.

Food Plants: Fagaceae - *Quercus virginiana, Q. marilandica*.

Life History: Multivoltine (Feb–Oct); hairy, pale green larvae with dark green dorsal stripe, slanted side bars.

Range: South America to eastern U.S.; Texas—East; eastern halves of North Central, Central, and Coastal Margin.

Comments: Striking butterfly that appears to be a small Great Blue Hairstreak (*Atlides halesus*) from above.

94 A

GRAY HAIRSTREAK
Strymon melinus

Description: 1–1¼ in (25–32 mm); one tail; above dark gray-brown with distinctive orange patch near eye spot on hindwing; below gray with white-edged black postmedian line and thin dark gray outer margins; BHW with submarginal line of black dashes and two orange spots near tail.

Food Plants: Fabaceae - *Lespedeza hirta, Lupinus texensis, Sesbania drummondii*; Zygophyllaceae - *Guaiacum angustfolia*; Malvaceae - *Gossypium*; Ebenaceae - *Diospyros texana*; Verbenaceae - *Lantana macropoda*; Bignoniaceae - *Tecoma stans*. Approximately 50 different food plants from more than 20 families have been recorded.

Life History: Multivoltine (Apr–Oct); polymorphic larva varying between deep green to light green with slanted side bars varying between white to mauve; commonly seen in backyard bean patches on which eggs are laid.

Range: Southern Canada, entire U.S., Mexico; Texas—entire.

Comments: Larva known as Cotton Square Borer when feeding on cotton; Texas subspecies -*franki* (Frank's Common Hairstreak).

95

REDDISH HAIRSTREAK
Strymon rufofuscus

Description: ⅞–1 in (22–25 mm); one tail; above tan with small red-capped black eye spot near tail; female darker with additional row of outer margin dots on AHW; below light gray-tan with row of white-capped red postmedian crescents and thin rust outer margins; BHW with orange-capped black spot near tail and larger black spot at outer angle.

Food Plants: Unknown; Malvaceae - *Malvastrum coromandelianum* in Mexico.

Life History: Multivoltine (Mar–Dec).

Range: South America to West Indies and extreme southern U.S.; Texas–Rio Grande Valley.

96

MEXICAN GRAY HAIRSTREAK
Strymon bebrycia

Description: 1 in (25 mm); one tail; above gray with dark gray outer margin spots and small red spot near tail (female darker above with hazy blue areas); below light gray with white-edged red postmedian line becoming jagged on hindwing and thin red outer margins; BHW with two orange-capped black spots near tail and outer angle.

Food Plants: Sapindaceae - *Cardiospermum halicacabum*; Rosaceae - *Prunus havardii*.

Life History: Multivoltine (all year in Rio Grande Valley; Mar-Sep in Big Bend).

Range: Northern Mexico and extreme southern U.S.; Texas–stray to Rio Grande Valley, Trans-Pecos.

97

YOJOA HAIRSTREAK
Strymon yojoa

Description: 1–1⅛ in (25–28 mm); one tail; above dark gray-brown with darker spots on hindwing margin; below light gray-brown with white-edged brown postmedian line becoming jagged on hindwing separating hazy white bands; BHW with orange-capped black spots at tail and outer angle.

Food Plants: Unknown; Malvaceae - *Hibiscus tubiflorus;* Fabaceae - *Desmodium axillare;* Gesneriaceae - *Kohleria tubiflora* in Central America, possibly uses these non-native ornamentals in Texas.

Life History: Multivoltine; larvae eat flowers and fruits.

Range: Central America to extreme southern U.S.; Texas–Rio Grande Valley.

Comments: Apparent resident in Rio Grande Valley.

98   A

WHITE HAIRSTREAK
Strymon albatus

Description: ⅞–1 in (22–25 mm); one tail; above white; AFW with dark gray-brown costal margin, apex, and outer margin; AHW with several small dark eye spots at outer angle; below gray-brown and white separated by jagged brown postmedian line and submarginal bands of hazy brown crescents; BHW with two dull orange and black spots near tail.

Food Plants: Unknown; Malvaceae - *Abutilon incanum* in Mexico.

Life History: Unknown; multivoltine in Mexico.

Range: Guatemala and Mexico; Texas–stray to Rio Grande Valley.

Comments: First record after Hurricane Beulah (1968), may periodically establish populations; Texas subspecies *-sedecia.*

99

LACEY'S HAIRSTREAK
Strymon alea

Description: ⅞ in (22 mm); seasonally dimorphic; one tail; above dark gray with dark spots near tail (summer form with paler hindwing, winter form pale only near spots); below gray with thin black and white postmedian line (summer form with red-

edged postmedian line); BHW with orange-capped black spot
near tail (winter form pale outside of postmedian line).

Food Plants: Euphorbiaceae - *Bernardia myricaefolia.*

Life History: Multivoltine in Rio Grande Valley, less common in
Central.

Range: Southern Mexico to extreme southern U.S.; Texas–Rio
Grande Valley, Southwest, and Central.

Comments: Summer form previously named *S. laceyi* after H. G.
Lacey, an early Texas naturalist.

100 A

COLUMELLA HAIRSTREAK
Strymon columella

Description: ⅞–1 in (22–25 mm); one tail; above gray-brown; male
with dark stigma on AFW; AHW with dark spots near tail; female
with pale blue AHW wedge on inner margin; below pale gray-
brown with incomplete postmedian line of white-edged dark
brown dashes and hazy bands of pale gray and brown crescents
between postmedian line and outer margins; BHW with orange-
capped black spot near tail.

Food Plants: Malvaceae - *Abutilon, Hibiscus, Sida.*

Life History: Multivoltine (all year); dark green larvae covered with
pale brown hair, dark dorsal stripe covered.

Range: Brazil to West Indies and extreme southern U.S.; Texas–
Rio Grande Valley; occasionally strays northward.

Comments: Texas specimens often lack orange cap on BHW eyespot while Florida specimens consistently have orange cap;
Texas subspecies -*istapa.*

101

CESTRI HAIRSTREAK
Strymon cestri

Description: ¾–1 in (19–25 mm); sexually dimorphic; tailless; above (male) gray-brown with dark stigma on AFW; or above (female) with pale blue haze restricted on AFW to inner half, almost entire AHW; with several small dark AHW marginal spots (obscure on male, distinct on female); below paler brown with pale gray outer margins; BHW mottled with bands of brown and pale gray spots and one small black spot near outer angle.

Food Plants: Unknown.

Life History: Multivoltine (Mar–Oct).

Range: Central America to extreme southern U.S.; Texas–Rio Grande Valley, southern area of South.

Comments: Uncommon; recorded in different months in different years.

102

BAZOCHII HAIRSTREAK
Strymon bazochii

Description: ⅞–1 in (22–25 mm); similar to Cestri Hairstreak (*S. cestri*) but more blue above and less distinct mottling below with faint white streaks; tailless; above dark gray-brown; male with dark stigma on AFW; AHW pale blue-gray with dark costal margin and row of dark marginal dots; below pale gray mottled with pale brown and white streaks.

Food Plants: Verbenaceae - *Lantana camara*, *Lippia alba*, *L. graveolens*.

Life History: Multivoltine (Feb–Dec).

Range: Brazil to West Indies and Mexico to extreme southern U.S.; Texas–Rio Grande Valley.

Comments: Introduced into Hawaii (known as Smaller Lantana Butterfly) to control introduced *Lantana*.

103

SERAPIO HAIRSTREAK
Strymon serapio

Description: 1 in (25 mm); above gray-brown with narrow blue streaks; below gray-brown with faint brown mottling.
Food Plants: Unknown.
Life History: Unknown.
Range: Panama to Mexico and extreme southern U.S.; Texas–Big Bend.
Comments: Recent records from Big Bend National Park, Brewster Co. (Apr).

104

ARIZONA HAIRSTREAK
Erora quaderna

Description: ¾–1 in (19–25 mm); tailless; above brown with pale blue patches from base outward (female with more violet-blue and dark brown restricted to apex and outer margins) and narrow cream fringes; below turquoise speckled with gray and open rows of small orange spots.
Food Plants: Fagaceae - *Quercus emoryi*.
Life History: Multivoltine.
Range: Guatemala to southwestern U.S.; Texas–Big Bend.
Comments: Prefers higher altitudes; Texas subspecies *-sanfordi* (Sanford's Hairstreak).

105

ENDYMION HAIRSTREAK
Electrostrymon endymion

Description: ¾–1 in (19–25 mm); two tails of unequal length; above yellow-orange with brown base, brown AFW costal margin, and outer margins of both wings; below gray-brown; BFW with faint postmedian and submarginal lines; BHW with wavy black and white-edged red postmedian band and blue patch at outer angle flanked by red-capped black spots.

Food Plants: Unknown, possibly Anacardiaceae.

Life History: Unknown.

Range: Brazil to extreme southern U.S.; Texas–Rio Grande Valley.

Comments: May be resident in Rio Grande Valley; Texas subspecies -*cyphara* (Ruddy Hairstreak).

106

MUTED HAIRSTREAK
Electrostrymon canus

Description: 1–1¼ in (25–32 mm); similar to Endymion Hairstreak (*E. endymion*) except that male above is pale orange-brown; female is difficult to separate from female Endymion Hairstreak.

Food Plants: Unknown; Anacardiaceae - *Mangifera indica* in South America.

Life History: Unknown.

Range: Peru to extreme southern U.S.; Texas–Rio Grande Valley.

Comments: Only recently recognized as separate from Endymion Hairstreak (*E. endymion.*)

BLUES—SUBFAMILY POLYOMMATINAE

Approximately 1,000 species are included in this subfamily with 32 of these in North America and 13 of these occurring in Texas. This subfamily includes the smallest butterfly in the world, the Pygmy Blue (*Brephidion exile*), which also occurs in Texas. Sexual dimorphism is often very striking with the male being shiny blue and the female brown. Eggs are laid singly on food plants from a number of families, but Fabaceae (legume family) is most commonly used. Larvae secrete a sugary liquid to attract ants. Some larvae are raised in ant nests. Overwintering is usually accomplished by the larva or the pupa, but a few species overwinter in the egg stage. Adults of all species visit flowers and most fly low around the larval foodplant. Hindwing rubbing is common and a few species are migratory, including the Pygmy Blue. The male is usually the flying partner of a disturbed mating pair.

107   A

PYGMY BLUE
Brephidium exile

> **Description:** ½–¾ in (13–19 mm); above golden brown to gray-brown with blue base area and thin white fringes (larger female with less blue); below gray-brown deepening to golden brown past rows of broken white postmedian dashes; BHW with row of black submedian oblongs and black outer margin spots.
>
> **Food Plants:** Chenopodiaceae - *Chenopodium album, Atriplex, Salicornia.*
>
> **Life History:** Multivoltine (all year in Rio Grande Valley); larvae varying between pale green to cream dotted with tiny brown bumps, yellow stripes on sides and back.
>
> **Range:** Venezuela to southern U.S.; Texas—entire, more common in South and Coastal Texas; strong annual migrant northward.
>
> **Comments:** Considered to be the smallest butterfly in the world; often common in saline habitats (especially Coastal Margin and Trans-Pecos).

108 A

EASTERN PYGMY BLUE
Brephidium isophthalma

Description: ½–1 in (13–25 mm); similar to Pygmy Blue (*B. exile*), but less blue or lacking blue above, darker fringes and below lacks pale base area (female may be red-brown).
Food Plants: Chenopodiaceae - *Salicornia*; Batidaceae - *Batis*.
Life History: Unknown; multivoltine outside of Texas.
Range: West Indies and southeastern U.S.; Texas–rare in extreme eastern Coastal Margin.
Comments: Apparently a stray in Coastal Margin, dispersing from resident range in eastern Louisiana; some workers think the stray Eastern Pygmy Blues recorded in Texas are variations of the Pygmy Blue (*B. exile*); Texas subspecies -*pseudofea*.

109

CASSIUS BLUE
Leptotes cassius

Description: ½–¾ in (13–19 mm); wings somewhat translucent; sexually dimorphic; above (male) pale blue striated with pale lavender, thin black outer margins; or above (female) white with pale blue bases, dark brown AFW costal margin and outer margin, AHW striated with pale brown and black outer margin spots; below white with extensive mottling of narrow brown lines and scallops; BHW with row of brown marginal spots before two prominent pale yellow-ringed black spots at outer angle.
Food Plants: Fabaceae - *Phaseolus vulgaris*; Malpighiaceae - *Malpighia glabra*.
Life History: Multivoltine (all year in Rio Grande Valley).

Range: Argentina to West Indies and southern U.S.; Texas–Rio Grande Valley, Southwest, South, and southern half of Coastal Margin; strays northward.

Comments: Texas subspecies -*striata* (Striated Blue).

110 A

MARINE BLUE
Leptotes marina

Description: ¾–1 in (19–25 mm); similar to Cassius Blue (*L. cassius*) but more purple above and more extensive mottling below; sexually dimorphic; above (male) lavender-blue, darker on basal area; or above (female) dull lavender with broad brown on AFW costal and outer margins; below off white extensively mottled with pale brown bars and scallops; BHW with two yellow-ringed black spots at outer angle.

Food Plants: Fabaceae - *Acacia, Amorpha, Dalea, Lathyrus, Lotus, Phaseolus, Prosopis, Wisteria.*

Life History: Multivoltine (Feb–Nov); polymorphic larvae varying between deep green to deep brown.

Range: Central America to central U.S.; Texas–entire, more common in southern and coastal Texas.

Comments: Regularly disperses and breeds in Kansas and Nebraska but cannot overwinter in these latitudes.

111

CYNA BLUE
Zizula cyna

Description: ⅝–¾ in (19–25 mm); slender forewing and shorter rounded hindwing; above pale lilac-blue with hazy gray-brown outer margins; below light gray speckled with small dark gray spots.

Food Plants: Unknown.

Life History: Bivoltine (Mar–Sep).

Range: Northern South America to southwestern U.S.; Texas—Big Bend, southern third of Trans-Pecos, Southwest, South, Rio Grande Valley, and southern half of Coastal Margin; straying northward.

Comments: Formerly thought to represent an introduced population of the African butterfly *Z. gaika.*

112 A

CERAUNUS BLUE
Hemiargus ceraunus

Description: ¾–1 in (19–25 mm); sexually dimorphic; above (male) lavender-blue with narrow dark brown outer margins; or above (female) deep gray-brown with blue highlights; both sexes with white fringes; AHW with vague dark spot at outer angle; below pale gray-brown with rows of white crescents; BHW with several small black spots at outer angle.

Food Plants: Fabaceae - *Acacia angustissima, Rhynchosia minima, Medicago, Prosopis, Senna.*

Life History: Multivoltine; polymorphic larvae varying from green to yellow or red with short hairs.

Range: Central America to West Indies and southern U.S.; Texas—Rio Grande Valley, southern halves of South and Coastal Margin; straying northward.

Comments: Texas subspecies *-zachaeina* (Zachaeina Blue).

113 A

REAKIRT'S BLUE
Hemiargus isola

Description: 1–1⅛ in (25–28 mm); similar to Ceraunus Blue (*H. ceraunus*) but brighter above with darker margins and additional black spots on BFW; below light gray-brown with hazy white submarginal bands; BFW with white-edged black cell bar and row of white-ringed black postmedian oblong spots; BHW with several small scattered white-ringed dark brown spots and two black spots at outer angle.

Food Plants: Fabaceae - *Acacia angustissima, A. roemeriana, Dalea pogonathera, Indigofera lindheimeriana, I. miniata* var. *leptosepala, Melilotus indicus, Prosopis glandulosa, Desmanthus, Medicago, Mimosa, Trifolium.*

Life History: Multivoltine; larvae feed on flowers and fruits.

Range: Central America to Canada; Texas—entire but resident only in Far West, Trans-Pecos, Southwest, South, Rio Grande Valley, and southern half of Coastal Margin.

Comments: Records north of Texas (to southern Canada) represent migrating individuals and reproducing populations that do not survive winter; Texas subspecies *-alce.*

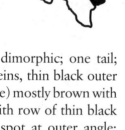

114   A

EASTERN TAILED BLUE
Everes comyntas

Description: ⅞–1 in (22–25 mm); sexually dimorphic; one tail; above (male) bright blue with fine silver veins, thin black outer margins, and white fringes; or above (female) mostly brown with blue base area and white fringes; AHW with row of thin black margin dashes and orange-capped black spot at outer angle; below (male) pale gray or (female) pale brown with scattered black dots, dark cell bar on both wings, irregular row of black postmedian dots, and two close rows of dark outer margin markings; BHW with two orange-capped black spots (larger orange caps on female) near tail.

Food Plants: Fabaceae - *Astragalus, Baptisia, Desmodium, Lathyrus, Lespedeza, Lotus, Lupinus, Phaseolus, Medicago, Melilotus, Trifolium, Vicia.*

Life History: Multivoltine (all year in eastern half of Coastal Margin).

Range: Eastern North America, isolated populations in West; Texas—East; eastern halves of North Central, Central, and Coastal Margin; northern area in Trans-Pecos.

Comments: Texas subspecies -*texanus* (Texas Tailed Blue).

115   A

SPRING AZURE
Celastrina argiolus

Description: 1–1¼ in (25–32 mm); seasonally and sexually dimorphic; above spring form silvery blue (male) or silvery blue with mostly black forewing and black hindwing outer margin (female); below spring form slate gray with variable dark brown spots, large dark brown hindwing median patch, and broad brown outer margins (paler on BFW); above summer form pale violet-blue with pale blue AFW base area and paler AHW (male) or very pale blue with black margins (female); below summer form white with faint pale brown markings.

Food Plants: Fagaceae, Rosaceae, Fabaceae, Aceraceae, Rhamnaceae, Aquifoliaceae, and Asteraceae.

Life History: Multivoltine; larvae variable from lime green, cream, or pink; flowers and buds eaten.

Range: North Africa, Eurasia, North America; Texas—East; eastern halves of North Central, Central, and Coastal Margin; and Big Bend.

Comments: Texas subspecies -*cinerea* in Chisos Mountains; -*gozora* in central Texas; -*ladon* in eastern Texas; some workers restrict *C. argiolus* to Old World populations and use *C. ladon* as name of this species.

116

RITA BLUE
Euphilotes rita

Description: ⅞–1 in (19–25 mm); sexually dimorphic; above (male) light blue with brown-gray outer margins, small outer margin

AHW spots, and occasionally short orange submarginal band; or above (female) brown, spotted with small black dots, large AHW yellow-orange submarginal band above black outer margin spots; below gray-white with dark gray spots; BHW with orange submarginal band and black marginal dots.

Food Plants: Polygonaceae - *Eriogonum* .

Life History: Univoltine (Jun–Sep).

Range: Northern Mexico and southwestern U.S.; Texas–Big Bend.

Comments: Texas subspecies -*rita*.

117   A

SILVERY BLUE
Glaucopsyche lygdamus

Description: 1–1¼ in (25–32 mm); sexually dimorphic; above (male) silver-blue with thin black outer margins, white AHW inner margin, white fringes; or above (female) dark brown with restricted blue basal area, pale gray AHW inner margin, white fringes; below pale gray with white-ringed black spots forming curved postmedian band and thin brown outer margins.

Food Plants: Fabaceae - *Astragalus, Lathyrus, Lotus, Lupinus, Medicago, Melilotus, Vicia.*

Life History: Univoltine (Mar–Jun); polymorphic larvae varying between green to light brown with dark brown dorsal stripe, lighter tan side dashes.

Range: Northern, western, and parts of eastern North America; Texas–northeastern corner of East.

Comments: One of the earliest spring butterflies; one Texas specimen collected in Cass Co.; Texas subspecies -*lygdamus*; another subspecies -*oro*, commonly found in western U.S., could occur periodically in western Panhandle.

118

MELISSA BLUE
Lycaeides melissa

Description: 1–1¼ in (25–32 mm); sexually dimorphic; above (male) silvery blue-violet with thin black outer margins, white fringes; or above (female) brown with variable yellow-orange submarginal bands before black outer margin spots, white fringes; below pale gray turning pale tan with scattered black median and postmedian spots, yellow-orange submarginal band, and thin black outer edges; BHW with small metallic dark green outer margin spots.

Food Plants: Fabaceae - *Astragalus, Lotus, Lupinus, Medicago, Oxytropis, Vicia.*

Life History: Multivoltine (Apr–Oct); green larvae covered with short soft brown hair, obscure light side stripes.

Range: Western North America and northern margins of U.S.; Texas–western half of Panhandle, montane areas in Trans-Pecos and Big Bend.

Comments: Closely related Karner's Blue (*L. m. samuelis*) in northern margins of U.S., which is now considered endangered; Texas subspecies -*melissa.*

119 A

ACMON BLUE
Icaricia acmon

Description: ¾–1 in (19–25 mm); similar to Melissa Blue (*Lycaeides melissa*) but not as bright; sexually dimorphic; above (male) lavender-blue with narrow black outer margins, orange AHW submarginal band with small black dots; or above (female) deep brown with broad orange AHW submarginal band before row of black dots; both with white fringes; below pale gray with scattered black dots, submarginal and outer marginal lines of dark spots and thin black wing edge; BHW with orange band between dark spots and marginal spots capped with metallic green.

Food Plants: Polygonaceae - *Eriogonum, Polygonum,* Fabaceae - *Lotus, Lupinus, Melilotus.*

Life History: Multivoltine (Feb–Oct).

Range: Western North America, Canada to Mexico; Texas—Panhandle, High Plains, Trans-Pecos, Big Bend, Far West, and northwestern corner of Central.

Comments: Flies close to the ground; Texas subspecies *-texana* (Texas Blue).

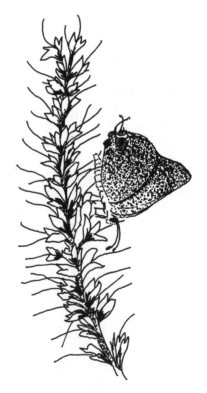

Gray Hairstreak (*Strymon melinus*)

METALMARKS—FAMILY RIODINIDAE

The majority of the 1,500 worldwide species of metalmarks are found in the tropics with a concentration in the New World tropics. Only 20 riodinid species are known from North America with the majority of these species being found in the southern United States; 16 of these occur in Texas. Only a single species is known from Canada. The metalmarks are closely related to the gossamer wings, but the foreleg of male metalmarks is reduced to half the length of the other legs.

Larvae use a variety of dicotyledonous plants, and some species are associated with ants. Unlike the small-headed, thick-bodied larvae of the gossamer wings, the metalmark larvae are longer with long hairs and larger heads. The typical metalmark chrysalis is less rounded than that of the gossamer wings.

Adult flight pattern is usually swift and erratic but the *Calephelis* spp. flight is weaker. Most species are found in localized colonies and migration is essentially unknown. Adults rest, bask, and feed with the wings held open. A few species rest underneath leaves with the wings held open.

This family has also been called the Nemeobiidae in the past, but the name Riodinidae has been conserved by the International Council on Zoological Nomenclature. The common family name, metalmarks, refers to the metallic marks on most species in this family. All Texas species belong to the subfamily Riodininae.

120   A

LITTLE METALMARK
Calephelis virginiensis

Description: ½–¾ in (13–19 mm); body colored same as wings with distinct dark abdominal bars; above varying between deep rust to orange with black bars, two dark metallic bands (wavy postmedian and curved submarginal) with row of dark spots between, and dark brown fringes; below similar but dull orange.

Food Plants: Asteraceae - *Cirsium horridulum*.

Life History: Multivoltine.

Range: Coastal Plain of southeastern U.S.; Texas—eastern half of Coastal Margin.

Comments: Found in various humid habitats such as pine forest, savannah, prairie, salt-meadow.

121   A

FATAL METALMARK
Calephelis nemesis

Description: ¾–1 in (19–25 mm); male with pointed forewing; above dull dark brown with hazy dark marks, wide smudged dark median band, thin metallic marginal line, and irregular checkered fringes; below pale orange-brown with scattered dark spots and faint thin metallic lines.

Food Plants: Ranunculaceae - *Clematis drummondii, C. henryi.*

Life History: Multivoltine (all year in south Texas); dark gray larvae with silver bumps, long light yellow hair.

Range: Mexico to south-central and southwestern U.S.; Texas—Far West, Trans-Pecos, Big Bend, Southwest, South, southwestern half of Central, southern half of Coastal Margin, and Rio Grande Valley.

Comments: Only *Calephelis* food plant not in Asteraceae. Texas subspecies *-australis* (Southern Metalmark).

122   A

LOST METALMARK
Calephelis perditalis

Description: ¾–⅞ in (19–22 mm); rounded forewing less pointed than other metalmarks; above dull dark brown with narrow broken black bands, jagged postmedian metallic band, submarginal metallic band before narrow dull orange outer margins, and dark smudged fringes; below bright orange-brown with metallic spots.

Food Plants: Asteraceae - *Eupatorium odoratum.*
Life History: Multivoltine.
Range: Central America to southern U.S.; Texas—Rio Grande Valley, southern halves of Coastal Margin and South.
Comments: Some workers consider this form to be a subspecies of Rounded Metalmark (*C. nilus*).

123 A

RAWSON'S METALMARK
Calephelis rawsoni

Description: ¾–1 in (19–25 mm); above dull brown with wide diffuse black median band, two narrow dark metallic lines (wavy postmedian, curved submarginal) before narrow dull orange outer margins, and irregularly checkered dark fringes; below bright orange-brown with dark spots and metallic lines past median.
Food Plants: Asteraceae - *Eupatorium greggii, E. havanense.*
Life History: Multivoltine (Feb–Nov).
Range: Mexico to southwestern U.S.; Texas—Big Bend, Southwest, South, Rio Grande Valley, and southern halves of Trans-Pecos, Central, and Coastal Margin.
Comments: Populations restricted to moist areas in more arid regions.

124

FREEMAN'S METALMARK
Calephelis freemani

Description: ¾–1 in (19–25 mm); very similar to Rawson's Metalmark (*C. rawsoni*) but paler brown; identification based on examination of male genitalia.
Food Plants: Unknown, possibly Asteraceae.
Life History: Unknown.

Range: Texas–Trans-Pecos, known only from type locality, 12.5 mi. (20 km) northwest of Alpine.

Comments: Considered by some as subspecies of Rawson's Metalmark (*C. rawsoni*); named for Texas skipper authority H. A. Freeman.

125 A

RED-BORDERED METALMARK
Caria ino

Description: ¾–1 in (19–25 mm); sexually dimorphic; elongated pointed forewing with slight dip in costal margin, usually held more perpendicular to body than other metalmarks; above (male) dark brown with wide dark red outer margin divided by narrow dark metallic line, may have green AFW costal margin; or above (female) lighter brown progressing from orange-brown on base to darker gray-brown with narrow curved dark brown bands, wide dark red outer margin divided by narrow dark metallic line; below red-brown (male redder) with dark spots and silver-blue metallic crescents.

Food Plants: Ulmaceae - *Celtis pallida*.

Life History: Multivoltine; larvae make nests of leaves with silk in which they pupates.

Range: Mexico to extreme southern U.S.; Texas–Rio Grande Valley; strays northward into South and southern half of Coastal Margin.

Comments: Texas subspecies *-melicerta* (Small Curvy Wing).

126 A

BLUE METALMARK
Lasaia sula

Description: ¾–1 in (19–25 mm); sexually dimorphic; above (male) iridescent green-blue; or above (female) pale gray-brown with narrow broken black bands (more on female); below banded light brown and white with submarginal row of dark brown spots.

Food Plants: Unknown.

Life History: Multivoltine (Apr–Nov).

Range: Central America to extreme southern U.S.; Texas–Rio Grande Valley.

Comments: Texas subspecies -*peninsularis*.

127 A

PIXIE
Melanis pixe

Description: 1⅜–2 in (41–51 mm); unmistakable; above velvet black; AFW with red-orange basal spot and yellow apex; AHW with red-orange basal spot and band of red-orange outer margin spots; below similar with more red in basal area.

Food Plants: Fabaceae - *Pithecellobium dulce*.

Life History: Multivoltine (Jan–Nov); hairy larvae.

Range: South America to extreme southern U.S.; Texas–Rio Grande Valley.

Comments: Spectacularly colored; established in Brownsville, Cameron Co. on ornamental plantings of guamuchil (*Pithecellobium dulce*).

128 A

EMESIA METALMARK
Emesis emesia

Description: 1–1⅛ in (25–28 mm); elongated, pointed forewing with dip in costal margin; above pale brown with translucent white crescent on AFW costal margin; below similar.

Food Plants: Fabaceae - *Caesalpinia mexicana*.

Life History: Unknown; multivoltine in Mexico.

Range: Central America to extreme southern U.S.; Texas—rare stray to Rio Grande Valley.

Comments: May periodically breed in Texas; recorded (Oct–Nov).

129 A

FALCATE EMESIA
Emesis tenedia

Description: 1¼–1½ in (32–38 mm); sexually dimorphic; above dark brown (male) or orange-brown (female) with light patch past discal cell; below orange-brown (male) or yellow-brown (female) with subtle dark dashes.

Food Plants: Unknown.

Life History: Unknown.

Range: Mexico and extreme southern U.S.; Texas—very rare stray to Rio Grande Valley.

Comments: One record in 1987.

130 A

MORMON METALMARK
Apodemia mormo

Description: 1–1¼ in (25–32 mm); sexually and geographically dimorphic; above dark brown with orange-brown from base to median on forewing only (male) or on both wings (female), several bright white spots on median and two rows of postmedian and submarginal white oblong spots, and distinct checkered fringes; below paler brown and orange with larger white spots.

Food Plants: Polygonaceae - *Eriogonum;* Krameriaceae - *Krameria pauciflora.*

Life History: Bivoltine at lower altitudes (Mar–Jun, Aug–Oct); univoltine (Aug–Sep) at higher altitudes.

Range: Western U.S.; Texas—Far West,Trans-Pecos, Big Bend; one report from Bastrop Co. in Central.

Comments: Overlapping geographic variations make subspecies identification difficult; Texas subspecies *-mejicana* (Mexican Metalmark) found in Trans-Pecos with orange-red band on AHW; *-mormo,* two specimens from Bastrop Co. in 1912(?) with distinct white spots.

131

NARROW-WINGED METALMARK
Apodemia multiplaga

Description: 1–1¼ in (25–32 mm); pointed forewing with concave outermargin below apex; above dark brown with large white spots and checkered outer margins; below pale brown with yellow-brown BFW basal area, small white spots including distinct black-edged white BFW cell bar.
Food Plants: Unknown.
Life History: Unknown.
Range: Mexico to extreme southern U.S.; Texas—rare stray to Rio Grande Valley.
Comments: Recorded (Nov).

132

HEPBURN'S METALMARK
Apodemia hepburni

Description: ¾ in (19 mm); above brown with few small white spots, row of black outer margin dots ; AHW with pale orange costal margin wedge (narrow at base, widest on median); below similar but yellow-orange.
Food Plants: Unknown.
Life History: Unknown.
Range: Mexico to extreme southern U.S.; Texas—Chisos Mountains in Big Bend.
Comments: Recorded (Jul).

133

PALMER'S METALMARK
Apodemia palmerii

Description: ¾–1 in (19–25 mm); elongated forewing; above gray-brown with red-orange median patches, white spots, narrow orange outer margin band, and checkered fringes; below dull orange with extensive cream patches, spots, and wing margins.

Food Plants: Fabaceae - *Prosopis glandulosa* var. *torreyana, P. pubescens.*

Life History: Multivoltine (Apr–Nov); dull blue-green larvae with yellow stripes, a line of short white hair.

Range: Mexico and southeastern U.S.; Texas–Trans-Pecos, Far West, and Big Bend.

134

WALKER'S METALMARK
Apodemia walkeri

Description: ¾–1 in (19–25 mm); similar to Palmer's Metalmark (*A. palmerii*) but lacks orange; above gray-brown with white blotches; below white with small brown marks and pale orange margin.

Food Plants: Unknown.

Life History: Bivoltine (May–Jun, Oct–Dec).

Range: Mexico to extreme southern U.S.; Texas–Rio Grande Valley.

135

CHISOS METALMARK
Apodemia chisosensis

Description: 1–1¼ in (25–32 mm); above pale orange with dark brown spots, two white AFW spots (male) or white band (female), checkered fringes; BFW pale orange with white apical patch; BHW off-white with scattered small oblong black spots, small black outer margin spots.

Food Plants: Rosaceaea-*Prunus havardii.*
Life History: Bivoltine (May–Aug).
Range: Texas–Chisos Mountains in Big Bend.

Zela Metalmark (*Emesis zela*)

SNOUT BUTTERFLIES—FAMILY LIBYTHEIDAE

Only eight to ten species of this very distinctive family exist in the entire world, generally in subtropical and tropical areas. These few species have been divided into two genera: *Libythea* in the Old World and *Libytheana* in the New World. Three species of *Libytheana* have been reported from North America with all known from Texas.

The immature stages combine characteristics of the immature forms of the Pieridae and Satyridae. The elongate eggs are deposited singly on various species of *Celtis* (hackberries or sugarberries in North America). The larvae are similar in shape to those of the Pieridae (cylindrical without spines) but have an enlarged thorax. The chrysalis has a crest on the abdomen and two points on the head. It hangs upside down from a cremaster.

Adult males have reduced forelegs. The adults rest with upright closed wings but bask with open wings. With the wings closed above the abdomen, the adults look like a leaf with the elongated palps (the "snout") looking like the petiole (a leaf stalk) of a leaf. Flight pattern is fluttery but very strong, and most species are known to migrate for long distances.

The most interesting biological characteristic of the snout butterflies is their habit of migrating in incredible numbers. Certain climatic conditions, such as severe drought followed by heavy rains over a large area in southern Texas, produce massive amounts of leaves on the foodplants. This leaf production allows a major buildup in population numbers of larvae and, subsequently, adults. The new generation of adults emerges at a time when the foodplants have been stripped of most of their leaves. The lack of leaves and the dense concentrations of adults trigger a migration involving masses of butterflies that easily number in the hundreds of thousands and even in the millions of individuals.

136 A

SNOUT BUTTERFLY
Libytheana bachmanii

Description: 1½–1⅞ in (38–48 mm); extended forewing with squared apex; above deep brown with large orange patches; AFW with short cream-white band of postmedian spots at end of discal cell with one separate squared spot, one cream-white subapical spot, and narrow cream wing edges; below gray-brown mottling; BFW with orange base and broad dark brown band with cream blotches and spots.

Food Plants: Ulmaceae - *Celtis laevigata, C. reticulata, C. pallida, C. occidentalis.*

Life History: Multivoltine; dark green larvae with yellow stripes, pair of black tubercles behind head.

Range: Central America to southern U.S.; Texas—entire, less common in High Plains and Panhandle.

Comments: Usually present in low numbers, can be extremely abundant following heavy rains, resulting in impressive migrations of thousands of adults; Texas subspecies -*bachmanii* (Snout Butterfly) in eastern Texas is smaller, lighter, and more angular; -*larvata* (Southern Snout) in central and south Texas is larger, darker, and less angular.

137

TROPICAL SNOUT
Libytheana carinenta

Description: 1½–1¾ in (38–44 mm); similar to Snout (*L. bachmanii*), but duller more diffuse orange with pale cocoa spots; below mottled with gray, brown, and rose speckled with dark brown; BFW with dull orange base and few cream spots.

Food Plants: Ulmaceae - *Celtis.*

Life History: Multivoltine.

Range: Paraguay to extreme southern U.S.; Texas—occasional migrant to Rio Grande Valley.

Comments: Texas subspecies *-mexicana* (Mexican Snout).

138

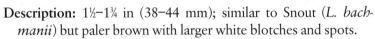

CUBAN SNOUT BUTTERFLY
Libytheana motya

Description: 1½–1¾ in (38–44 mm); similar to Snout (*L. bach-manii*) but paler brown with larger white blotches and spots.

Food Plants: Ulmaceae - *Celtis* spp.

Life History: Unknown.

Range: West Indies to extreme southern U.S.; Texas—Rio Grande Valley, Boca Chica Beach in Cameron Co.

Comments: Two specimens (Jun 1968), possibly strays from Cuba.

Gulf Fritillary *(Argraulis vanillae)*

LONGWING BUTTERFLIES—FAMILY HELICONIIDAE

This family contains 76 species of medium-sized tropical butterflies. Sixty-five species occur in the New World tropics with 11 additional species known from tropical Asia. The 7 species that are known from North America, all of which occur in Texas, are generally restricted to the southern United States. Eggs may be laid singly or in small clusters. Larvae have distinctive branching spines on the body and the head. Most species feed on members of the Passifloraceae (passion flowers) or, rarely, on the related family Turneraceae. Especially in the tropics, a particular longwing may use only a few related passion flower species as larval food plants. The chrysalids, which hang upside down, are generally cryptic and often have projections or spines.

Adults are characterized by large eyes, long antennae, and elongated forewings. The head and eyes of longwings are the largest in proportion to body size of all the Lepidoptera. Adults generally flutter slowly and are typically local in distribution, although a few species are known to migrate. Males locate the females by pheromones and mate with the female immediately following and sometimes even before emergence from the chrysalis. All species feed on nectar, and some species are able to feed on pollen gathered by their probosces.

Adults of this family are generally considered to be the "smartest" of the butterflies with much scientific research focusing on the behavior of these species. Visual search behavior for oviposition sites on suitable food plants by female longwings has led to the evolution of leaf shapes by various passion flowers that resemble leaf shapes of non-food plant species living in the same area. Many female longwings will not lay eggs on tips of passion flowers that already have an egg. This avoidance by female longwings has led to the evolution of small colored bumps on some of these plants that function as permanent egg mimics.

Longwings have no true overwintering stage and can die during freezing weather. The population may be reestablished by migrants in the next warm season. Many of the adult longwings are believed to be distasteful to potential predators. The noxious chemicals causing the distastefulness are apparently manufactured during the larval stage, rather than merely collected from the larval food plant.

139   C,L,A

GULF FRITILLARY
Agraulis vanillae

Description: 2½–3 in (64–76 mm); long pointed curved forewing; above red-orange with dark brown vein lines; AFW with small black rimmed white spots near middle of costal margin; below yellow-brown with large oblong metallic silver spots (most rimmed with black); BFW with large orange-pink discal cell and black-rimmed white spots near costal margin.

Food Plants: Passifloraceae - *Passiflora* spp.

Life History: Multivoltine; shiny black larvae with red lateral stripes, purple-gray band down back, and black spines.

Range: Argentina to West Indies and southern U.S.; Texas–Southwest, South, Central, Rio Grande Valley, Coastal Margin, and southern half of East; migrates northward.

Comments: Migrates northward; Texas subspecies -*incarnata*.

140   A

MEXICAN SILVERSPOT
Dione moneta

Description: 2½–3 in (64–76mm); similar to Gulf Fritillary (*Agraulis vanillae*) but above yellow-brown without white spots; below with more silver spots without black rims.

Food Plants: Passifloraceae - *Passiflora* spp.

Life History: Multivoltine (Apr–Dec).

Range: Brazil north to extreme southern U.S.; Texas–rare migrant to Rio Grande Valley; very rare in Far West, Big Bend.

Comments: Texas subspecies -*poeyi*.

141

BANDED ORANGE
Dryadula phaetusa

Description: 3–3½ in (76–89 mm); above orange and orange-brown bands; below with series of dark brown, yellow-brown and orange stripes; BHW with small white spot band on outer margin.

Food Plants: Passifloraceae - *Passiflora*.

Life History: Unknown; multivoltine in Mexico.

Range: Paraguay to extreme southern U.S.; Texas–rare stray to Rio Grande Valley.

Comments: Collected near Sarita in Kenedy Co., (1933) after severe hurricane; another record from Garland in Dallas Co. (1981).

142   L,C,A

JULIA
Dryas iulia

Description: 3–3½ in (76–89 mm); long narrow forewing; sexually dimorphic; above (male) orange with dark brown AFW cell spot, yellow AHW inner margin; or above (female) pale yellow-brown with large black spot on AFW costal margin, hazy brown streaks and outer margins, narrow scalloped yellow-brown AHW submarginal band; below pale yellow-brown mottling with silver streak on BHW costal margin.

Food Plants: Passifloraceae - *Passiflora*.

Life History: Multivoltine; pale tan larva with red and brown patches, fine dark lines, black spines except three white pairs.

Range: Paraguay to West Indies and southern U.S.; Texas–Rio Grande Valley and southern halves of South and Coastal Margin; occasional migrant northward through eastern half of state.

Comments: Texas subspecies *-moderata*.

143

ISABELLA TIGER
Eueides isabella

Description: 2½–3 in (64–76 mm); similar to Large Tiger (*Lycorea cleobaea*), but much smaller and dark bands on hindwing are separate, do not form loop; elongated forewing with rounded apex; above orange with brown-black banding; AFW yellow on outer half with dark banding; below similar.

Food Plants: Passifloraceae - *Passiflora*.

Life History: Unknown; multivoltine in tropics.

Range: Brazil to West Indies and extreme southern U.S.; Texas–stray to South, rare into Central.

Comments: Observed as far north as Austin in 1971; recorded (Apr–Jul); Texas subspecies -*zoracaon*.

144   L,C,A

ZEBRA
Heliconius charitonius

Description: 3–3½ in (76–89 mm); long narrow forewing with rounded apex; above jet black with narrow yellow stripes and rows of yellow AHW submarginal spots; below dark velvet brown with similar stripes and spots; BHW with small crimson spots near base.

Food Plants: Passifloraceae - *Passiflora*.

Life History: Multivoltine; white larvae with light yellow heads, small red-brown spots, and black spines.

Range: Peru to West Indies and southern U.S.; Texas–Rio Grande Valley, southern areas of South and Coastal Margin.

Comments: Adults roost communally, returning to same roost nightly; Texas subspecies -*vazquezae*.

145 A

CRIMSON-PATCHED LONGWING
Heliconius erato

Description: 2½–3 in (64–76 mm); long narrow forewing with rounded apex; above black with broad red postmedian AFW band and narrow yellow AHW line; below similar but brown with pink BFW band and paler yellow BHW line.

Food Plants: Passifloraceae - *Passiflora*.

Life History: Unknown; multivoltine in tropics.

Range: Paraguay to southern U.S.; Texas—rare stray to Rio Grande Valley.

Comments: Recorded (Aug–Sep); Texas subspecies -*petiveranus*.

American Painted Lady (*Vanessa virginiensis*)

BRUSHFOOTED BUTTERFLIES—FAMILY NYMPHALIDAE

Brushfoots get their family name from the reduced forelegs that characterize this group, although many other families share this characteristic. A total of 1,100 species are known worldwide, of which 123 occur in North America and 73 of these are found in Texas. This family has long been a "dumping ground" for groups that obviously did not belong to the other recognized families of butterflies. Indeed, this family in the past has also included many groups recognized as separate families in this book, such as Libytheidae, Heliconiidae, Satyridae, Danaidae, and Ithomiidae. Many respected workers place these families in Nymphalidae.

Due to the variety in appearance of adult and immature forms in this family, there are no obvious characteristics separating this group from the other families of butterflies. Eggs are barrel- or spindle-shaped with prominent vertical ribbing. Eggs may be deposited singly, in small clusters, or in masses of up to 500 eggs. Larvae are found on various species of dicots and are often covered with complex spines. The chrysalis hangs upside down and is often cryptically patterned to blend with its background.

Both sexes have forelegs that are very reduced in length and covered with spines (especially spiny in the male). Adults usually rest with the wings folded above the body, but they bask with the wings held out flat. Generally, the female is the flying member of a mating pair that has been disturbed.

Even with the above five groups removed from the Nymphalidae in this treatment, the remaining nymphalids known from Texas are still divided into seven subfamilies: Argynninae (fritillaries), Melitaeinae (checker spots), Nymphalinae (anglewings), Limenitidinae (admirals), Marpesiinae (daggerwings), Charaxinae (goatweeds), and Apaturinae (hackberry butterflies).

FRITILLARIES—SUBFAMILY ARGYNNINAE

This small subfamily contains the *Argynnis* and a few related genera in the Old World; *Speyeria* and *Euptoieta* in North America. The genera *Argynnis* and *Speyeria* use Violaceae (violet family) as larval food plants. *Euptoieta* use plants in the Passifloraceae (passion flower family) and Turneraceae (turnera family), indicating its transitional position between the boreal *Speyeria* and the neotropical Heliconiidae (longwings). Only three species of this subfamily are known from Texas: one is statewide in occurrence; one is found in the Lower Rio Grande Valley (and southward); and one is a temporary accidental introduction. The *Euptoieta* species in Texas lack the distinctive silver spots below that the other Texas fritillaries possess. The larvae in this subfamily are vividly colored with many spines.

146 L,C,A

VARIEGATED FRITILLARY
Euptoieta claudia

> **Description:** 2–2¼ in (51–57 mm); elongated forewing with rounded apex and angled hindwing; above yellow-brown with dark brown lines, submarginal spots, and two outer margin lines; below pale brown and hazy white with orange BFW basal area and white veins.
> **Food Plants:** Linaceae; Violaceae; and Passifloraceae.
> **Life History:** Multivoltine (Feb–Dec); red-headed larvae with two long spines, white body with red bands and black spines.
> **Range:** Argentina to West Indies and U.S.; Texas—entire.
> **Comments:** Yearly springtime migration north from Texas.

147 A

MEXICAN FRITILLARY
Euptoieta hegesia

> **Description:** 2–2¼ in (51–57 mm); similar to Variegated Fritillary (*E. claudia*) but hindwing less angled, two black-ringed pale orange spots in AFW discal cell, more orange (clear orange AHW from base to postmedian); below similar but duller with fainter markings.

Food Plants: Passifloraceae - *Passiflora foetida;* also Turneraceae - *Turnera ulmnifolia* in Costa Rica.

Life History: Multivoltine (Jul–Dec); shiny red larva with black and silver lines, black spines, and black clubbed horns on head.

Range: Argentina to West Indies and extreme southern U.S.; Texas–Rio Grande Valley.

Comments: Occasional northward migration; Texas subspecies *-hoffmanni.*

148

GREAT SPANGLED FRITILLARY
Speyeria cybele

Description: 3½–3¾ in (89–95 mm); above tawny orange with dusty brown basal area and complex pattern of black lines, crescents, and spots; below yellow-orange with scattered silver spots; BHW darker orange on inner third.

Food Plants: Violaceae - *Viola.*

Life History: Univoltine (Jun–Sep).

Range: Southern Canada and northern U.S.; Texas–Central, Bexar Co.

Comments: Accidental introduction when several adults developed from eggs on violets from Maryland transplanted into yard in Bexar Co.; natural migrants from Arkansas expected in northeast Texas; Texas subspecies *-cybele.*

CHECKERSPOTS—SUBFAMILY MELITAEINAE

The Melitaeinae contains more species (28) than any other subfamily of the Nymphalidae in Texas. The subfamily is almost worldwide in distribution, although species in this group have not been able to invade and establish species in tropical areas except in the New World. These small to medium-sized butterflies often exhibit a bewilderingly complex pattern of bands, spots, stripes, and patches. Larval food plants used by species in this subfamily include members of

several plant families, of which Asteraceae (sunflowers), Scrophulariaceae (snapdragons), Verbenaceae (vervains), and Acanthaceae
(acanthus) are the most commonly used in North America.

The species in this subfamily appear to be a rapidly evolving group
with often unclear boundaries between species. Beyond this confu-
sion concerning species, the generic classification within this subfamily has undergone considerable revision during the last few
decades. At present, the species in Texas have been placed into the
tribe Melitaeini.

149 A

DOTTED CHECKERSPOT
Poladryas minuta

> **Description:** 1¼–1½ in (32–38 mm); above orange with dark brown
> bars and patches, orange-brown patches, and creamy spots in
> vague AHW band; below mottled orange with yellow bands and
> cream crescents.
> **Food Plants:** Scrophulariaceae - *Penstemon cobaea.*
> **Life History:** Multivoltine (May–Sep) in Central; univoltine
> (Jun–Sep) in other localities.
> **Range:** Mexico and southwestern U.S.; Texas–High Plains, western
> area of North Central, southern area of Panhandle, and area in
> Central.
> **Comments:** Populations are in disjunct localities; Texas subspecies
> *-minuta.*

150   L,C,A

THEONA CHECKERSPOT
Thessalia theona

> **Description:** 1¼–1½ in (32–38 mm); above dark brown bases with
> dark brown vein markings through bands of pale orange, one

pale yellow postmedian band, and dark outer margins with two bands of white spots; below almost solid cream with orange bands and black veins.

Food Plants: Scrophulariaceae - *Castilleja, Leucophyllum.*

Life History: Multivoltine (Apr–Oct).

Range: Venezuela to southwestern U.S.; Texas–Far West, Trans-Pecos, Big Bend, Southwest, South, Rio Grande Valley, southern half of Coastal Margin, and western half of Central.

Comments: Texas subspecies *-thekla* (Thekla Checkerspot) in west; *-bolli* (Boll's Checkerspot) in south and central Teas.

151   A

CHINATI CHECKERSPOT
Thessalia chinatiensis

Description: 1¼–1½ in (32–38 mm); above pale orange with brown base, dark brown veins, and white-spotted dark brown outer margins; below with dark brown veins; BFW pale orange with two dark brown costal margin marks, brown submarginal and outer margin lines with cream spots between; BHW yellow-cream with dark brown-edged orange submarginal band.

Food Plants: Scrophulariceae - *Leucophyllum minus.*

Life History: Multivoltine (Jun–Oct).

Range: Texas–Chinati Mountains in Trans-Pecos.

152   A

FULVIA CHECKERSPOT
Thessalia fulvia

Description: 1¼–1½ in (32–38 mm); similar to Chinati Check-erspot (*T. chinatiensis*) but paler above with yellow median streaks and below without orange BHW band.

Food Plants: Scrophulariceae - *Castilleja.*

Life History: Multivoltine (Apr–Oct).
Range: Northern Mexico, southwestern U.S.; Texas–Far West, Trans-Pecos, Big Bend.
Comments: Texas subspecies *-fulvia.*

153 A

BORDERED PATCH
Chlosyne lacinia

Description: 1½–2 in (38–51 mm); geographic variations; above black-brown with small orange spots, wide curved yellow-orange median band, small white spot lines, and white dotted outer margins (*-adjutrix*); or above black-brown with curved broken band of white median spots, small white AFW subapical spots, and white dotted outer margins (*-crocale*); below dark brown with white dotted outer margins; BFW with orange streak on costal margin near body and scattered pale yellow spots; BHW with pale yellow basal area, median bands, submarginal band of crescents, and orange at outer angle.

Food Plants: Asteraceae - *Ambrosia trifida, Helianthus annuus, Verbesina encelioides, Viguiera dentata, Zexmenia hispida.*

Life History: Multivoltine (Mar–Nov); polymorphic larvae in three colors–black, orange, black with orange stripe.

Range: Argentina to southwestern U.S.; Texas–Far West, Trans-Pecos, Big Bend, Southwest, South, Rio Grande Valley, western half of Central, and southern half of Coastal Margin.

Comments: Has most variable wing pattern of all North American butterflies; Texas subspecies *-adjutrix* (Adjutrix Patch) in South, Central, Rio Grande Valley, Coastal Margin, and Southwest; *-crocale* (Crocale Patch) in Far West, Big Bend, and Trans-Pecos.

154   A

DEFINITE PATCH
Chlosyne definita

Description: 1¼–1½ in (32–38 mm); above dark brown with odd-shaped cream spot with curved orange spot on either side in AFW discal cell, curved postmedian band of pale yellow spots followed by submarginal band of orange spots, and vague pale brown marginal spots; below orange with brown veins and marginal bands of oblong cream spots; BHW with cream median band followed by orange band with one white spot.

Food Plants: Acanthaceae - *Stenandrum*.

Life History: Multivoltine (Apr–Oct).

Range: Mexico to southwestern U.S.; Texas–Rio Grande Valley, South, Southwest, Big Bend, and southern fourth of Trans-Pecos and Coastal Margin.

155

ENDEIS PATCH
Chlosyne endeis

Description: 1½–1¾ in (38–44 mm); above brown-black; AFW with one orange and one cream spot in discal cell, postmedian and submarginal bands of pale cream spots; AHW with deep yellow postmedian band and orange submarginal band; BFW orange with dark brown outer half with bands of cream spots; BHW cream with orange base, submedian and submarginal bands; one dark-rimmed cream spot in submedian band.

Food Plants: Unknown.

Life History: Multivoltine (Mar–Nov).

Range: Mexico and extreme southern U.S.; Texas–Rio Grande Valley, rare stray to Central.

156
ERODYLE PATCH
Chlosyne erodyle

Description: 1½–2 in (38–51 mm); above black with small white AFW spots; AHW with yellow patch postbasal to postmedian and red outer angle spot; below similar with more red on BHW.
Food Plants: Unknown.
Life History: Unknown.
Range: Central America to extreme southern U.S.; Texas–rare stray into Rio Grande Valley.
Comments: No confirmed records, some reports may refer to subspecies -*melitaeoides*.

157   E,LC,A
JANAIS PATCH
Chlosyne janais

Description: 2¼–2½ in (57–64 mm); above black-brown with small white AFW spots, distinct large red AHW patch, and narrow white outer margin dashes; below black with white BFW spots; BHW with large cream patch dotted with dark brown followed by short orange band, cream oblong submarginal band, and narrow white outer margin crescents.
Food Plants: Acanthaceae - *Anisacanthus quadrifidus* var. *wrightii*; also *Odontonema callistachus* in Mexico.
Life History: Multivoltine (Jul–Nov); metallic silver-green larvae with black rings and spines.
Range: Colombia to southwestern U.S.; Texas–Rio Grande Valley, South, Southwest, into Central.
Comments: One stray to High Plains, Lubbock in Lubbock Co. (1977).

158

ROSITA PATCH
Chlosyne rosita

Description: 2–2¼ in (51–57 mm); similar to Janais Patch (*C. janais*) but AHW patch yellow and orange, no marginal spots, and less detail on BHW.
Food Plants: Acanthaceae - *Dicliptera, Siphonoglossa.*
Life History: Multivoltine.
Range: Central America to southwestern U.S.; Texas–Rio Grande Valley.
Comments: Texas subspecies *-browni.*

159

STRIPED PATCH
Chlosyne ehrenbergi

Description: 1¾–2¼ in (44–57 mm); above black with cream lines along veins, expanding toward margin.
Food Plants: Unknown Loganiaceae - *Buddleia* in Mexico.
Life History: Unknown.
Range: Mexico and extreme southern U.S.; Texas–rare stray to Rio Grande Valley.
Comments: One unsubstantiated Texas record.

160

YELLOW PATCH
Chlosyne melitaeoides

Description: 1½–1¾ in (38–44 mm); similar to Janais Patch (*C. janais*) but BHW yellow is restricted to the basal third of wing, separated from the red spots by a series of black dashes.

Food Plants: Unknown; possibly Acanthaceae.
Life History: Unknown; multivoltine in Mexico.
Range: Mexico and extreme southern U.S.; Texas—rare stray to Rio Grande Valley.
Comments: Often considered to be a subspecies of Checkered Patch (*C. marina*).

161 A

GORGONE CHECKERSPOT
Charidryas gorgone

Description: 1¼–1½ in (32–44 mm); above banded brown-black and orange with submarginal AHW band of square orange-rimmed black spots and white-checkered outer margins; BFW orange through postmedian then complex pattern of white, cream, and brown oblong spots; BHW brown with white spots, broad jagged median band (often referred to as "arrowheads"), narrow lines, and oblong spotted outer margin.
Food Plants: Asteraceae - *Ambrosia trifida, Helianthus annuus, H. petiolaris, Viguiera dentata.*
Life History: Multivoltine (Apr–Sep); polymorphic larvae in three color forms—black, orange, black with orange stripe.
Range: South central Canada, southeastern and central U.S.; Texas—Panhandle, High Plains, North Central, East, eastern halves of Central and Coastal Margin.
Comments: Texas subspecies -*carlota* (Carlota Checkerspot).

162 A

SILVERY CHECKERSPOT
Charidryas nycteis

Description: 1½–1¾ in (38–44 mm); elongated forewing; above black-brown with orange mottled area from base to median, broad orange irregular curved postmedian to submarginal band,

and crescent-checkered outer margins; black spot AHW band inside orange band (one black spot with cream center); below orange BFW with dark brown mottling and white apex spot; BHW pale tan with brown lines, bars, strip with orange-ringed black spots postmedian to outer margin; both wings with white spots centered on outer margins next to narrow orange margins and checkered fringes.

Food Plants: Asteraceae - *Verbesina virginica, Aster, Helianthus, Rudbeckia.*

Life History: Bivoltine (Mar–Sep).

Range: Eastern North America; Texas–East, eastern halves of North Central, Central, and Coastal Margin.

Comments: Texas subspecies *-nycteis.*

163   A

ELF
Microtia elva

Description: ¾–1 in (19–25 mm); narrow, elongated wings; above dark brown with orange band; AFW with large cone-shaped orange spot on inner margin; below similar.

Food Plants: Unknown.

Life History: Unknown.

Range: Venezuela to Mexico and extreme southern U.S.; Texas– rare stray to Rio Grande Valley.

Comments: Common at mud puddles in Mexico; recorded (Aug).

164

DYMAS CHECKERSPOT
Dymasia dymas

Description: ¾–1 in (19–25 mm); above orange with network of dark lines forming blocks and circles (some filled with brown) and small white bar on AFW costal margin; below similar but BHW with cream-white bands and white-checkered fringes.

Food Plants: Acanthaceae - *Beloperone, Siphonoglossa.*
Life History: Multivoltine (Feb–Nov).
Range: Mexico to southwestern U.S.; Texas–Far West, Trans-Pecos, Big Bend, Southwest, South, Rio Grande Valley, western third of Central, and southern half of Coastal Margin.
Comments: Texas subspecies -*dymas.*

165 A

ELADA CHECKERSPOT
Texola elada

Description: 1–1¼ in (25–32 mm); similar to Dymas Checkerspot (*T. dymas*) but larger, without white AFW costal margin bar, and BHW outer margin band is red-orange; more distinct checkered fringes.
Food Plants: Acanthaceae - *Anisacanthus quadrifidus* var. *wrightii, Siphonoglossa.*
Life History: Multivoltine (Apr–Oct).
Range: Mexico to southwestern U.S.; Texas–Far West, Trans-Pecos, Big Bend, Southwest, South, Rio Grande Valley, western third of Central, and southern half of Coastal Margin.
Comments: Texas subspecies -*ulrica* (Ulrica Checkerspot).

166 A

TEXAN CRESCENT
Anthanassa texana

Description: 1¼–1½ in (32–44 mm); above dark brown with orange basal area through submedian, open curved white spot bands, and thin crescent-spotted fringes; BFW orange with wide dark brown postmedian band with white spots; BHW pale brown mottled with cream; both wings with crescent-spotted wing fringes.
Food Plants: Acanthaceae - *Beloperone guttata, Dicliptera dibrachiata, Jacobinia carnea, Ruellia.*

Life History: Multivoltine (Mar–Nov).

Range: Guatemala to southern U.S.; Texas–Far West, Trans-Pecos, Big Bend, Southwest, South, Rio Grande Valley, western half of Central, and southern half of Coastal Margin.

Comments: Very closely related to Seminole Crescent (*A. seminole*).

167

SEMINOLE CRESCENT
Anthanassa seminole

Description: 1¼–1½ in (32–44 mm,); similar to Texan Crescent (*A. texana*), but white spots more prominent and more numerous on AFW, orange AFW base.

Food Plants: Acanthaceae - *Dicliptera, Jacobinia, Ruellia.*

Life History: Multivoltine (Mar–Nov).

Range: West Indies to southeastern U.S.; Texas eastern fourth of Coastal Margin.

Comments: Very closely related to Texan Crescent (*A. texana*) and has been considered a subspecies of *A. texana* by some workers.

168

FALSE BLACK CRESCENT
Anthanassa ptolyca

Description: ¾–1 in (19–25 mm); above brown-black with light cream spots and bands; below pale gray-brown with orange BFW discal cell band; BHW with small brown spots.

Food Plants: Unknown, possibly Acanthaceae.

Life History: Unknown; multivoltine in Mexico.

Range: Nicaragua to Mexico and extreme southern U.S.; Texas– rare stray to Rio Grande Valley.

Comments: Recorded (Mar, Dec).

169   A

TULCIS CRESCENT
Anthanassa tulcis

Description: 1–1⅛ in (25–28 mm); similar to False Black Crescent (*A. ptolyca*) but has orange highlights on AFW base; BFW pale yellow through median then brown with cream blotches; BHW yellow-cream with cream postmedian band and vague brown semi-circle middle of outer margin.

Food Plants: Acanthaceae - *Beloperone, Dicliptera, Ruellia.*

Life History: Unknown; multivoltine in Mexico.

Range: Argentina to extreme southern U.S.; Texas–Rio Grande Valley.

Comments: Formerly considered a subspecies of Black Crescent (*A. frisia*).

170   A

VESTA CRESCENT
Phyciodes vesta

Description: 1–1¼ in (25–32 mm); above orange with scalloped dark brown lines, yellow submarginal crescent band; below pale orange with scalloped dark brown BFW postmedian lines; BHW with white spot in middle of brown patch on outer margin.

Food Plants: Acanthaceae - *Siphonoglossa pilosella.*

Life History: Multivoltine (Apr–Oct).

Range: Guatemala to southwestern U.S.; Texas–Far West, Trans-Pecos, Big Bend, Southwest, South, Rio Grande Valley, western half of Central, and southern half of Coastal Margin; strays to High Plains and Panhandle.

Comments: Rare strays to Nebraska.

171 A

PHAON CRESCENT
Phyciodes phaon

> **Description:** 1–1¼ in (25–32 mm); above brown at base with orange bands divided by black lines, black from postmedian to outer margin; AFW with crooked pale cream postmedian band divided by black lines; BFW orange with crooked brown median and submarginal bands, cream blotch on costal margin, and cream spot middle of outer margin; BHW yellow-cream with dark veins, postmedian band of black spots (large orange-ringed spot in middle); spring or fall individuals with gray-brown BHW with cream blotches and bands.
>
> **Food Plants:** Verbenaceae - *Phyla nodiflora.*
>
> **Life History:** Multivoltine; eggs laid in clusters up to 100; olive larvae with brown and cream stripes and spines.
>
> **Range:** Guatemala to West Indies and southern U.S.; Texas–Big Bend, Southwest, South, Rio Grande Valley, Coastal Margin, and southern fourth of Trans-Pecos; strays throughout remainder of state.
>
> **Comments:** Somewhat migratory, strays throughout north Texas to Nebraska and Iowa.

172 A

PEARL CRESCENT
Phyciodes tharos

> **Description:** 1¼–1½ in (32–38 m); geographically and seasonally variable; above orange with black-brown dagger-shaped AFW costal marks, lines (including a black submedian chain on both wings), and broad jagged outer margins; AHW with black spot submarginal band; below yellow or cream with brown lines, BHW with brown patch with white crescent on outer margin; spring or fall individuals with mottled gray-brown BHW.

Food Plants: Asteraceae - *Aster. drummondii*; also *A. praeltus* in eastern U.S.

Life History: Multivoltine (Apr–Nov); brown larva with white dots, white dashes on back, cream lines on side, and brown branched spines with white tips.

Range: Mexico to eastern and southern U.S.; Texas—entire.

Comments: Texas subspecies *-tharos* (Pearl Crescent).

173   A

PAINTED CRESCENT
Phyciodes pictus

Description: 1–1¼ in (25–32 mm); similar to Pearly Crescent (*P. tharos*) but more brown; BFW apex and BHW clear yellow (male) or cream (female).

Food Plants: Asteraceae - *Aster*; Convolvulaceae - *Ipomoea*; also Acanthaceae - *Siphonoglossa* in lab.

Life History: Multivoltine (Apr-Oct).

Range: Northern Mexico and southwestern U.S.; Texas—Panhandle, High Plains, Trans-Pecos, Far West, Big Bend, Southwest, western edge of South and Rio Grande Valley (close to Rio Grande River).

Comments: Texas subspecies *-pictus*.

174

ANIETA
Tegosa anieta

Description: ¾–1 in (19–25 mm); elongated forewing; above orange with brown outer margins becoming very narrow on AHW.

Food Plants: Asteraceae - *Mikania, Vernonia*.

Life History: Unknown.

Range: Venezuela to Mexico and extreme southern U.S.; Texas-very rare stray to Rio Grande Valley.

Comments: Texas subspecies *-luka*.

175

CHALCEDON CHECKERSPOT
Euphydryas chalcedona

Description: 1¼–2¼ in (32–57 mm); geographically variable; above black with bands of orange and yellow divided by black bars and lines (darker individuals with less orange and more yellow), and checkered fringes; below red-orange with yellow BFW submarginal spot bands; BHW with cream bands ending with red-orange outer margin.

Food Plants: Boraginaceae; Scrophulariaceae; Plantaginaceae; Caprifoliaceae.

Life History: Unknown; univoltine outside Texas.

Range: Western North America—Alaska to northern Mexico; Texas—rare stray to Panhandle.

Comments: Single female in Palo Duro Canyon in Randall Co.; Texas subspecies -*chalcedona*.

176   A

BALTIMORE
Euphydryas phaeton

Description: 1½–3 in (45–70 mm); yellow-clubbed black antennae and orange palps; above black with orange cell spots, several postmedian and submarginal lines of white spots, and orange outer margin spot band; below orange with white spots, black lines, and wide orange outer margin band divided by black lines.

Food Plants: Scrophulariaceae; Plantaginaceae; Caprifoliaceae.

Life History: Unknown; univoltine outside Texas; white chrysalis with orange dots, black dots and blotches.

Range: Eastern North America—Nova Scotia to Minnesota and south to Georgia and Oklahoma; Texas—rare stray to North Central.

Comments: Single Texas record in Collin County, 19th century; Texas subspecies -*ozarkae* (Baltimore Checkerspot).

ANGLEWINGS—SUBFAMILY NYMPHALINAE

The Nymphalinae are generally medium-sized butterflies that are characteristically patterned in earth tones of brown, cream, black, and red. The brighter colored of the 14 Texas species in this group are the tropical members of the genus Anartia. These butterflies range over most of the world but are especially represented in the northern hemisphere. Several species have very extensive geographical ranges including the most widely distributed butterfly species in the world, the Painted Lady (*Vanessa cardui*). The Texas Nymphalinae contains species that have worldwide affinities, others with more restricted North American distributions, and still others with tropical American distributions.

177   L,C,A

QUESTION MARK
Polygonia interrogationis

Description: 2–2½ in (51–64 mm); elongated forewing with square apex and angulated hindwing with short tail in middle of outer margin; seasonal variations; above red-orange with black blotches and outer margins (narrow violet outer margin in fall and spring); AHW black with brown basal area (summer); below mottled red-brown, cream, and gray (spring and fall) or brown suffused with lavendar-blue (summer); BHW with silver comma and dot at end of cell (all seasons).

Food Plants: Ulmaceae - *Ulmus, Celtis*.

Life History: Multivoltine (Mar–Nov); black larvae with yellow lengthwise lines, orange-based branched yellow spines on body, and two branched black spines on head.

Range: Mexico to eastern North America; Texas—entire.

Comments: Common name refers to shape of silver spots on BHW; common in urban areas with elms or hackberries.

178   A

HOP MERCHANT
Polygonia comma

Description: 1⅝–2 in (41–51 mm); similar to Question Mark (*P. interrogationis*) but smaller with shorter tail, lacking silver dot at end of BHW cell; seasonal variation but summer variation more similar to Question Mark (*P. interrogationis*) than spring and fall; above orange with black-brown median spots, AFW costal margin blotches, apex, and outer margin (spring and fall); AHW with pale orange submarginal marks in broad dark orange band (spring and fall); below mottled yellow-brown (spring and fall) or more brown and cream mottling (summer).

Food Plants: Ulmaceae - *Ulmus*; Urticaceae - *Urtica*.

Life History: Multivoltine (May–Sep).

Range: Eastern North America; Texas–East.

Comments: Previously referred to as the Comma, a name that refers to the shape of silver spot on BHW.

179   C,A

MOURNING CLOAK
Nymphalis antiopa

Description: 2¾–3¼ in (70–82 mm); elongated forewing with squared apex and irregular outer margin with several short projections; above deep purple-brown, band of bright blue submarginal spots, and bright cream-yellow outer margin band flecked with brown; below gray-brown with dark brown striations, a cream outer margin band with brown marks.

Food Plants: Salicaceae - *Salix, Populus*; Betulaceae - *Betula*; Ulmaceae - *Celtis, Ulmus*; Moraceae - *Morus*.

Life History: Multivoltine; black larvae with short hairs, red spots down back, and black branched spines.

Range: Venezuela to Alaska, also Eurasia; Texas—entire except less common in Coastal Margin and Rio Grande Valley.

Comments: Known as Camberwell Beauty in Britain where it is an occasional stray from continental Europe; below is cryptic on tree trunk, when disturbed it flashes upper coloration and produces a noticeable "click" as its flies away; individual adults may live up to ten months; Texas subspecies *-antiopa*.

180 L,A

AMERICAN PAINTED LADY
Vanessa virginiensis

Description: 1¾–2 in (44–51 mm); above orange with brown-orange basal area; AFW with black marks, gold bar on costal margin, black apex with white spots, single white dot in orange below apical patch, and black outer margin; AHW with black-ringed blue postmedian spots, scalloped black submarginal line bordering black outer margin spots; below gray-brown with complex pattern of cream and black; BFW with large pink patch; BHW with two large black-ringed eyespots.

Food Plants: Asteraceae - *Artemesia, Cirsium, Gnaphalium, Helianthus;* Also Scrophulariaceae and Malvaceae in tropics.

Life History: Multivoltine; black larvae with yellow bands with black lines alternating with black with red and white spots, yellow branched spines on side and black branched spines on top.

Range: Venezuela to southern Canada; Texas—entire.

Comments: Somewhat migratory; active year-round in Rio Grande Valley.

181   L,C,A

PAINTED LADY
Vanessa cardui

Description: 2–2½ in (51–64 mm); above similar to American Painted Lady (*V. virginiensis*) but forewing more elongated, no white dot on AFW, white costal margin bar, and without large eyespots on BHW; above orange variable from dark to pale with rose-orange on AFW; BHW with four small black-ringed eyespots.

Food Plants: Asteraceae - *Cirsium, Helianthus;* Malvaceae.

Life History: Multivoltine; dark headed larvae variable between green to lavender-brown with yellow dorsal stripe, branched spines.

Range: Venezuela to Canada, Eurasia, Africa, India (absent from Australia, New Zealand, Antarctica); Texas; most common in Southwest, South, Rio Grande Valley, and Coastal Margin; strong migrant through remainder of state.

Comments: Considered to be the most widely distributed butterfly in the world; in North America overwinters only in far south, migrates northward each spring and southward in fall.

182

WEST COAST LADY
Vanessa annabella

Description: 1½–2 in (38–51 mm); similar to American Painted Lady (*V. virginiensis*) but smaller, forewing apex more squared, above with white crescent outer margin spots, and without large eyespots on BHW; AHW with four black-ringed blue spots, brown costal margin band curving onto upper third of outer margin; below gray-brown and yellow with orange patch and black lines on BFW; BHW with less distinct spot band.

Food Plants: Malvaceae - *Alcea, Malvastrum, Sida;* Urticaceae - *Urtica.*

Life History: Univoltine (Aug–Sep).

Range: Central America to western North America; Texas—Far West, Trans-Pecos, Big Bend, High Plains, Panhandle.

Comments: Migratory as far north as British Columbia.

183   A

RED ADMIRAL
Vanessa atalanta

Description: 1¾–2 in (44–51 mm); above brown-black with red-orange AFW postmedian band curving onto AHW outer margin and thin white crescents on outer edges; AFW with white subapical and apical spots; below reticulated dark brown; BFW with deep coral patch and cream bar on costal margin above cream spot.

Food Plants: Urticaceae - *Parietaria, Urtica.*

Life History: Multivoltine; larvae varying between shiny black with narrow yellow stripes to brown with tan stripes, bumpy with many branched spines.

Range: Guatemala to Alaska and Iceland, also northern Africa, Eurasia; Texas—entire.

Comments: Texas subspecies -*rubria.*

184

ORANGE MAP WING
Hypanartia lethe

Description: 2½ in (64 mm); small bump on forewing outer margin and short projection in middle of hindwing outer margin; above orange with brown-black AFW stripes; below complex "map" or "bark" like pattern of cream, brown, and orange with short band of blue-gray triangles on BHW from projection to outer angle.

Food Plants: Unknown; Urticaceae - *Boehmeria;* Ulmaceae - *Celtis, Trema* in tropics.

Life History: Unknown; multivoltine in Mexico.

Range: South America to Mexico and extreme southern U.S.; Texas—very rare stray to Rio Grande Valley.

Comments: Single specimen in Snow Museum, University of Kansas, figured by Ehrlich and Ehrlich 1961.

185   L,C,A

BUCKEYE
Junonia coenia

Description: 1½–2½ in (38–64 mm); above yellow-brown with four eyespots (AFW with one small above one large dark eyespot, AHW with one larger eyespot with magenta crescent above smaller spot); AFW with two black-edged orange-red cell bars and broad wavy cream band surrounding larger eyespot; AHW with cream outer margin band edged and dissected with brown lines; below similar but muted; BHW with faint eyespots.

Food Plants: Acanthaceae; Plantaginaceae; Scrophulariaceae - *Agalinus, Castilleja, Linaria, Maurandya antirrhiniflora*; Verbenaceae.

Life History: Multivoltine; spiny black larvae with two rows of orange spots on back, two rows of cream spots on sides, orange prolegs, black branched spines with blue bases on back and orange bases on sides.

Range: Mexico and West Indies to southern U.S. (strays northward to southern Canada); Texas—Far West, Trans-Pecos, Big Bend, Central, Southwest, South, Rio Grande Valley, Coastal Margin, and East; migrates through remainder of state.

Comments: Typically found in wide open habitats; the dark *Junonia* in Texas has been called Dark Buckeye (*J. nigrosuffusa*), but it is now considered a subspecies of *J. coenia*.

186

GENOVEVA
Junonia genoveva

Description: 1½–2½ in (38–64 mm); similar to Buckeye (*J. coenia*) but AFW band light orange, not surrounding eyespot; upper AHW eyespot not as large and lacking magenta; BFW with orange apex; BHW with distinct black-ringed eyespots.

Food Plants: Avicenniaceae - *Avicennia*; Verbenaceae - *Lippia*.

Life History: Multivoltine (Mar–Oct).

Range: Gulf coastal Mexico, West Indies, and extreme southern U.S.; Texas–stray to Rio Grande Valley.

Comments: Some workers state that this species has become a breeding resident along extreme southern coast; Texas subspecies *-zonalis* (Tropical Buckeye).

187

WEST INDIAN BUCKEYE
Junonia evarete

Description: 1½–2½ in (38–64 mm); similar to Genoveva (*J. coenia*) but AFW band orange, surrounding smaller eyespots and continuing across AHW between eyespots and outer margin band; AHW eyespots almost equal in size.

Food Plants: Scrophulariaceae; Verbenaceae; Acanthaceae.

Life History: Multivoltine.

Range: Argentina to southern U.S.; Texas–Rio Grande Valley, southern half of South; strays to Central and Trans-Pecos.

Comments: Prefers mangrove swamps and tidal flats; these three buckeye species confused the author while collecting in the Valley in his younger days, confused several taxonomists, and continue to perplex collectors; suspected hybridization is likely cause of unclear species boundaries.

188   A

WHITE PEACOCK
Anartia jatrophae

Description: 2¼–2½ in (57–64 mm); extended forewing and short projection in middle of hindwing outer margin; above clear white deepening to pale orange-brown at outer margin with brown lines and three black spots (one on forewing, two on hindwing); below similar but off-white with orange-edged brown lines, brown band from BFW costal through postmedian BHW, and orange-ringed black spots.

Food Plants: Verbenaceae - *Lippia, Phyla;* Scrophulariaceae - *Bacopa, Lindernia;* Acanthaceae - *Blechum, Ruellia occidentalis.*

Life History: Multivoltine.

Range: Argentina to southern U.S.; Texas–Rio Grande Valley; strays north to Central.

Comments: Prefers moist habitats; Texas subspecies *-luteipicta.*

189   A

FATIMA
Anartia fatima

Description: 2–2½ in (51–64 mm); extended forewing and short tail in middle of scalloped hindwing outer margin; above brown-black with curving yellow-cream band from AFW costal margin tapering through AHW postmedian; AFW with three white subapical spots; AHW with red median band and small triangle near outer angle; below similar but orange-brown with all bands and spots paler.

Food Plants: Acanthaceae - *Blechum, Dicliptera, Justicia, Ruellia.*

Life History: Bivoltine (Mar–May, Oct–Dec); black larvae with purple-black head, rows of pale dots, and red-brown spines.

Range: Panama to extreme southern U.S.; Texas–Rio Grande Valley.

Comments: Usually resident in Rio Grande Valley but apparently absent some years.

190   A

MALACHITE
Siproeta stelenes

Description: 3¼–3¾ in (82–95 mm); extended forewing, scalloped outer margins, and short tail in middle of hindwing outer margin; female paler than male; above black-brown with broad bands and spots of semitransparent green varying from pale jade to deep lime; below pale green with pale brown-edged white stripes and pale brown outer margin bands.

Food Plants: Acanthaceae - *Justicia, Ruellia*; also *Blechum, Justicia* in Latin America.

Life History: Multivoltine; black larva with red divisions, two red horns on head curving backwards, and pink prolegs.

Range: Brazil to West Indies and southern U.S.; Texas–Rio Grande Valley; strays north.

Comments: Rare migrant to Kansas; Texas subspecies *-biplagiata*.

ADMIRALS–SUBFAMILY LIMENITIDINAE

The Limenitidinae are worldwide in distribution and are well-represented in northern latitudes. However, the majority of the 25 species known from Texas are tropical species and several of these are present in Texas only as rare strays. This subfamily is divided into five tribes: Limenitidini (*Basilarchia, Adelpha*); Epicalini (*Epiphile, Myscelia, Eunica, Dynamine, Diaethria*); Eurytelini (*Mestra, Biblis*); Ageronini (*Hamadryas*); and Coloburini (Historis, Smyrna). Only the two species of *Basilarchia*, one of the species of *Adelpha*, and the single species of *Mestra* can be regularly found far north of the Rio Grande. The crackers (*Hamadryas*) found in Texas are unusual temporary colonists. The adults do not visit flowers, perch head down with spread wings on tree trunks, and produce a loud "click" or "crack" when darting away.

191   A

RED-SPOTTED PURPLE
Basilarchia arthemis

Description: 2½–2¾ in (64–70 mm); elongated forewing and angulated hindwing with scalloped outer margin; above blue-black becoming iridescent blue to blue-green (broader, more pronounced on AHW), AHW with black veins and submarginal band dividing iridescent blue; below deep brown with basal area red spots and red spot submarginal band bordering black-lined iridescent blue outer margin.

Food Plants: Salicaceae - *Salix*; Betulaceae - *Carpinus*; Fagaceae - *Quercus*; Rosaceae - *Crataegus, Prunus*.

Life History: Multivoltine.

Range: Eastern North America, isolated populations in Southwest; Texas—East; eastern halves of North Central, Central and Coastal Margin; isolated population in Trans-Pecos.

Comments: Mimics Pipevine Swallowtail (Battus *philenor*); classification of these subspecies varies among field guides; Texas subspecies *-arizonensis* (Arizona Admiral) in Trans-Pecos without red spots on BFW; *-astyanax* (Red-spotted Purple) in east and central Texas with red spots on BFW.

192   A

VICEROY
Basilarchia archippus

Description: 2¾–3 in (70–76 mm); similar to Monarch (*Danaus plexippus*) but smaller, more black, deeper orange, curved black postmedian AHW line, and BHW more orange; above deep orange with black veins and wide black bands on all margins (outer margins with white spots); AFW with small white apical spots; below similar but slightly paler.

Food Plants: Salicaceae - *Populus, Salix.*

Life History: Multivoltine; larvae similar to Giant Swallowtail (*Heraclides cresphontes*) but smaller with two branched spines on head without osmeterium.

Range: Mexico to Canada; Texas—East, Coastal Margin, Rio Grande Valley, eastern halves of Central and South Far West, Trans-Pecos, Big Bend.

Comments: Mülerian mimic with Monarch; previously considered to be a Batesian mimic but recent research indicates that willow has foul-tasting phytochemicals that "flavor" the Viceroy larva; Texas subspecies -*obsoleta* (Arizona Viceroy) in west Texas with white spots along curved black BHW postmedian band; -*watsoni* (Watson's Viceroy) in east and south Texas without white spots on BHW black postmedian band.

193   A

MEXICAN SISTER
Adelpha fessonia

Description: 2½–2¾ in (64–70 mm); above brown with black lines, broad white median band from forewing costal margin through hindwing tapering to point above orange spot at outer angle, and scalloped outer margins; below white with orange-brown lines, broad white median band bordering gray-brown postmedian to outer margin band with brown lines and orange outer margin dots.

Food Plants: Ulmaceae - *Celtis laevigata, C. lindheimeri;* also Rubiaceae - *Randia* in Central America.

Life History: Unknown.

Range: Costa Rica to Mexico; extreme southern U.S., Texas—regular stray to Rio Grande Valley.

Comments: Recorded all year.

194

TROPICAL SISTER
Adelpha basiloides

Description: 2¼–2½ in (57–64 mm); similar to Mexican Sister (*A. fessonia*) but darker, smaller AFW orange apical patch, and white band does not reach costal margin.

Food Plants: Unknown; Rubiaceae - *Alibertia, Faramea, Ixora* in tropics.

Life History: Unknown; multivoltine (Mar–Nov) in Mexico.

Range: Panama to Mexico and extreme southern U.S.; Texas—rare stray to Rio Grande Valley.

Comments: Single record.

195   A

CALIFORNIA SISTER
Adelpha bredowii

Description: 2¾–3¼ in (70–82 mm); extended forewing and scalloped outer margins; above dark brown with white AFW postmedian spots becoming a white median stripe through AHW to inner margin; AFW with large orange apical patch not touching margins; below similar but with pale blue-gray basal area, pale orange stripes, and pale blue-gray scalloped submarginal band.

Food Plants: Fagaceae - *Quercus* .

Life History: Univoltine (May–Jun) in west Texas; Bivoltine (Apr–Oct) in central Texas; humped larvae, green or yellow-orange, with narrow dark line on sides above brown or tan, six pairs of bristly tubercles, and covered with short bristles.

Range: Honduras to southwestern U.S.; Texas—Far West, Big Bend, Trans-Pecos; strays to Central.

Comments: Migrates eastward during droughts; Texas subspecies -*eulalia* (Arizona Sister).

196

DIMORPHIC BARK WING
Epiphile adrasta

Description: 2¼–2½ in (57–64 mm); forewing with projection below apex on outer margin; above golden brown with black-brown stripe, white AFW band from costal to tornus, black-brown apical area with white spots; below similar but mottled brown.

Food Plants: Unknown; Sapindaceae - *Paullinia, Serjania* in Mexico.

Life History: Unknown; multivoltine in Mexico.

Range: South America to Mexico and extreme southern U.S.; Texas—rare stray to Rio Grande Valley.

Comments: Only single female from Texas, Hidalgo Co., but suitable food plant common in Rio Grande Valley; Texas subspecies -*adrasta*.

197   A

BLUE WING
Myscelia ethusa

Description: 2½–3 in (64–76 mm); squared forewing apex; above iridescent blue with black stripes, white AFW apical spots; below mottled dark brown and black with white BFW apical spots.

Food Plants: Euphorbiaceae - *Dalechampia*.

Life History: Multivoltine.

Range: Central America to southern U.S.; Texas—Rio Grande Valley.

Comments: Difficult to find due to cryptic bark-like pattern below; Texas subspecies -*ethusa*.

198

CYANANTHE BLUE WING
Myscelia cyananthe

> Description: 2–2¼ in (51–57 mm); similar to Blue Wing (*M. ethusa*) but wider black bands and lacking white forewing spots.
> Food Plants: Unknown, possibly Euphorbiaceae.
> Life History: Unknown.
> Range: Mexico; Texas–rare stray to Rio Grande Valley.
> Comments: Texas subspecies -*skinneri* (Mengel's Mycelia).

199

DINGY PURPLE WING
Eunica monima

> Description: 1⅝–2 in (41–51 mm); above brown, iridescent purple on basal area, white AFW apical spots.
> Food Plants: Unknown; Burseraceae - *Bursera simaruba* in Central America; report on Rutaceae - *Zanthoxylum* in Mexico requires confirmation.
> Life History: Unknown.
> Range: Venezuela to West Indies and extreme southern U.S.; Texas–stray to Rio Grande Valley.
> Comments: Adults feed on dung, fruit, sap, mud, rarely flowers; recorded (Jun–Sep).

200

FLORIDA PURPLE WING
Eunica tatila

> Description: 1¾–2 in (44–51 mm); similar to Dingy Purple Wing (*E. monima*) but larger, more white AFW spots, forewing outer

margin concave below apex, BHW with postmedian band of small brown spots.

Food Plants: Unknown, possibly Euphorbiaceae or Burseraceae.

Life History: Unknown.

Range: Argentina to extreme southern U.S.; Texas–stray to Rio Grande Valley.

Comments: One migrant to Kansas is known; recorded (Aug–Sep); Texas subspecies *tatila.*

201

BLUE-EYED GREEN WING
Dynamine dyonis

Description: 1½–1¾ in (38–44 mm); sexually dimorphic; above (male) green with black lines and outer margins or (female) black-brown with open white median band and white AFW margin spots; below brown with white bands, two BHW submarginal orange-ringed dark blue eyespots.

Food Plants: Unknown; Euphorbiaciae - *Tragia; Dalechampia* in Central America.

Life History: Multivoltine (May–Nov).

Range: Central America to southern U.S.; Texas–Rio Grande Valley, strays to Central.

Comments: Periodically migrates north and breeds as far north as Austin, in Austin in Travis Co. (1899, 1968).

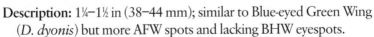

202

SPOTTED GREEN WING
Dynamine tithia

Description: 1¼–1½ in (38–44 mm); similar to Blue-eyed Green Wing (*D. dyonis*) but more AFW spots and lacking BHW eyespots.

Food Plants: Unknown; Euphorbiaceae - *Dalechampia* in Central America.

Life History: Unknown.

Range: Brazil, possibly Mexico, and extreme southern U.S.; Texas—rare stray to Big Bend.

Comments: Single Texas capture in Brewster Co. is puzzling as there are no records from Mexico.

203

MEXICAN EIGHTY-EIGHT BUTTERFLY
Diaethria asteria

Description: 1½–1¾ in (38–44 mm); above violet with white post-median AFW oblong spot, dark brown through submarginal area to outer margin with one white apical spot; BFW brown with pink costal margin wedge (narrow at base, widest on median), broad white postmedian band, and white apex curving down outer margin; BHW off-white with four dark rings forming "88", scalloped brown submarginal line.

Food Plants: Unknown, probably Sapindaceae or Ulmaceae.

Life History: Unknown.

Range: Tropical America to Mexico and extreme southern U.S.; Texas—very rare stray to Rio Grande Valley.

Comments: One Texas specimen, Hidalgo Co., 1939.

204 A

EIGHTY-EIGHT BUTTERFLY
Diaethria clymena

Description: 1½–1¾ in (38–44 mm); above black-brown with pale green AFW diagonal band from costal margin to tornus, white subapical spot; BFW red with broad black diagonal band from costal margin to tornus, white apical area with black lines; BHW white with "88" pattern and concentric black circles.

Food Plants: Unknown; Ulmaceae - *Trema micrantha* in Brazil.

Range: Tropical America to Mexico and extreme southern U.S.; Texas—very rare stray to Big Bend.

Life History: Unknown.

Comments: One specimen, now lost, from Big Bend National Park (1973).

205   A

AMYMONE
Mestra amymone

Description: 1½–1¾ in (38–44 mm); rounded wings with scalloped outer margins; above very pale gray with brown veins, broad hazy white median through postmedian band; AFW with brown-orange outer margin; AHW with large bright orange patch on outer third; below bright orange with submedian and postmedian bands of white oblongs (white smudged near BFW subapical area).

Food Plants: Euphorbiaceae - *Tragia ramosa;* also *Dalechampia* in Costa Rica.

Life History: Multivoltine.

Range: Central America to southern U.S.; Texas–Southwest, South, Rio Grande Valley, southern halves of Coastal Margin and Central; migrating through remainder of state.

Comments: Resident as far north as Austin, in Travis Co., occasionally migrates to Kansas, even Minnesota; recorded (Jun–Nov).

206   A

RED RIM
Biblis hyperia

Description: 2–2⅝ in (51–65 mm); extended forewing with deeply scalloped hindwing; above black with red-pink AHW submarginal band; below similar but more brown than black, BHW band smaller and pink; BHW with small red basal dots.

Food Plants: Euphorbiaceae - *Tragia.*

Life History: Unknown; multivoltine in Mexico.

Range: Paraguay to West Indies and southern U.S.; Texas–Rio Grande Valley, Big Bend National Park; rare stray to Central.

Comments: Recorded (Feb, Jul–Nov); Texas subspecies *-aganisa* (Hyperia).

207 A

GRAY CRACKER
Hamadryas februa

Description: 2½–2¾ in (64–70 mm); above pale brown and pale gray with complex pattern of rippling brown and dark brown lines, submarginal row of spots with dark brown crescents in one AFW eyespot and in four AHW eyespots; below similar but with unmarked pale gray to median on BFW, to postmedian on BHW.

Food Plants: Unknown; Euphorbiaceae - *Dalechampia scandens, Tragia volubilis* in Latin America.

Life History: Unknown; multivoltine in tropics; black larvae with light green spines, and six lengthwise stripes, red-brown head with two long curved knobbed spines.

Range: Argentina to Mexico and extreme southern U.S.; Texas–Rio Grande Valley.

Comments: Recorded (Aug–Oct); Texas subspecies *-ferentina* (Ferentine Calico).

208

BLUE CRACKER
Hamadryas feronia

Description: 2½–2¾ in (64–76 mm); similar to Gray Cracker (*H.februa*) but with dull red AFW-discal cell bar, above eyespots ringed with blue having white spotted black centers; below chalk white, red BFW discal cell bar, more distinct dark brown lines, and boldly checkered outer margins; BHW with black submarginal circles.

Food Plants: Unknown; Euphorbiaceae - *Dalechampia* in tropics.
Life History: Unknown; multivoltine in tropics.
Range: Paraguay to extreme southern U.S.; Texas–rare stray to Rio Grande Valley.
Comments: Recorded (Jul–Dec); Texas subspecies *-farinulenta*.

209 A

CENTRAL AMERICAN CRACKER
Hamadryas guatamalena

Description: 2½–3¼ in (64–82 mm); similar to Blue Cracker (*H. feronia*) but darker, submarginal eyespots pale blue-ringed black with pale blue-ringed brown centers; AFW with two gray subapical oblongs on costal margin; below off-white unmarked through median, jagged dark brown bands, black submarginal BHW circles, and boldly checkered outer margins.
Food Plants: Unknown; Euphorbiaceae - *Dalechampia* in tropics.
Life History: Unknown; multivoltine in tropics.
Range: Costa Rica to extreme southern U.S.; Texas–rare stray to Rio Grande Valley.
Comments: Single female known from Hidalgo Co., recorded (Aug); Texas subspecies *-marmarice*.

210

RINGLESS BLUE CRACKER
Hamadryas iphthime

Description: 2½–3 in (64–76 mm); similar to Central American Cracker (*H. guatamelena*) but paler above, lacking red AFW discal cell bar, and AHW eyespots smaller.
Food Plants: Unknown; Euphorbiaceae - *Dalechampia* in tropics.
Life History: Unknown; multivoltine in tropics.
Range: Brazil to extreme southern U.S.; Texas–rare stray to Rio Grande Valley.

Comments: Single specimen from Burnet Co., recorded (Aug); Texas subspecies *-joannae.*

211

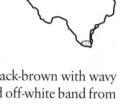

RED CRACKER
Hamadryas amphinome

Description: 2½–2¾ in (64–70 mm); above black-brown with wavy pattern of pale blue marks; AFW with broad off-white band from costal margin to lower outer margin and subapical spot; AHW with submarginal band of circles with pale blue centers; below with brick red BFW basal area, white band and subapical spots, and both wings with boldly checkered outer margins; brick red BHW through submargin without circles.

Food Plants: Unknown; Euphorbiaceae - *Dalechampia scandens* in El Salvador.

Life History: Unknown; multivoltine in tropics.

Range: Argentina to extreme southern U.S.; Texas—stray to Rio Grande Valley.

Comments: Recorded (Sep); Texas subspecies *-mexicana.*

212

STINKY LEAF WING
Historis odius

Description: 3¾–4½ in (95–114 mm); extended forewing with rounded apex and hindwing with pointed outer angle; above brown-black with orange bases (brighter, more extensive on AFW); below orange-brown to purple-brown with leaf-like reticulated pattern.

Food Plants: Unknown; Moraceae - *Cecropia peltata* in Central America.

Life History: Unknown; multivoltine in tropics.

Range: Argentina to West Indies and extreme southern U.S.; Texas—rare stray to Rio Grande Valley.

Comments: Adults feed at dung, fruit, sap, mud, rarely visit flowers.

213

DASH-WING
Historis acheronta

Description: 3¼–3½ in (82–89 mm); similar to Stinky Leaf Wing (*H. odius*) but hindwing outer angle point longer; below with white BFW spots.

Food Plants: Unknown; Moraceae - *Cecropia* in Central America.

Life History: Unknown.

Range: Brazil to West Indies and extreme southern U.S.; Texas— very rare stay to Rio Grande Valley.

Comments: One verified Texas specimen in Presidio Co.; old records from Valley not verified; Texas subspecies *-cadmus* (Cadmus).

214

KARWINSKI'S BEAUTY
Smyrna karwinskii

Description: 3¼–3½ in (82–89 mm); above orange with black AFW apex; BFW with broad diagonal yellow-cream band, broad diagonal dark brown band and pale brown apex with hazy white spots; BHW white with complex of brown oblong spots and lines, two black-ringed submarginal eyespots (upper with white centered black, lower with white-centered brown).

Food Plants: Unknown; Urticaceae - *Myriocarpa, Urera, Urticastrum* in El Salvador.

Life History: Unknown.

Range: Central America to Mexico and extreme southern U.S.; Texas—rare stray to Rio Grande Valley.

Comments: Old records from Brownsville, Cameron Co., no specimens available.

215   A

BLOMFILD'S BEAUTY
Smyrna blomfildia

Description: 3–3¼ in (76–82 mm); sexually dimorphic with more orange (male) or more brown (female); similar to Karwinski's Beauty (*S. karwinksii*) but hindwing outer angle tail shorter, blunted; both BHW eyespots black-centered.

Food Plants: Unknown; Urticaceae - *Urera, Urticastrum* in El Salvador.

Life History: Unknown; multivoltine in tropics.

Range: Brazil to Mexico and extreme southern U.S.; Texas—rare stray to Rio Grande Valley.

Comments: Two Texas records, Hidalgo Co., (Nov 1983, Dec 1978); Texas subspecies -*datis.*

DAGGER WINGS—SUBFAMILY MARPESIINAE

This small subfamily contains two genera: Marpesia (dagger wings) of the New World tropics and *Cyrestis* (map butterflies) of the Old World tropics. Only three species of this subfamily occur in Texas; none have a broad range within the state, being restricted to occasional strays to the Rio Grande Valley and rarely further northward. Larvae are very distinctive among the nymphalids, being very colorful as well as having two long spines on the head capsule and a row of single spines down the middle of the back. All species use members of Moraceae (mulberry family), preferably *Ficus* (figs), for larval foodplants. Adults visit flowers, rotting fruit, and mammal dung.

216 A

WAITER
Marpesia zerynthia

Description: 2–2½ in (51–64 mm); extended curved forewing with squared apex, hindwing with one long white-tipped tail above one short reddish outer angle tail; above dark brown; below chalk white through median then brown, separated by narrow red-brown line.

Food Plants: Unknown.

Life History: Unknown; multivoltine in Mexico.

Range: Brazil to Mexico and extreme southern U.S.; Texas–rare stray to Rio Grande Valley, Far West.

Comments: Formerly known as *M. coresia;* recorded (Jul, Oct).

217 A

MANY-BANDED DAGGER WING
Marpesia chiron

Description: 2–2⅜ in (51–60 mm); extended forewing with blunt apex and hindwing with two white-tipped tails, longer tail above shorter outer angle tail; above brown with dark brown dagger-like stripes; AFW with two rows of three faint white apical spots; below pale gray through median then pale brown with red-edged white stripes (most distinct through median), gray AFW spots and hazy stripes.

Food Plants: Unknown, probably Moraceae - *Ficus, Morus;* also *Artocarpus, Chlorophora* in tropics.

Life History: Unknown; multivoltine in Mexico.

Range: Argentina to West Indies and southern U.S.; Texas–occasional migrant to Rio Grande Valley.

Comments: Rare migrant to Kansas; recorded (Feb, Jul–Oct).

218 A

RUDDY DAGGER WING
Marpesia petreus

Description: 2½–3 in (64–76 mm); very extended forewing with squared apex held apart from hindwing with two tails (long tail above short outer angle tail); above orange with narrow dark brown stripes and outer margins (margins darker on AHW); below light brown with narrow white basal stripe, brown lines, and brown-gray mottling past postmedian with submarginal line of black dots.

Food Plants: Unknown; probably Moraceae - *Ficus;* also *Arctocarpus, Chlorophora* in tropics.

Life History: Multivoltine.

Range: Brazil to West Indies and southern U.S.; Texas–regular migrant to lower Rio Grande Valley.

Comments: Rare migrant to Nebraska.

GOATWEED BUTTERFLIES—SUBFAMILY CHARAXINAE

About 400 species are known in this subfamily, mostly from tropical areas of the world. Of the five species known from North America and Texas, only one occurs as far north as Canada. The Texas species are included in the tribe Anaeini. All North American species are found on plants of Euphorbiaceae (spurges), although tropical species are found on a variety of plant families, including Poaceae (grasses).

The spherical eggs are flattened from top to bottom and are laid singly. None of the New World charaxids have gregarious larvae. Found in nests made from rolled leaves, the larvae generally have horns or bumps on the head capsules, smooth or hairy bodies with no spines, and a divided tail. The pupa is suspended upside down from a cremaster.

The medium-sized adults rest with the wings closed above the body, and bask with the wings open flat. Wing pattern may be brightly colored or dull on the upper surface, but the underside is generally cryptic and resembles bark or dead leaves. The typical species has a stout body, short proboscis, and large palps. Adults readily feed on carrion, rotting fruit, and dung; most species never visit flowers. Flight is strong with a powerful wing beat. Some species are migratory.

219

TROPICAL LEAF WING
Anaea aidea

Description: 2¼–3 in (57–76 mm); seasonal variation (winter form with hooked forewing apex), hindwing with toothed outer wing edges and one tail; above yellow-orange to red-orange with hazy dark brown outer margins (female with bands of yellow submarginal spots); below grainy gray-brown.

Food Plants: Unknown; Euphorbiaceae - *Croton soliman* in Mexico.

Life History: Multivoltine (Apr–Nov).

Range: Honduras to Southwestern U.S.; Texas—Big Bend, along Texas-Mexico border to Southwest, southwestern half of South, Rio Grande Valley.

Comments: Occasionally migrates to Kansas and Illinois; recorded (Apr–Nov).

220   L,C,A

GOATWEED BUTTERFLY
Anaea andria

Description: 2–2½ in (51–64 mm); similar to Tropical Leaf Wing (*A. aidea*) but with wider range, larger, less red, less outer marginal marking, and smooth wing edges with one hindwing tail; above orange-red with short black costal margin line connected to black bar at end of cell, hazy dark brown outer bands; AHW with more brown, occasionally submarginal row of small faint orange dots; below grainy gray-brown.

Food Plants: Euphorbiaceae - *Croton capitatus, C. monanthogynous, C. texensis.*

Life History: Multivoltine; gray-green larvae covered with short tubercles.

Range: Mexico to central and southeastern U.S.; Texas—entire.

Comments: Strong flier, migrates northward yearly.

221

ANGLED LEAF WING
Memphis glycerium

Description: 2¼–3 in (57–76 mm); falcate forewing with squared apex and concave outer wing edge, hindwing with toothed wing edge and one short tail; above pale orange with jagged yellow postmedian band (fading on AHW), brown-orange veins, and hazy brown-orange outer margin bands; AFW with short dark brown costal margin line connected to distinct black bar at end of cell; below grainy yellow-brown mottling with narrow dark brown median line (incomplete on BFW).

Food Plants: Unknown; Euphorbiaceae - *Croton jalapensis* in Central America.

Life History: Unknown; multivoltine in Mexico.

Range: Argentina to West Indies and extreme southern U.S.; Texas-stray to Rio Grande Valley.

222   A

BLUE LEAF WING
Memphis pithyusa

Description: 2–2¾ in (51–70 mm); extended forewing, one short narrow tail on hindwing; above iridescent blue-black over brown; AHW with small white spots near tail; below mottled gray.

Food Plants: Unknown; Euphorbiaceae - *Croton reflexifolius, C. niveus* in El Salvador.

Life History: Unknown.

Range: Bolivia to extreme southern U.S.; Texas—lower Rio Grande Valley.

Comments: Only iridescent leaf wing in U.S., many other iridescent species in tropical America.

223

CHESTNUT LEAF BUTTERFLY
Memphis echemus

Description: 2¼–2¾ in (57–70 mm); above brown with yellow wash; AHW with dark spots near tail; below pale brown with reticulated lines; BHW with two dark brown spots near tail.

Food Plants: Unknown.

Life History: Unknown.

Range: Central America, West Indies; Texas—southeastern Central, Colorado Co.

Comments: Single specimen (1938).

HACKBERRY BUTTERFLIES—SUBFAMILY APATURINAE

Most of the 50 worldwide species occur in temperate and tropical portions of the Old World. Only five species are known from North America, all of which occur in Texas. North American species use various members of *Celtis* (hackberries) as their larval food plant.

The spherical eggs are laid in small to large clusters. The larvae have branching spines on the head (sometimes referred to as "antlers"), smooth or slightly hairy body, and two short "tails" projecting from the rear of the body. Overwintering larvae cluster inside rolled dead leaves. The typical chrysalis has horns on the head end, is laterally compressed, and (in our species) rests horizontally against a leaf or branch.

The adults are swift and powerful fliers but do not migrate. Adults generally prefer sap, fruit, or dung to flowers. Sexual dimorphism in wing pattern and shape is typical. In tropical species the male frequently has highly reflective patches or stripes on the upper side of the wings; the female is generally non-iridescent but may possess a complex pattern.

224   A

HACKBERRY BUTTERFLY
Asterocampa celtis

Description: 1¾–2¼ in (40–55 mm); geographic and sexual variation (male smaller, female paler); extended forewing; above
brown turning yellow-brown past cell; AFW with dark brown discal cell bar past two small cell spots, black-brown postmedian to
wing edge with orange marks, light oblong subapical spots, and
distinct black postmedian spot; AHW with black postmedian
spot band, several black submarginal lines; below pink-brown
bands with pale gray spots; BFW with black spot; BHW with
brown lines, postmedian band black spots.

Food Plants: Ulmaceae - *Celtis laevigata, C. occidentalis, C. reticulata.*

Life History: Multivoltine (Mar–Oct).

Range: Northern Mexico to southwest and eastern U.S.; Texas–
entire.

Comments: Texas subspecies *-antonia* (Antonia) is west of Corpus
Christi to Austin to Fort Worth line with two dark AFW spots;
-celtis (Hackberry Butterfly) is east of Corpus Christi to Austin to
Fort Worth line with one dark AFW spot; subspecies -may
hybridize in blend zone along above mentioned line.

225   L,A

EMPRESS LEILIA
Asterocampa leilia

Description: 1¾–2¼ in (44–57 mm); similar to Hackberry Butterfly
(*A. celtis*) but slightly smaller, more orange and without lines,
without cell spots; AFW with faint brown cell bars, two distinct
black postmedian spots; AHW with black postmedian spot band;
below darker pink-brown with darker, more complex pattern;
BFW with off-white cell bar and spots, two yellow-ringed black

postmedian eyespots with white centers; BHW with submarginal row of smaller yellow-ringed black eyespots with white centers.

Food Plants: Ulmaceae - *Celtis pallida.*

Life History: Bivoltine.

Range: Northern Mexico and south central, southwestern U.S.; Texas—Big Bend, along Texas-Mexico border through Southwest, South, Rio Grande Valley.

Comments: Very similar to Antonia (*A. celtis antonia*).

226   C,A

TAWNY EMPEROR
Asterocampa clyton

Description: 1¾–2¼ in (44–57 mm); geographic and sexual variations (smaller male with angulated wings, larger female with rounded wings); extended forewing; above dull orange and yellow-brown; AFW orange with two wavy black cell bars, wavy smudged black postmedian band before yellow spots, smudged black submarginal line; AHW brown-orange with orange-ringed black submarginal eyespots in broad hazy black area; below pale pink-brown with brown veins; BFW with wavy black cell bars, wavy black postmedian line; BHW with white postmedian band, row of small white-centered submarginal black eyespots.

Food Plants: Ulmaceae - *Celtis laevigata, C. occidentalis, C. reticulata.*

Life History: Bivoltine, possibly multivoltine in south.

Range: Northeastern Mexico to southwestern and eastern U.S.; Texas—entire except for northern half of Panhandle, southern half of High Plains, or western third of Central.

Comments: Texas subspecies *-clyton* (Tawny Emperor) is east of Freeport to Austin to Fort Worth line with unringed white lower submarginal BFW spot; *-louisa* (Empress Louisa) in Rio Grande Valley with black-brown AFW apex, less dark on AHW, and below less patterned; *-texana* (Texan Emperor) is west of Freeport to Austin to Fort Worth line and north of Rio Grande Valley with brown-ringed white lower submarginal BFW spot. Field identification relies as much on location as markings.

227 A

PAVON
Doxocopa pavon

> **Description:** 2¼–2¾ in (57–70 mm); sexually dimorphic; above (male) brown with purple iridescent haze, vague pale median and submarginal bands; or above (female) paler brown with white bands; both with two wavy black cell bars, large orange AFW subapical patch, black scalloped outer margin lines; below light brown with broad white median band, black dots and bar on BFW cell, brown scalloped outermargin lines.
>
> **Food Plants:** Unknown; Ulmaceae - *Celtis pallida, C. iguanaea* in Mexico.
>
> **Life History:** Unknown; multivoltine in Mexico.
>
> **Range:** Mexico and extreme southern U.S.; Texas–Rio Grande Valley.
>
> **Comments:** Regular stray to Rio Grande Valley; female similar to Mexican Sister (*Adelpha fessonia*) but without AHW outer angle orange spot.

228

LAURE
Doxocopa laure

> **Description:** 2¾–3 in (70–76 mm); extended curved forewing with squared apex and hindwing with extended outer angle; sexually dimorphic; above (male) deep brown with black mottling, broad median band orange on AFW turning to white on AHW (blue iridescence along median band in newly emerged males), light orange AFW apex; or above (female) brown with broad white median band, large pale orange AFW costal margin patch, scalloped dark brown submarginal and outer margin lines; below hazy broad bands of brown and iridescent white.

Food Plants: Unknown; Ulmaceae - *Celtis pallida, C. iguanaea* in Mexico.

Life History: Unknown; multivoltine in Mexico.

Range: Venezuela to West Indies, Mexico, and extreme southern U.S.; Texas—stray to Rio Grande Valley.

Comments: Regular stray to southern Texas; female similar to Mexican Sister (*Adelpha fessonia*) but more angulated wings, lacks rust stripes below.

Hackberry (*Asterocampa celtis*)

Morpho Butterflies—Family Morphidae

The morphos are best known as the large, incredibly iridescent blue butterflies from the tropical rain forests of Central and South America. Wingspans of the various species vary from 3 in (76 mm) to 8 in (204 mm). Approximately 80 species have been identified. Some of these are white or brown in general color on the above wing surfaces rather than the iridescent blue of the best-known species. All species have a series of prominent eyespots on the below side of the wings. Eggs are hemispherical in shape and the larvae are gregarious during the early instars. The pupa is suspended upside down and possesses small but distinctive projections on the head. Three species occur in Mexico and one of these has resident populations less than 200 miles south of the Rio Grande. One sight record of a species of this family exists for Texas. Normally, sight records without at least one specimen in a museum or private collection are not listed in this book. However, the significance of the sighting and the veracity of the observer are such that this record is repeated here.

229   A

COMMON MORPHO
Morpho peleides

> **Description:** 3¾–4½ in (95–114 mm); Very shiny blue above and orange below.
>
> **Food Plants:** Unknown; Fabaceae - *Machaerium seemannii, Lonchocarpus* in Mexico.
>
> **Life History:** Unknown; multivoltine in Mexico.
>
> **Range:** Mexico, West Indies, and extreme southern U.S.; Texas—single stray to Rio Grande Valley.
>
> **Comments:** Single sight record afternoon of 25 Mar 1945 by H. A. Freeman, two miles north of Hidalgo, Hidalgo Co.; description indicates that Freeman observed a worn *M. peleides* with below faded from its original dark brown; Texas subspecies probably *-montezuma.*

SATYR BUTTERFLIES—FAMILY SATYRIDAE

Although there are about 2,000 species of satyrs worldwide, only 43 species are known from North America, of which 10 occur in Texas. Larvae generally feed on monocotylenous plants, specifically Poaceae (grass family) and Cyperaceae (sedge family). A few species even feed on mosses or club mosses (plants on which few insects feed). No satyr has been reported to feed on a dicotyledonous plant.

Eggs are spherical with a flattened bottom. The eggs may be deposited directly on the proper food plant, on vegetation (dead or alive) near the food plant, or even dropped in flight over suitable habitat for the proper food plant. Generally, the larvae have horns on the head, two posterior "tails," but no spines on the body. The typical chrysalis has a humped thorax with two horns (but no spiny projection) and hangs upside down.

Texas satyrs are largely brown with eyespots occurring in most species, but more tropical species can be quite colorful or possess transparent areas on the wings. Similar to the brushfoots (Nymphalidae), the forelegs are greatly reduced in length. The base of the forewing costal vein is generally swollen to form a readily visible bubble that is diagnostic for this family. The antennal club is reduced in width and much less obvious than in many butterfly families. Adults rest with the wings closed, but they bask with the wings held out flat. Arctic satrys (*Oeneis*) and the northern ringlets (*Coenonympha*) will bask with wings closed above the body as the butterfly rests sideways to the sun. Adults rarely visit flowers, preferring rotting fruit, tree sap, dung, and fungi. The flight pattern of most species is a distinctive "hop." Most satyrs fly close to the ground and many prefer wooded habitats. The female is the flying partner if a mating pair is disturbed. Migratory behavior is unknown in this family, although local populations may disperse during population peaks.

PEARLY EYES—SUBFAMILY ELYMNIINAE

Of the five species of this subfamily in North America, only two occur in restricted eastern areas of Texas. Pearly eyes are always found in moist habitats, generally around swamps, marshes, glades, and riparian bottoms. They feed on Poaceae (grasses) as larvae. Adults have a darting flight pattern that is swift but erratic. Adults do not visit flowers, but may be observed at tree sap, carrion, and dung. Wing patterns are dominated by light brown coloration with large to medium-sized eyespots in a row near the outer margins of both forewing and hindwing, above and below.

230 A

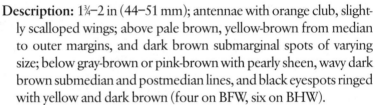

PEARLY EYE
Enodia portlandia

> **Description:** 1¾–2 in (44–51 mm); antennae with orange club, slightly scalloped wings; above pale brown, yellow-brown from median to outer margins, and dark brown submarginal spots of varying size; below gray-brown or pink-brown with pearly sheen, wavy dark brown submedian and postmedian lines, and black eyespots ringed with yellow and dark brown (four on BFW, six on BHW).
>
> **Food Plants:** Poaceae - *Arundinaria gigantea.*
>
> **Life History:** Multivoltine (Mar–Oct); light green larvae with two pairs of red-capped horns (one pair at each end).
>
> **Range:** Southeastern U.S.; Texas–East, eastern third of Coastal Margin.
>
> **Comments:** Males aggressively territorial; Texas subspecies *-missarkae.*

231 A

CREOLE PEARLY EYE
Enodia creola

> **Description:** 2–2¼ in (51–57 mm); similar to Pearly Eye (*E. portlandia*) but slightly larger, more extended forewing, BFW with five eyespots; above more olive-brown; below more gray-brown.
>
> **Food Plants:** Poaceae - *Arundinaria gigantea.*
>
> **Life History:** Multivoltine (Apr–Sep).
>
> **Range:** Southeastern U.S.; Texas–East, eastern third of Coastal Margin.
>
> **Comments:** Males aggressively territorial, fly in deep forest, also at dusk.

SATYRS AND WOOD NYMPHS—SUBFAMILY SATYRINAE

Of the 45 species of this subfamily known from North America, eight have been reported from Texas. These species are found in various habitat types, usually at least semi-woody. However, several species have adapted to now-common very open habitat-type residential lawns. Larvae have only been found feeding on Poaceae (grass family). The adults have an erratic, bobbling flight pattern; some species visit flowers. Wing patterns vary but are mostly brown with light yellow and brick red highlights or patches common. A few eyespots of varying sizes are common and usually possess a metallic center.

232

WARM BROWN
Cyllopsis pertepida

Description: 1½–1¾ in (38–44 mm); above and below red-brown; BHW red-brown (male) or purple-brown (female) with distinct silver patch surrounding two oblong black spots on upper half of outer margin bordered by wavy red postmedian line.

Food Plants: Unknown; feeds on Poaceae - *Cynodon, Poa* in lab.

Life History: Univoltine at higher altitudes (Jul–Aug); bivoltine at lower altitudes (May–Jun, Aug–Oct).

Range: Mexico to southwestern U.S.; Texas—Far West, Big Bend, western half of Trans-Pecos.

Comments: Texas subspecies -*avicula* (Texas Brown).

233   A

GEMMED SATYR
Cyllopsis gemma

> **Description:** ¾–1 in (19–25 mm); above dusty brown, with a few very small black AHW submarginal spots; below brown with wavy dark brown lines; BHW with reflective black oblong spots in small silver outer margin patch.
> **Food Plants:** Unknown; Poaceae - *Cynodon dactylon* in lab.
> **Life History:** Multivoltine (Feb–Nov); light green larvae with dark green stripes (summer) or brown with dark brown stripes (fall) with long brown horns at both ends.
> **Range:** Guatemala to southeastern U.S.; Texas–East, Coastal Margin, Rio Grande Valley, South, eastern halves of Central and North Central.
> **Comments:** Larval color dimorphism may be linked to seasonal changes in the grass color; Texas subspecies *-freemani* in south Texas with ground color more red-brown; *-gemma* in east and central Texas with ground color more yellow-brown.

234   A

HERMES SATYR
Hermeuptychia hermes

> **Description:** 1–1¼ in (25–32 mm); above brown with faint lines; below brown with grainy white haze, several wavy narrow dark brown lines, small submarginal eyespots (five of BFW, six on BHW with second and fifth most distinct).
> **Food Plants:** Poaceae - *Axonopus compressus, Cynodon dactylon.*
> **Life History:** Multivoltine.
> **Range:** South America to southeastern U.S.; Texas–East, Coastal Margin, Rio Grande Valley, South, eastern halves of Central and North Central.

Comments: Some workers restrict Hermes Satyr to south Texas and classify east Texas populations as Carolina Satyr (*H. sosybius*); adults visit sap, fruit, mud, dung, but rarely flowers; common in urban lawns.

235 A

GEORGIA SATYR
Neonympha areolata

Description: ¾–1 in (19–25 mm); above unmarked brown; below brown with two wavy red median lines and two red outer margin lines; BHW with row of postmedian yellow-ringed dark metallic oblong eyespots.
Food Plants: Poaceae - *Sorghastrum nutans*.
Life History: Bivoltine (Apr–Sep).
Range: Southeastern U.S.; Texas—East, eastern third of Coastal Margin.
Comments: Texas subspecies -*areolata*.

236 A

LITTLE WOOD SATYR
Megisto cymela

Description: 1⅜–1⅝ in (35–41 mm); above brown with yellow-ringed black submarginal eyespots (two on each wing), two narrow dark brown outer margin lines; below similar but with narrow dark brown submedian and postmedian lines, metallic centers in eyespots.
Food Plants: Poaceae - *Dactylis, Eremochloa*.
Life History: Bivoltine (Mar–Sep); light olive larvae with black lengthwise stripes, brown patches on sides, off-white head, and two tails with red tips.
Range: Eastern North America; Texas—East; eastern halves of North Central, Central, and Coastal Margin.
Comments: Texas subspecies -*cymela*.

237   A

RED SATYR
Megisto rubricata

Description: 1½–1¾ in (38–44 mm); above deep brown with pale orange area next to yellow-ringed submarginal black eyespots (one on each wing) and two narrow dark brown outer margin lines; below similar but orange restricted to BFW.

Food Plants: Unknown; Poaceae - *Stenotaphrum secundatum*, *Cynodon dactylon* in lab.

Life History: Bivoltine (Apr–Sep).

Range: Guatemala to southwestern U.S.; Texas—entire except East; eastern halves of North Central, Central, and Coastal Margin.

Comments: Texas subspecies *-rubricata* (Red Satyr) in north, central, and south Texas with diffuse red-orange BFW patch; *smithorum* (Smith's Red Satyr) in more western Texas with distinct red-orange BFW patch.

238   A

COMMON WOOD NYMPH
Cercyonis pegala

Description: 1¾–2½ in (44–64 mm); geographic variation and sexual dimorphism (larger paler female with larger eyespots); above brown with broad yellow postmedian through submargin band with black eyespots (two on AFW; usually one, sometimes two, on AHW); below brown, heavily striated with dark brown; BFW with (or without) yellow band, two black eyespots with (or without) yellow rings; BHW with (or without) smaller black centered eyespots with (or without) yellow rings.

Food Plants: Poaceae - *Andropogon, Stipa, Tridens.*

Life History: Univoltine (Jun–Sep); light green larvae with four lengthwise yellow lines and fine, short hairs.

Range: Southern Canada, most U.S.; Texas–Panhandle; North Central; East; eastern halves of Coastal Margin, Central, High Plains; and western Big Bend.

Comments: Large, showy butterfly seen crossing highways during population peaks; Texas subspecies -*texana* (Texas Wood Nymph).

239

MEAD'S WOOD NYMPH
Cercyonis meadii

Description: 1½–1¾ in (38–44 mm); above brown; AFW with large orange-brown patch surrounding or next to two yellow-ringed black submarginal eyespots (larger eyespot above smaller); AHW may have one orange-ringed black submarginal eyespot; below similar but striated with brown and gray-brown (heaviest on BHW); two small black BHW spots on lower submargin.

Food Plants: Poaceae - *Bouteloua*.

Life History: Univoltine (Aug–Sep).

Range: Mountain areas of western U.S. and adjacent Mexico; Texas–mountain areas in Far West, Big Bend, and western half of Trans-Pecos.

Comments: Texas subspecies -*melania* (Winds Satyr).

MONARCHS AND QUEENS—FAMILY DANAIDAE

Generally large in size and tropical in occurrence, this family contains approximately 200 species. However, only four species are known from North America, all of which have been reported from Texas.

In Texas, the food plants are Asclepiadaceae (milkweeds) and Apocynaceae (dogbane), although tropical Danaidae may feed on plants in the Caricaceae, Moraceae, Loganiaceae, and Theophrastaceae families. Phytochemicals, specifically cardiac glycosides, in these plant families include a number of compounds that are toxic to vertebrates. During the larval stage, these compounds are stored in the body tissues and retained in the adult's body tissues. The adult will be poisonous only if the larva ate a poisonous plant. Since both larval and adult milkweed butterflies are frequently poisonous, other butterflies, for example the Viceroy (*Basilarchia archippus*), mimic them for protection.

Eggs are spindle-shaped and are deposited singly. Larvae are usually striped or banded in colorful patterns dominated by black, white, yellow, and red. Spines are absent but long, fleshy tubercles (like tentacles) are usually present. The chrysalis, which hangs upside down, is usually a stout cylinder of green or golden color. Metallic golden spots are present on the chrysalids of the genus *Danaus*.

The large adults are strong fliers that flap strongly at a slow rate. Female Danainae have reduced forelegs and both sexes lack scales on their antennae. Adult males visit plants that contain phytochemicals known as pyrrolizidine alkaloids in the nectar or on the surfaces of the leaves. These alkaloids are used in the production of male sex pheromones, which are produced and released by a patch of black androconial scales on the hindwing or from "hair pencils," an organ that can be extruded from the abdomen. Male butterflies use pheromones to attract females as part of the courtship behavior.

MONARCHS —SUBFAMILY DANAINAE

Members of this subfamily are found worldwide in tropical and subtropical areas. The three Texas species are largely orange or gold-brown and black in color, but many of the tropical species are more colorful and some of these exhibit ornate patterns of black and white. The most readily recognized butterfly in North America, the Monarch (*Danaus plexippus*), belongs to this subfamily.

240 A

MONARCH
Danaus plexippus

Description: 3½–4¼ in (89–108 mm); above orange with black vein
markings, broad black marginal bands with white spots in outer
margin bands (female dull orange with thicker vein markings);
male with androconial scales in spot near end of AHW cell;
below similar but yellow with orange restricted to BFW except
for yellow subapical area.

Food Plants: Asclepiadaceae - *Asclepias*; Apocynaceae - *Apoc-
ynum*.

Life History: Multivoltine; smooth white larvae with yellow and
black rings, two pairs of black tentacles (one behind head, one
near tail).

Range: South America to southern Canada; Texas–entire, mostly
as migrants in spring and fall.

Comments: Millions of monarchs from eastern and central U.S.
overwinter in central Mexico after migrating through Texas;
rarely a few individuals in coastal south Texas during mild winters; possibly a summer breeding resident in Texas but probably
only along northern border with Oklahoma, in the Red River
Valley area; Müllerian mimic with Viceroy (*Basilarchia archippus*); Texas subspecies -*plexippus*.

241 C,A

QUEEN
Danaus gilippus

Description: 2¾–3½ in (70–89 mm); above deep gold-brown
becoming paler past discal cell with black-brown costal and
outer margins, white spots scattered from cell to wing edge
(heavier on AFW); male with AHW androconial patch; below
similar but more brown and BHW with black vein lines.

Food Plants: Asclepiadaceae - *Asclepias, Sarcostemma.*

Life History: Multivoltine; smooth black larvae with alternating black-striped white bands, yellow dashes in black bands, and three pairs of tentacles (pair behind head, pair in middle, pair near tail).

Range: Argentina to southern U.S.; Texas—entire, resident in Rio Grande Valley, Southwest, South, Coastal Margin, and southern third of Central.

Comments: Texas subspecies *-strigosus* (Striated Queen).

242   A

SOLDIER
Danaus eresimus

Description: 2½–3 in (64–76 mm); similar to Queen (*D. gilippus*) but slightly smaller, brown-black veins above and below (restricted to BHW on Queen); fewer white AFW spots.

Food Plants: Asclepiadaceae - *Asclepias.*

Life History: Multivoltine (Aug–Dec).

Range: Brazil to West Indies and extreme southern U.S.; Texas—Rio Grande Valley.

Comments: Texas subspecies *-montezuma* (Montezuma).

TIGERS—SUBFAMILY ITUNINAE

The Tigers are restricted to the New World tropics. Only a single species is known to have strayed into North America and Texas. The wings are longer than observed in the subfamily Danainae, but are not as extended as seen in the longwings (Heliconiidae). Many species are involved in the "tiger-stripe" mimicry complex of tropical America.

PLATE 1

LIFE CYCLE

157. JANAIS PATCH Breeding Pair
Chlosyne janais

157. JANAIS PATCH Eggs
Chlosyne janais

157. JANAIS PATCH Larva
Chlosyne janais

157. JANAIS PATCH Chrysalis
Chlosyne janais

157. JANAIS PATCH Adult
Chosyne janais

PLATE 2

EGGS

4. ZEBRA SWALLOWTAIL
Eurytides marcellus

2. PIPEVINE SWALLOWTAIL
Battus philenor

16. SPICEBUSH SWALLOWTAIL
Pterourus troilus

157. JANAIS PATCH
Chlosyne janais

247. GUAVA SKIPPER
Phocides polybius

PLATE 3

LARVAE

4. ZEBRA SWALLOWTAIL
Eurytides marcellus

2. PIPEVINE SWALLOWTAIL
Battus philenor

4. ZEBRA SWALLOWTAIL (dark form)
Eurytides marcellus

6. BLACK SWALLOWTAIL
Papilio polyxenes

PLATE 4

13. TIGER SWALLOWTAIL
Pterourus glaucus

8. GIANT SWALLOWTAIL
Heraclides cresphontes

16. SPICEBUSH SWALLOWTAIL
Pterourus troilus

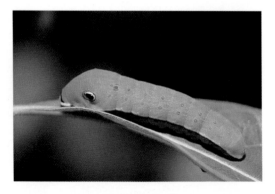

17. PALAMEDES SWALLOWTAIL
Pterourus palamedes

PLATE 5

34. DOG FACE
Zerene cesonia

37. CLOUDLESS SULPHUR
Phoebis sennae

139. GULF FRITILLARY
Agraulis vanillae

142. JULIA
Dryas iulia

PLATE 6

144. ZEBRA
Heliconius charitonius

146. VARIEGATED FRITILLARY
Euptoieta claudia

150. THEONA CHECKERSPOT
Thessalia theona

157. JANAIS PATCH
Chlosyne janais

PLATE 7

177. QUESTION MARK
Polygonia interrogationis

181. PAINTED LADY
Vanessa cardui

180. AMERICAN PAINTED LADY
Vanessa virginiensis

185. BUCKEYE
Junonia coenia

PLATE 8

220. GOATWEED BUTTERFLY
Anaea andria

225. EMPRESS LEILIA
Asterocampa leilia

226. TAWNY EMPEROR
Asterocampa clyton texana

PLATE 9

247. GUAVA SKIPPER
Phocides polybius

441. WEST TEXAS GIANT SKIPPER
Agathymus gilberti

PLATE 10

CHRYSALIDS

2. PIPEVINE SWALLOWTAIL
Battus philenor

8. GIANT SWALLOWTAIL
Heraclides cresphontes

16. SPICEBUSH SWALLOWTAIL
Pterourus troilus

PLATE 11

25. GREAT SOUTHERN WHITE
Ascia monuste

33. ALFALFA BUTTERFLY
Colias eurytheme

34. DOG FACE
Zerene cesonia

37. CLOUDLESS SULPHUR (green form)
Phoebis sennae

PLATE 12

37. CLOUDLESS SULPHUR (Brown Form)
Phoebis sennae

49. LITTLE YELLOW
Eurema lisa

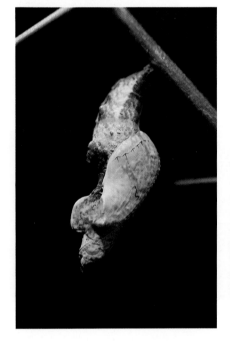

139. GULF FRITILLARY
Agraulis vanillae

142. JULIA
Dryas iulia

PLATE 13

144. ZEBRA
Heliconius charitonius

146. VARIEGATED FRITILLARY
Euptoieta claudia

150. THEONA CHECKERSPOT
Thessalia theona

157. JANAIS PATCH
Chlosyne janais

PLATE 14

177. QUESTION MARK
Polygonia interrogationis

179. MOURNING CLOAK
Nymphalis antiopa

181. PAINTED LADY
Vanessa cardui

185. BUCKEYE
Junonia coenia

PLATE 15

220. GOATWEED BUTTERFLY
Anaea andria

226. TAWNY EMPEROR
Asterocampa clyton

241. QUEEN
Danaus gilippus

PLATE 16

ADULTS

3. POLYDAMAS SWALLOWTAIL
Battus polydamas

2. PIPEVINE SWALLOWTAIL
Battus philenor

6. BLACK SWALLOWTAIL
Papilio polyxenes

4. ZEBRA SWALLOWTAIL
Eurytides marcellus

8. GIANT SWALLOWTAIL
Heraclides cresphontes

PLATE 17

13. TIGER SWALLOWTAIL (male)
Pterourus glaucus

14. TWO-TAILED SWALLOWTAIL
Pterourus multicaudatus

13. TIGER SWALLOWTAIL
(female—dark form)
Pterourus glaucus

16. SPICEBUSH SWALLOWTAIL
Pterourus troilus

PLATE 18

17. PALAMEDES SWALLOWTAIL
Pterourus palamedes

20. TROPICAL WHITE
Appias drusilla

22. CHECKERED WHITE
Pontia protodice

24. CABBAGE BUTTERFLY
Pieris rapae

PLATE 19

25. GREAT SOUTHERN WHITE
Ascia monuste

27. PEARLY MARBLE
Euchloe hyantis

26. GIANT WHITE
Ganyra josephina

31. FALCATE ORANGE TIP
Paramidea midea

PLATE 20

32. CLOUDED SULPHUR
Colias philodice

34. DOG FACE
Zerene cesonia

33. ALFALFA BUTTERFLY
Colias eurytheme

36. YELLOW BRIMSTONE
Anteos maerula

PLATE 21

38. ORANGE-BARRED SULPHUR
Phoebis philea

37. CLOUDLESS SULPHUR
Phoebis sennae

39. ARGANTE GIANT SULPHUR
Phoebis argante

40. LARGE ORANGE SULPHUR
Phoebis agarithe

PLATE 22

43. LYSIDE
Kricogonia lyside

46. MEXICAN YELLOW
Eurema mexicanum

44. BARRED YELLOW
Eurema daira

48. TAILED ORANGE
Eurema proterpia

PLATE 23

49. LITTLE YELLOW
Eurema lisa

53. DAINTY SULPHUR
Nathalis iole

52. SLEEPY ORANGE
Eurema nicippe

55. HARVESTER
Feniseca tarquinius

PLATE 24

56. GREAT COPPER
Gaeides xanthoides

58. GREAT BLUE HAIRSTREAK
Atlides halesus

57. CYCAD BUTTERFLY
Eumaeus toxea

61. SOAPBERRY HAIRSTREAK
Phaeostrymon alcestis

PLATE 25

62. CORAL HAIRSTREAK
Harkenclenus titus

67. STRIPED HAIRSTREAK
Satyrium liparops

65. BANDED HAIRSTREAK
Satyrium calanus

69. CLYTIE HAIRSTREAK
Ministrymon clytie

Plate 26

79. DUSKY-BLUE HAIRSTREAK
Calycopis isobeon

**78. RED-BANDED
HAIRSTREAK**
Calycopis cecrops

83. JUNIPER HAIRSTREAK
Mitoura siva

84. OLIVE HAIRSTREAK
Mitoura grynea

PLATE 27

87. FROSTED ELFIN
Incisalia irus

89. EASTERN PINE ELFIN
Incisalia niphon

88. HENRY'S ELFIN
Incisalia henrici

93. WHITE-M HAIRSTREAK
Parrhasius m-album

91. NORTHERN HAIRSTREAK
Fixsenia ontario

PLATE 28

94. GRAY HAIRSTREAK
Strymon melinus

100. COLUMELLA HAIRSTREAK
Strymon columella

98. WHITE HAIRSTREAK
Strymon albatus

107. PYGMY BLUE
Brephidium exile

PLATE 29

108. EASTERN PYGMY BLUE
Brephidium isophthalma

112. CERAUNUS BLUE
Hemiargus ceraunus

110. MARINE BLUE
Leptotes marina

113. REAKIRT'S BLUE
Hemiargus isola

PLATE 30

115. SPRING AZURE
Celastrina argiolus

114. EASTERN TAILED BLUE
Everes comyntas

119. ACMON BLUE
Icaricia acmon

117. SILVERY BLUE
Glaucopsyche lygdamus

PLATE 31

120. LITTLE METALMARK
Calephelis virginiensis

121. FATAL METALMARK
Calephelis nemesis

123. RAWSON'S METALMARK
Calephelis rawsoni

122. LOST METALMARK
Calephelis perditalis

PLATE 32

125. RED-BORDERED METALMARK
Caria ino

127. PIXIE
Melanis pixe

126. BLUE METALMARK
Lasaia sula

128. EMESIA METALMARK
Emesis emesia

PLATE 33

129. FALCATE EMESIA
Emesis tenedia

136. SNOUT BUTTERFLY
Libytheana bachmanii

130. MORMON METALMARK
Apodemia mormo

139. GULF FRITILLARY
Agraulis vanillae

PLATE 34

140. MEXICAN SILVERSPOT
Dione moneta

144. ZEBRA
Heliconius charitonius

142. JULIA
Dryas iulia

145. CRIMSON-PATCHED LONGWING
Heliconius erato

PLATE 35

146. VARIEGATED FRITILLARY
Euptoieta claudia

149. DOTTED CHECKERSPOT
Poladryas minuta

147. MEXICAN FRITILLARY
Euptoieta hegesia

150. THEONA CHECKERSPOT
Thessalia theona

PLATE 36

151. CHINATI CHECKERSPOT
Thessalia chinatiensis

152. FULVIA CHECKERSPOT
Thessalia fulvia

153. BORDERED PATCH
Chlosyne lacinia

154. DEFINITE PATCH
Chlosyne definita

PLATE 37

157. JANAIS PATCH
Chlosyne janais

162. SILVERY CHECKERSPOT
Charidryas nycteis

161. GORGONE CHECKERSPOT
Charidryas gorgone

163. ELF
Microtia elva

PLATE 38

165. ELADA CHECKERSPOT
Texola elada

169. TULCIS CRESCENT
Anthanassa tulcis

166. TEXAN CRESCENT
Anthanassa texana

170. VESTA CRESCENT
Phyciodes vesta

PLATE 39

171. PHAON CRESCENT
Phyciodes phaon

173. PAINTED CRESCENT
Phyciodes pictus

172. PEARL CRESCENT
Phyciodes tharos

176. BALTIMORE
Euphydryas phaeton

PLATE 40

177. QUESTION MARK
Polygonia interrogationis

179. MOURNING CLOAK
Nymphalis antiopa

178. HOP MERCHANT
Polygonia comma

180. AMERICAN PAINTED LADY
Vanessa virginiensis

PLATE 41

181. PAINTED LADY
Vanessa cardui

185. BUCKEYE
Junonia coenia

183. RED ADMIRAL
Vanessa atalanta

188. WHITE PEACOCK
Anartia jatrophae

PLATE 42

189. FATIMA
Anartia fatima

191. RED-SPOTTED PURPLE
Basilarchia arthemis

190. MALACHITE
Siproeta stelenes

192. VICEROY
Basilarchia archippus

Plate 43

193. MEXICAN SISTER
Adelpha fessonia

197. BLUE WING
Myscelia ethusa

195. CALIFORNIA SISTER
Adelpha bredowii

204. EIGHTY-EIGHT BUTTERFLY
Diaethria anna

PLATE 44

206. RED RIM
Biblis hyperia

205. AMYMONE
Mestra amymone

207. GRAY CRACKER
Hamadryas februa

209. CENTRAL AMERICAN CRACKER
Hamadryas guatamalena

PLATE 45

215. BLOMFILD'S BEAUTY
Smyrna blomfildia

217. MANY-BANDED DAGGER WING
Marpesia chiron

216. WAITER
Marpesia zerynthia

218. RUDDY DAGGER WING
Marpesia petreus

PLATE 46

220. GOATWEED BUTTERFLY
Anaea andria

222. BLUE LEAF WING
Memphis pithyusa

224. HACKBERRY BUTTERFLY
Asterocampa celtis

224. HACKBERRY BUTTERFLY
Asterocampa celtis antonia

PLATE 47

225. EMPRESS LEILIA
Asterocampa leilia

226. TEXAN EMPEROR
Asterocampa clyton texana

226. TAWNY EMPEROR
Asterocampa clyton

227. PAVON
Doxocopa pavon

PLATE 48

229. COMMON MORPHO
Morpho peleides

231. CREOLE PEARLY EYE
Enodia creola

230. PEARLY EYE
Enodia portlandia

233. GEMMED SATYR
Cyllopsis gemma

PLATE 49

234. HERMES SATYR
Hermeuptychia hermes

236. LITTLE WOOD SATYR
Megisto cymela

235. GEORGIA SATYR
Neonympha areolata

237. RED SATYR
Megisto rubricata

PLATE 50

238. COMMON WOOD NYMPH
Cercyonis pegala

241. QUEEN
Danaus gilippus

240. MONARCH
Danaus plexippus

242. SOLDIER
Danaus eresimus

PLATE 51

244. KLUG'S DIRCENNA
Dircenna klugii

250. SILVER-SPOTTED SKIPPER
Epargyreus clarus

247. GUAVA SKIPPER
Phocides polybius

254. WHITE-STRIPED LONGTAIL
Chioides catillus

PLATE 52

265. LONG-TAILED SKIPPER
Urbanus proteus

272. BROWN LONGTAIL
Urbanus procne

268. DORANTES SKIPPER
Urbanus dorantes

274. FLASHING ASTRAPTES
Astraptes fulgerator

PLATE 53

279. GOLDEN-BANDED SKIPPER
Autochton cellus

287. CONFUSED CLOUDY WING
Thorybes confusis

281. HOARY EDGE
Achalarus lyciades

305. SOUTHERN SCALLOPED SOOTY WING
Staphylus mazans

PLATE 54

312. TEXAS POWDERED SKIPPER
Systasea pulverulenta

314. SICKLE-WINGED SKIPPER
Achlyodes mithridates

316. BROWN-BANDED SKIPPER
Timochares ruptifasciatus

317. ASYCHIS SKIPPER
Chiomara asychis

320. JUVENAL'S DUSKY WING
Erynnis juvenalis

PLATE 55

323. HORACE'S DUSKY WING
Erynnis horatius

331. CHECKERED SKIPPER
Pyrgus communis

328. FUNEREAL DUSKY WING
Erynnis funeralis

332. WESTERN CHECKERED SKIPPER
Pyrgus albescens

PLATE 56

333. TROPICAL CHECKERED SKIPPER
Pyrgus oileus

339. STREAKY SKIPPER
Celotes nessus

336. LAVIANA SKIPPER
Heliopetes lavianus

341. COMMON SOOTY WING
Pholisora catullus

PLATE 57

353. JULIA'S SKIPPER
Nastra julia

352. SWARTHY SKIPPER
Nastra lherminier

355. FAWN-SPOTTED SKIPPER
Cymaenes odilia

356. CLOUDED SKIPPER
Lerema accius

PLATE 58

361. PERCOSIUS SKIPPER
Decinea percosius

366. ORANGE SKIPPERLING
Copaeodes aurantiacus

363. LEAST SKIPPER
Ancyloxypha numitor

367. SOUTHERN SKIPPERLING
Copaeodes minimus

PLATE 59

369. FIERY SKIPPER
Hylephila phyleus

372. COMMON BRANDED SKIPPER
Hesperia comma

370. MORRISON'S SKIPPER
Stinga morrisoni

380. PECK'S SKIPPER
Polites peckius

PLATE 60

386. WHIRLABOUT
Polites vibex

388. NORTHERN BROKEN DASH
Wallengrenia egremet

387. BROKEN DASH
Wallengrenia otho

389. LITTLE GLASSYWING
Pompeius verna

PLATE 61

390. SACHEM
   Atalopedes campestris

392. DELAWARE SKIPPER
   Atrytone logan

396. ZABULON SKIPPER (male)
   Poanes zabulon

396. ZABULON SKIPPER (female)
   Poanes zabulon

PLATE 62

398. YEHL SKIPPER
Poanes yehl

412. BRONZE ROADSIDE SKIPPER
Amblyscirtes aenus

416. LACE-WINGED ROADSIDE SKIPPER
Amblyscirtes aesculapius

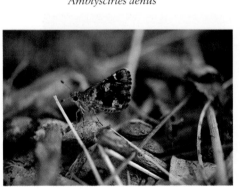

418. NYSA ROADSIDE SKIPPER
Amblyscirtes nysa

419. EOS ROADSIDE SKIPPER
Amblyscirtes eos

PLATE 63

423. LEAST FLORIDA SKIPPER
Amblyscirtes alternata

426. EUFALA SKIPPER
Lerodea eufala

428. TWIN-SPOT SKIPPER
Oligoria maculata

429. BRAZILIAN SKIPPER
Calpodes ethlius

PLATE 64

430. SALT MARSH SKIPPER
Panoquina panoquin

431. OBSCURE SKIPPER
Panoquina panoquinoides

441. WEST TEXAS GIANT SKIPPER
Agathymus gilberti

444. STRECKER'S GIANT SKIPPER
Megathymus streckeri

243

LARGE TIGER
Lycorea cleobaea

Description: 3½–4 in (89–102 mm) similar to Isabella Tiger (*Eueides isabella*) but much larger and dark BHW stripes form loop; long narrow body with black hair pencils protruding at tip of abdomen, extended rounded wings, and slightly scalloped hindwing edges; above orange except yellow through forewing subapical to apex with horizontal black-brown stripes and narrow outer margin band; AHW with two horizontal black-brown stripes joined to form loop, black-brown outer margin band with one row of cream dots; below similar.

Food Plants: Unknown; Asclepiadaceae - *Asclepias curassavica;* Caricaceae - *Carica papaya;* Moraceae - *Ficus mexicana, F. maxima* in Latin America.

Life History: Unknown; multivoltine in tropics; white-green larvae with black head, black rings, and one pair black tentacles behind head.

Range: Argentina to West Indies and extreme southern U.S.; Texas—rare stray to Big Bend.

Comments: Texas subspecies -*atergatis* (Ceres).

Viceroy (*Basilarchia archippus*)

ITHOMIID BUTTERFLIES—FAMILY ITHOMIIDAE

This family of slightly over 400 species is restricted to the tropical areas of the New World, except for one species known from Australia and New Guinea. Only two species are reported from North America based on rare occurrences in the Lower Rio Grande Valley of Texas. Both of the alleged Texas species are in the subfamily Ithomiinae.

Eggs may be laid singly or in masses. The typical larva is dull translucent green and has large fleshy projections along the side of the body. Many species feed on members of Solanaceae (potato). The chrysalis is silver or gold in color and often twisted and almost ornate in appearance; it hangs upside down.

Wings of many species are mostly transparent, because most of the wing surface contains no scales. However, the wings usually have scales on restricted portions, most commonly with dark markings that are associated with the veins of the wings. Adult males collect pyrrholizodine alkaloids from plants to use in the production of pheromones.

244 A

KLUG'S DIRCENNA
Dircenna klugii

> **Description:** 3–3¼ in (76–82 mm); long slender transparent wings (brown tinted wings on darker female), very few scales except for dark band on hindwing costal margin.
>
> **Food Plants:** Unknown; possibly Solanaceae - *Solanum erianthum*; also *S. lanceifolium*, *S. umbellatum* in Mexico.
>
> **Life History:** Unknown.
>
> **Range:** Mexico and extreme southern U.S.; Texas–Rio Grande Valley.
>
> **Comments:** Recorded (1877, 1902) Brownsville area in Cameron Co.

245

POLIS TRANSPARENT
Greta polissena

Description: 2⅜–2½ in (60–64 mm); long slender mostly transparent wings with dark scales at end of discal cell and on wing margins.

Food Plants: Unknown; Solanaceae - *Cestrum* in Central America.

Life History: Unknown.

Range: Central America and extreme southern U.S.; Texas–very rare; record does not indicate location.

Comments: Two specimens labeled "Texas" collected in 1869, all other records from Central America; Texas subspecies -*umbrana*.

Mottled Dusky Wing *(Erynnis matialis)*

SKIPPERS—FAMILY HESPERIIDAE

There are about 3,650 species of skippers in the world with 263 occurring in North America; 201 of these are known from Texas. In general, skippers are much less colorful than true butterflies. Skippers are more diverse in the New World tropics, where most of the colorful species occur.

Eggs are dome-shaped or globular and laid singly or dropped during flight in habitat suitable for the food plant. Larvae are generally long and slender with a constriction or "neck" at the first thoracic segment behind the large, often globular, head. Color is often green or brown, but many tropical species have brightly colored larvae. The pupa is enclosed in a shelter made from a leaf of the food plant or in a flimsy cocoon. The proboscis sheath of the pupa is typically free from the body and is frequently somewhat longer than the body.

Most adults have brown, gray, or orange as the dominant colors. A few of the tropical species are more colorfully patterned and may be involved in mimicry complexes. All six legs are fully developed and function as walking legs in both sexes. The adult's antennal club is bent from the general axis of the antenna and may have an extension called an apiculus. Most skippers have long probocises enabling them to feed at a wide variety of flowers. Large eyes, short antennae, and heavy, hairy bodies are typical skipper features. Due to a large muscle mass ratio to wing area, skippers tend to be very strong fliers, although very few are migratory. The flight pattern is usually jerky or skipping (hence the name "skippers"), but some species typically "float" around the proper food plant. Generally, skippers bask with both wings spread, but the subfamilies Hesperiinae and Megathyminae have an unusual basking posture in which the forewings are partially upright at a 45° angle with the hindwings spread.

FIRETAIL SKIPPERS—SUBFAMILY PYRRHOPYGINAE

This subfamily contains only 170 species, all of which are restricted to the tropics of the New World. Only one species is known from North America (including Texas). Males may have specialized cells on the hindwings, but this type of sexual dimorphism is very subtle. Larvae are generally very strikingly colored purple or red with yellow rings and long fine hairs. Adults spread the wings when they feed at flowers. Most species have reddish abdomens and iridescent blue or green on the wings. Our single species is much more drab than the typical firetail skipper but has the typical robust, broad thorax.

246

ARAXES SKIPPER
Pyrrhopyge araxes

> **Description:** 1¾–2½ in (44–64 mm); antennae strongly recurved at end, resembling golf putter; above brown with white median and postmedian AFW spots, white dashes on outer margins; below similar but darker with brown-orange wash near BFW base; BHW brown-orange with vague darker marks.
> **Food Plants:** Fagaceae - *Quercus arizonica.*
> **Life History:** Bivoltine (Jun–Sep); red-brown larvae with black head and yellow stripes.
> **Range:** Mexico to southern U.S.; Texas—rare stray to Big Bend.
> **Comments:** Texas subspecies *-arizonae* (Arizona Araxes Skipper).

PYRGINE SKIPPERS—SUBFAMILY PYRGINAE

This subfamily contains 1,150 species worldwide with 112 in North America and 97 of these in Texas. Most larvae of these species feed on dicotyledons including herbs, shrubs, and trees, although a few species of the genus *Urbanus* use Poaceae (grasses). Males in this subfamily never have a stigma, but they may have specialized scales in a costal fold, on the hind tibia, on the abdomen, or along the hindwing. The larva has a particularly large head. Adults may rest with the wings closed above the body or out flat and parallel to the surface. A few species rest on twigs with the wings opened so far that they close around the twig below the body.

247   E,L,A

GUAVA SKIPPER
Phocides polybius

Description: 2–2¾ in (51–70 mm); red ring forming "collar" behind head; above black with metallic blue-green stripes; AFW with red cell bar; below similar.

Food Plants: Myrtacaeae - *Pisidium guayava, P. cattleianum.*

Life History: Multivoltine; young larvae fold over a flap on a single leaf, but the mature larvae form a nest from three leaves that they fasten together; mature larvae are chalky white with maroon heads.

Range: South America to extreme southern U.S.; Texas–known only from the Lower Rio Grande Valley.

Comments: This colorful species has been known from the Brownsville area since the late nineteenth century. Breeding populations in Texas dependent upon ornamental plantings of *Pisidium* guavas; Texas subspecies *-lilea.*

248

URANIA SKIPPER
Phocides urania

Description: 2¼–2½ in (55–60 mm); above brown-black with iridescent blue or green stripes; AFW with white hyaline postmedian oblong spots (lacking in some populations); below similar.

Food Plants: Unknown.

Life History: Unknown.

Range: Costa Rica to Mexico and extreme southern U.S.; Texas– rare stray to lower Rio Grande Valley.

Comments: Several old records in Rio Grande Valley, needs modern verification.

249

MERCURIAL SKIPPER
Proteides mercurius

Description: 2½–2¾ in (64–70 mm); extended forewing, head and thorax yellow-brown; above brown with yellow-brown basal area; AFW with hyaline spots through median; below brown with gray haze on outer margins; BHW with dark brown basal area.

Food Plants: Unknown; Fabaceae - *Derris, Ecastophyllum, Rhyncosia, Senna* in Latin America.

Life History: Unknown; multivoltine in Mexico.

Range: Argentina to extreme southern U.S.; Texas—rare stray to Rio Grande Valley, Coastal Margin.

Comments: Texas subspecies -*mercurius*. Recorded (Apr–Oct).

250   A

SILVER-SPOTTED SKIPPER
Epargyreus clarus

Description: 1¾–2½ in (44–64 mm); small projection on hindwing outer angle; above brown with pale orange AFW median spots, small subapical bar, and checkered fringes; below similar; BHW with distinct bright white median patch, pale lavender overscaling on outer third of wing.

Food Plants: Fabaceae - *Robinia pseudo-acacia, Wisteria sinensis;* also *Acacia, Amorpha, Desmodium, Gleditsia, Lespedeza, Lotus, Phaseolus.*

Life History: Bivoltine; possibly multivoltine in more southern areas.

Range: Northern Mexico to southern Canada; Texas—East, North Central, Central, eastern half of Coastal Margin, and eastern halves of Panhandle and High Plains; restricted population northern Big Bend.

Comments: Texas subspecies -*clarus*.

251

EXADEUS SKIPPER
Epargyreus exadeus

Description: 2–2½ in (50–60 mm); similar to Silver-Spotted Skipper (*E. clarus*) but all spots smaller; BHW white patch much smaller.

Food Plants: Unknown; Fabaceae - *Senna, Phaseolus* in Latin America.

Life History: Unknown; multivoltine in Mexico.

Range: Argentina to Mexico and extreme southern U.S.; Texas—rare stray to Rio Grande Valley.

Comments: Texas subspecies *-cruza*.

252

HAMMOCK SKIPPER
Polygonus leo

Description: 1¾–2 in (45–50 mm); small projection on hindwing; above dark velvet brown with white hyaline AFW spots; below similar; BHW with violet highlights, dark spot near base.

Food Plants: Unknown; Fabaceae - *Piscidia, Pongamia* in Florida.

Life History: Unknown; multivoltine in Mexico; yellow-green larva with yellow lengthwise stripes and patches.

Range: Argentina to extreme southern U.S.; Texas—rare stray to Rio Grande Valley and Big Bend.

Comments: Texas subspecies *-histrio* (Skinner's Arizona Skipper).

253

MANUEL'S SKIPPER
Polygonus manueli

Description: 1½–1¾ in (38–44 mm); similar to Hammock Skipper (*P. leo*) but AFW more blue-black with larger white spots; below with slight blue haze; BHW with two vague dark brown bands.
Food Plants: Fabaceae - *Muellera*.
Life History: Multivoltine in Mexico.
Range: Argentina to West Indies and extreme southern U.S.; Texas—rare stray to Rio Grande Valley.
Comments: Rarely collected, found in tidal mud flats.

254   A

WHITE-STRIPED LONGTAIL
Chioides catillus

Description: 1¾–2 in (44–51 mm); long tail on hindwing angles away from body axis; above deep brown with square AFW cream hyaline median spots; below similar with dark purple-brown mottling; BFW with triangular black subapical mark on costal margin; BHW with long diagonal median white stripe.
Food Plants: Fabaceae - *Phaseolus atropurpureus, Rhyncosia minima; Tephrosia lindheimeri.*
Life History: Multivoltine; young larvae dull green turning to rose with orange lengthwise stripes on side when mature.
Range: Argentina to West Indies and extreme southern U.S.; Texas—Rio Grande Valley; record in Trans-Pecos; can migrate northeast.
Comments: Larvae survive in Rio Grande Valley during mild winters; breeding population in Brazoria Co. (1995); Texas subspecies -*albofasciatus.*

255

ZILPA LONGTAIL
Chioides zilpa

> **Description:** 2–2½ in (51–64 mm); similar to White-Striped Longtail (*C. catillus*) but AFW hyaline spots more golden; BHW with white patch instead of stripe.
> **Food Plants:** Unknown, probably Fabaceae..
> **Life History:** Unknown.
> **Range:** Ecuador to extreme southern U.S.; Texas–Rio Grande Valley.
> **Comments:** Recorded (Sep–Nov); Texas subspecies -*zilpa*.

256

GOLD-SPOT AGUNA
Aguna asander

> **Description:** 2–2¼ in (51–57 mm); similar to Silver-Spotted Skipper (*Epargyreus clarus*) especially above but checkered fringe restricted to hindwing; below similar but with more diffuse white band instead of bright patch (occasionally faint).
> **Food Plants:** Fabaceae.
> **Life History:** Unknown.
> **Range:** Argentina to West Indies and extreme southern U.S.; Texas–rare stray to Rio Grande Valley.
> **Comments:** Recorded (Apr–Nov).

257

EMERALD GREEN AGUNA
Aguna claxon

> **Description:** 2–2¼ in (51–57 mm); similar to Gold-Spot Aguna (*A. asander*) but above with blue-green overscaling on body and basal area on wings; below similar but with distinct bright white BHW stripe.
> **Food Plants:** Unknown, possibly Fabaceae.
> **Life History:** Unknown.
> **Range:** Brazil to extreme southern U.S.; Texas–rare stray to Rio Grande Valley.
> **Comments:** Recorded (Oct).

258

TAILED AGUNA
Aguna metophis

> **Description:** 1¾–2 in (44–51 mm); tail on hindwing; above brown with slight green highlights and hyaline AFW median spots; below similar but lacking green and BHW with narrow white postmedian line dividing dark brown median and lighter brown to outer margin.
> **Food Plants:** Unknown; Fabaceae - *Bauhinia mexicana* in Tamaulipas, Mexico.
> **Life History:** Unknown; multivoltine in Mexico.
> **Range:** Brazil to extreme southern U.S.; Texas–rare stray to Rio Grande Valley and southern half of Coastal Margin.
> **Comments:** Recorded (Aug–Oct).

259

MOTTLED LONGTAIL
Typhedanus undulatus

> **Description:** 1½–1¾ in (38–44 mm); similar to Tailed Aguna (*Aguna metophis*) but with longer tail and lacking green highlights; below without white BHW stripe but with dark brown BFW apical spot; BHW mottled with dark brown oblong spots.
> **Food Plants:** Unknown; Fabaceae - *Senna* in South America.
> **Life History:** Unknown; multivoltine in Mexico.
> **Range:** Argentina to extreme southern U.S.; Texas—rare stray to Rio Grande Valley.
> **Comments:** Recorded (Sep–Oct).

260

MEXICAN POLYTHRIX
Polythrix mexicana

> **Description:** 1½–1¾ in (38–44 mm); long black-brown tail with expanded club at end; above brown; AFW with cream hyaline spots in short median band from costal margin and shorter subapical bar; below similar.
> **Food Plants:** Unknown; Fabaceae - *Amerimnon, Ichthyomethia* in Mexico.
> **Life History:** Unknown; multivoltine in Mexico.
> **Range:** Mexico to extreme southern U.S.; Texas—rare stray to Rio Grande Valley.
> **Comments:** Recorded (Jun–Oct).

261

EIGHT-SPOTTED POLYTHRIX
Polythrix octomaculata

Description: 1½–1¾ in (38–44 mm); similar to Mexican Polythrix (*P. mexicana*) but with paler, shorter tail (especially in male), female below with silver BHW median patch.

Food Plants: Unknown; Fabaceae - *Muellera, Pterocarpus, Toluifera* in tropics.

Life History: Unknown; multivoltine in Mexico; white larvae with gray lengthwise stripes, yellow and red head.

Range: Argentina to West Indies and extreme southern U.S.; Texas—stray to Rio Grande Valley.

Comments: Recorded (Mar–Oct).

262

SHORT-TAILED ARIZONA SKIPPER
Zestusa dorus

Description: 1½–1¾ in (38–44 mm); above brown with checkered fringes; AFW with scattered cream hyaline median and submarginal spots and cream hyaline subapical spot on costal margin; AHW with single median cream hyaline oblong spot, vague darker brown bands; below similar.

Food Plants: Fagaceae - *Quercus arizonica, Q. emoryi.*

Life History: Bivoltine (Apr–Jul); light yellow-green larvae with orange-brown head.

Range: Mexico and southwestern U.S.; Texas—Trans-Pecos.

Comments: Adults rarely feed at flowers; preferring mud, sap, and spittlebug (Cercopidae) secretions.

263

ALCAEUS SKIPPER
Codatractus alcaeus

> **Description:** 2–2¼ in (51–57 mm); extended forewing, dark-tipped tail on hindwing angles away from body axis; above brown with cream hyaline AFW spots in band on median, one squared spot below end of cell, and small subapical bar on costal margin; below similar but purple-brown with darker purple-brown blotches; BHW with distinct white post median spot almost entering tail.
>
> **Food Plants:** Unknown; Fabaceae - *Amerimnon, Ichthyomethia* in Mexico.
>
> **Life History:** Unknown; multivoltine in Mexico; larvae eat and live in leaf nests.
>
> **Range:** Mexico and extreme southern U.S.; Texas–rare stray to Rio Grande Valley, Big Bend.
>
> **Comments:** Recorded (Oct).

264

ARIZONA SKIPPER
Codatractus arizonensis

> **Description:** 1¾–2¼ in (44–57 mm); above brown with paler basal areas and checkered fringes; AFW with diagonal line of white hyaline spots on median, one squared spot below end of cell, and short subapical bar on costal margin; below similar but mottled with darker purple-brown (heavier on BHW); hazy white submarginal BHW highlights.
>
> **Food Plants:** Fabaceae - *Eysenhardtia spinosa, E. texana.*
>
> **Life History:** Multivoltine (Apr–Oct).
>
> **Range:** Mexico and extreme southwestern U.S.; Texas–Big Bend.
>
> **Comments:** Found in desert mountains.

265   A

LONG-TAILED SKIPPER
Urbanus proteus

Description: 1½–2¼ in (38–57 mm); long dark brown tail on hindwing; above brown with iridescent green or blue-green on body and basal area (spreading on AHW toward tail) and checkered fringes; AFW with short line of off-white hyaline spots on median, one squared spot below end of cell, and few small scattered subapical spots; below similar but without green and with dark brown bands on BHW.

Food Plants: Fabaceae - *Clitoria ternata, Phaseolus limensis, P. vulgaris, Bauhinia, Desmodium, Prosopis, Pisum, Vigna.*

Life History: Multivoltine (Jul–Dec); green larvae with maroon and black heads, black dorsal stripe, yellow or orange side stripes, and yellow and black raised dots.

Range: Argentina to West Indies and southern U.S.; Texas–Rio Grande Valley, southern area of South; disperses to entire except High Plains or Panhandle.

Comments: Disperses to central U.S. each year; larva known as "Leaf-Bean Roller."

266

SHORT-TAILED GREEN LONGTAIL
Urbanus pronus

Description: 1½–1¾ in (38–44 mm); similar to Long-Tailed Skipper (*U. proteus*) but slightly smaller, shorter tail, and green does not reach margins on hindwing.

Food Plants: Unknown, possibly Fabaceae.

Life History: Unknown.

Range: Argentina to Mexico; Texas–rare stray to Rio Grande Valley.

Comments: Originally reported as the related *U. pronta* which is not known from U.S. as yet.

267

ESMERALDA LONGTAIL
Urbanus esmeraldus

Description: 1½–1¾ in (38–44 mm); similar to Long-Tailed Skipper (*U. proteus*) but dark BHW bands broken into spots near basal area.

Food Plants: Unknown; Fabaceae - *Desmodium neomexicanum* in Mexico.

Life History: Unknown; multivoltine in Mexico.

Range: Paraguay to extreme southern U.S.; Texas—very rare stray to Rio Grande Valley.

Comments: Recorded (Aug).

268   A

DORANTES SKIPPER
Urbanus dorantes

Description: 1½–2 in (38–51 mm); similar to Long-Tailed Skipper (*U. proteus*) but without green, smaller forewing white hyaline spots; below with dark purple-brown and hazy gray-purple bands (heavier on BHW).

Food Plants: Fabaceae - *Clitoria, Desmodium, Phaseolus.*

Life History: Multivoltine.

Range: Argentina to West Indies and southern U.S.; Texas—Rio Grande Valley, southern halves of South and Coastal Margin; disperses through central to northeastern areas of state.

Comments: Texas subspecies -*dorantes.*

269

TELEUS LONGTAIL
Urbanus teleus

Description: 1½–1¾ in (38–44 mm); slender tail on hindwing; above deep brown; AFW with very narrow white median line and short subapical line of four small dots; below similar but red-brown with dark brown BHW bands.

Food Plants: Unknown; Poaceae - *Paspalum ciliatifolium, Panicum maximum* in Mexico; Fabaceae - *Schrankia* in Brazil.

Life History: Unknown; multivoltine in Mexico.

Range: Argentina to southern U.S.; Texas–Rio Grande Valley.

Comments: One of the few Pyrgine Skippers to feed on moncotyledonous plants; flies year round.

270

TANNA LONGTAIL
Urbanus tanna

Description: 1½–1¾ in (38–44 mm); very similar to Teleus Longtail (*U. teleus*) but white AFW subapical line increased to five small dots.

Food Plants: Unknown.

Life History: Unknown.

Range: Ecuador to extreme southern U.S.; Texas–rare stray to Rio Grande Valley.

Comments: Also strays into southeastern Arizona; recorded (Jun).

271

PLAIN LONGTAIL
Urbanus simplicius

Description: 1½–1¾ in (38–44 mm); similar to Tanna Longtail (*U. tanna*) but above unmarked brown; similar to Brown Longtail (*U. procne*) but BHW with solid submedian dark brown band; difficult to identify as some individuals have small white subapical forewing spots.

Food Plants: Unknown; Fabaceae - *Phaseolus* in Mexico; *Schrankia* in Brazil.

Life History: Unknown; multivoltine in Mexico.

Range: Brazil to extreme southern U.S.; Texas—rare stray to Rio Grande Valley.

Comments: Recorded (Apr).

272   A

BROWN LONGTAIL
Urbanus procne

Description: 1½–1¾ in (38–44 mm); very similar to Plain Longtail (*U. simplicius*) but BHW submedian dark brown band separate from two dark brown costal margin spots; positive identification only by examination of male genitalia.

Food Plants: Poaceae - *Cynodon dactylon, Sorghum halepense, Stenotaphrum secundatum.*

Life History: Multivoltine.

Range: Argentina to extreme southern U.S.; Texas—Rio Grande Valley.

Comments: Strays northwest from Mexico to southern Arizona and California; one of the few Pyrgine Skippers to feed on monocotyledonous plants.

273

WHITE-TAILED SKIPPER
Urbanus doryssus

Description: 1⅛–1¾ in (28–44 mm); short blunt white tail; above brown with narrow white AFW hyaline median line; AHW with white submarginal wash extending into tail; below similar with less white on BHW.

Food Plants: Unknown, possibly Poaceae.

Life History: Unknown.

Range: Argentina to Mexico; Texas—rare stray to Rio Grande Valley.

Comments: Recorded (Mar, Oct).

274   A

FLASHING ASTRAPTES
Astraptes fulgerator

Description: 2–2½ in (51–64 mm); extended pointed forewing; above dark brown with metallic blue body and basal area of wing; AFW with band of rectangular hyaline spots through median and small subapical dots; below brown with blue restricted to BFW base, white line on BHW costal margin.

Food Plants: Rhamnaceae - *Karwinskia humboldtiana;*Verbenaceae. *Vitex* agnus-castus; also reportedly *Vitex* in Mexico.

Life History: Multivoltine; black larvae with maroon below, yellow bands, and curved white hairs.

Range: Argentina to extreme southern U.S.; Texas—Rio Grande Valley.

Comments: Texas subspecies *-azul.*

275

GREEN FLASHER
Astraptes egregius

Description: 1½–2 in (38–51 mm); similar to Flashing Astraptes (*A. fulgerator*) but slightly smaller, green metallic instead of blue, reduced hyaline forewing spots, and BHW costal line yellow.
Food Plants: Unknown.
Life History: Unknown.
Range: Brazil to extreme southern U.S.; Texas—rare stray to Rio Grande Valley.
Comments: Rarely found north of Veracruz, Mexico; recorded (Oct).

276

WHITE FLASHER
Astraptes alardus

Description: 2½–2¾ in (64–70 mm); similar to Flashing Astraptes (*A. fulgerator*) but without forewing spots; below without blue but with broad diffuse white outer margins; BHW with white fringe.
Food Plants: Unknown.
Life History: Unknown.
Range: Argentina to West Indies and extreme southern U.S.; Texas—rare stray to Rio Grande Valley.
Comments: Recorded (Jun–Oct);Texas subspecies -*latia*.

277

GILBERT'S FLASHER
Astraptes gilberti

Description: 1¾–2 in (44–51 mm); similar to Flashing Astraptes (*A. fulgerator*) but slightly smaller; above deep dark brown; AFW with green on base without spots; AHW more blue on base; below without green or blue; BHW with hazy white median area along inner margin.

Food Plants: Unknown; Fabaceae - *Bauhinia divaricata* in Mexico.

Life History: Unknown; multivoltine in Mexico.

Range: Mexico; Texas–stray to Rio Grande Valley.

Comments: Originally reported in Texas as *A. hopfferi*, a different species that has not yet been reported from Texas; several Hidalgo Co. records during widely scattered years; recorded (Oct).

278

YELLOW FLASHER
Astraptes anaphus

Description: 2–2¼ in (51–57 mm); above brown with dark brown bars; AHW with broad deep yellow patch near outer angle on outer margin; below similar but BHW yellow patch may be larger.

Food Plants: Unknown; Fabaceae - *lobata* in Tamaulipas, Mexico; *Phaseolus* in South America.

Life History: Unknown; multivoltine in Mexico.

Range: Argentina to West Indies and extreme southern U.S.; Texas–rare stray to Rio Grande Valley.

Comments: Texas subspecies -*annetta*.

279   A

GOLDEN-BANDED SKIPPER
Autochton cellus

Description: 1½–2 in (38–51 mm); extended forewing; above black-brown with checkered fringes (restricted to AHW on male); AFW with broad yellow band from costal margin almost to tornus and small white subapical bar; below similar but BHW with dark brown bars sometimes lightly overscaled with gray.

Food Plants: Fabaceae - *Amphicarpa, Clitoria, Phaseolus, Vigna.*

Life History: Multivoltine (Feb–Sep).

Range: Mexico to southwestern U.S., eastern U.S. (large gap between U.S. ranges); Texas–Big Bend; old records from Central.

Comments: Divided range suggested two species, but detailed work revealed population variations of a single species.

280

WHITE-BANDED SKIPPER
Autochton cinctus

Description: 1½–2 in (38–51 mm); similar to Golden-Banded Skipper (*A. cellus*) but darker with more narrow white forewing band; darker hindwing with bright unchecked white fringe.

Food Plants: Unknown, probably Fabaceae - *Desmodium grahamii.*

Life History: Multivoltine (Mar–Sep).

Range: South America to Mexico; Texas–Big Bend.

Comments: Texas records are adults from Big Bend National Park, probably a permanent resident there.

281   A

HOARY EDGE
Achalarus lyciades

Description: 1½–1¾ in (38–44 mm); straight edge on forewing outer margin; above brown with large yellow hyaline AFW spots in jagged band through median and lightly checkered fringes; below similar but grainy and paler on outer third; BHW with black-brown median bands and broad hazy white overscaling on outer third.

Food Plants: Fabaceae - *Desmodium ciliare, Lespedeza hirta, L. texana.*

Life History: Bivoltine, possibly multivoltine; green larvae with black heads, blue dorsal stripe, and small yellow dots.

Range: Eastern U.S.; Texas–East; eastern halves of North Central, Central, and Coastal Margin.

Comments: Univoltine in northeastern US.

282

DESERT HOARY EDGE
Achalarus casica

Description: 1½–2 in (38–51 mm); above brown with a few small scattered white AFW submarginal spots and checkered wing fringes; below similar to Hoary Edge (*A. lyciades*) but white BHW band more restricted and defined.

Food Plants: Unknown; *Fabaceae - Desmodium cinerascens, D. batocaulon* in Arizona; *Clitoria mariana* in Sonora, Mexico.

Life History: Bivoltine (May–Oct).

Range: Mexico to southwestern U.S.; Texas–Big Bend, southwestern corner of Trans-Pecos, disperses to Central.

Comments: Found in desert, evergreen woodland, and grassland.

283

COYOTE SKIPPER
Achalarus toxeus

Description: 1½–2 in (38–51 mm); forewing slightly pointed with straight outer margin edge; above brown with vague AFW bands or occasionally (female) lighter brown with more distinct bands; below brown mottled with darker brown; BHW with distinct white fringe.

Food Plants: Fabaceae - *Pithecellobium ebano*.

Life History: Unknown.

Range: Panama to extreme southern U.S.; Texas—stray to Rio Grande Valley.

Comments: Apparently not a permanent resident, but records year-round, occasionally common.

284

JALAPUS SKIPPER
Achalarus jalapus

Description: 1¾–2 in (44–51 mm); very similar to Coyote Skipper (*A. toxeus*), but lighter with small lobe on BHW outer angle.

Food Plants: Unknown, possibly Fabaceae.

Life History: Unknown; multivoltine in Mexico.

Range: Colombia to extreme southern U.S.; Texas—rare stray to Rio Grande Valley.

Comments: Recorded (Jul–Oct).

285

SOUTHERN CLOUDY WING
Thorybes bathyllus

Description: 1¼–1½ in (32–38 mm); above brown with distinct checkered fringes; white AFW hyaline spots through median and small subapical bar; below similar but BHW with two dark brown curved bands and frosty gray outer margin band.

Food Plants: Fabaceae - *Astragalus engelmannii, Centrosema virginianum, Desmodium ciliare, D. paniculatum, Lespedeza hirta.*

Life History: Bivoltine (Mar–Dec).

Range: Eastern U.S.; Texas–East; eastern halves of North Central, Central, and Coastal Margin.

Comments: Found in open habitats such as meadows, pastures, power line right-of-ways, and prairie hills.

286

NORTHERN CLOUDY WING
Thorybes pylades

Description: 1¼–1¾ in (32–44 mm); similar to Southern Cloudy Wing (*T. bathyllus*) but slightly larger and more olive-brown; above with less AFW spots; below more gray-brown and BHW bands only outlined; male with costal fold.

Food Plants: Fabaceae - *Astragalus nuttalianus, Desmodium paniculatum, Rhynchosia senna* var. *texana, Amorpha, Lathyrus, Lespedeza, Medicago, Trifolium, Vicia.*

Life History: Bivoltine, possibly multivoltine at lower altitudes (Mar–Dec).

Range: Western Mexico to Canada, eastern U.S.; Texas–East; eastern halves of North Central, Central, and Coastal Margin; Big Bend.

Comments: Found in wooded habitats.

287   A

CONFUSED CLOUDY WING
Thorybes confusis

> **Description:** 1¼–1½ in (32–38 mm); similar to Southern Cloudy Wing (*T. bathyllus*) but above with much less AFW spots and muted fringes; below similar but BFW gray-brown from submarginal to fringe and pale submarginal BHW band with dark outlines.
> **Food Plants:** Unknown, probably Fabaceae - *Lespedeza*.
> **Life History:** Multivoltine (Feb–Oct).
> **Range:** Southeastern U.S.; Texas–East; eastern halves of North Central, Central, and Coastal Margin.
> **Comments:** Found in clearings in woodlands.

288

DRUSIUS CLOUDY WING
Thorybes drusius

> **Description:** 1¼–1½ in (32–38 mm); above dark walnut brown with a few small scattered white hyaline AFW spots and fringes muted on AFW but white on AHW; below similar but paler; BFW with faint marks, darker outer margins; BHW with wavy brown bands, pale gray on outer third; male with costal fold.
> **Food Plants:** Unknown; Fabaceae - *Cologenia angustifolia* in Arizona.
> **Life History:** Univoltine (Apr–Jun).
> **Range:** Mexico to southwestern U.S.; Texas–Davis Mountains in Trans-Pecos.
> **Comments:** Found in open oak woodlands and desert grasslands.

289

POTRILLO SKIPPER
Cabares potrillo

Description: 1–1½ in (25–38 mm); hindwing with slight angle in middle of outer margin; above pale brown with irregular wavy white hyaline AFW spots (diagnostic cell spot formed like "u" turned sideways); below similar but paler with purple-gray overscaling and wavy dark bands.

Food Plants: Verbenaceae - *Priva lappulacea*.

Life History: Bivoltine, possibly multivoltine.

Range: Venezuela to West Indies and extreme southern U.S.; Texas–Rio Grande Valley; strays northward to Central.

Comments: Dependably observed at Santa Ana National Wildlife Refuge, Hidalgo Co.

290

FRITZ SKIPPER
Celaenorrhinus fritzgaertneri

Description: 1½–1¾ in (38–48 mm); above dark brown becoming darker past cell with large white AFW hyaline spot band in median, one small spot below cell, and small bar on costal margin; AHW paler brown with concentric dark brown ripples and distinct white checkered fringe; below similar.

Food Plants: Unknown; related species on Acanthaceae in Tamaulipas, Mexico.

Life History: Unknown.

Range: Costa Rica to extreme southern U.S.; Texas–rare stray to Rio Grande Valley.

Comments: Recorded (Feb).

291

STALLING'S SKIPPER
Celaenorrhinus stallingsi

Description: 1¼–1¾ in (32–44 mm); similar to Fritz Skipper (*C. fritzgaertneri*) but smaller with more extensive AFW median band extending to tornus, without small spot under cell, AHW more spotted than banded, and unmarked fringes; below similar but BFW with buff outer margin area.

Food Plants: Unknown; related species on Acanthaceae in Tamaulipas, Mexico.

Life History: Unknown.

Range: Costa Rica to extreme southern U.S.; Texas–stray to Rio Grande Valley.

Comments: Recorded (Jun, Nov).

292

EURIBATES SKIPPER
Dyscophellus euribates

Description: 2¼–3 in (57–76 mm); above brown with gold over-scaling, three large yellow hyaline AFW spots; angled hindwing with small black postmedian spots; below similar.

Food Plants: Unknown.

Life History: Unknown.

Range: Brazil to extreme southern U.S.; Texas–very rare stray to Rio Grande Valley.

Comments: Only recently reported from Texas; some workers doubt it occurs here.

293

FALCATE SKIPPER
Spathilepia clonius

Description: 1½–1¾ in (38–44 mm); extended forewing with squared apex, hindwing with small bump at outer angle, and body weakly iridescent blue; above black-brown with muted checkered fringes; AFW with diagonal band of white hyaline spots and small white subapical costal margin bar; below similar but BHW with vague violet or blue overcast and fine white wavy lines over dark brown mottling.

Food Plants: Unknown; Fabaceae - *Inga, Phaseolus* in Brazil.

Life History: Bivoltine; yellow larvae with dark "x" markings on back.

Range: Argentina to extreme southern U.S.; Texas—rare in Rio Grande Valley.

Comments: Recorded (Jun, Nov).

294

CALCHAS SKIPPER
Cogia calchas

Description: 1¼–1¾ in (32–44 mm); slightly extended forewing (especially on male) with rounded apex; above dark brown with gray fringes; AFW with vague pale median mark and distinct subapical bar; below with darker brown mottling, pale inner margins, and pale lavender overscaling on BHW with thin white lines.

Food Plants: Fabaceae - *Mimosa pigra* var. *berlandieri*.

Life History: Multivoltine (Mar–Nov).

Range: Argentina to extreme southern U.S.; Texas—Rio Grande Valley.

Comments: Usually found near water.

295

ACACIA SKIPPER
Cogia hippalus

Description: 1½–2 in (38–51 mm); above brown with checkered forewing fringe and unchecked hindwing fringe; distinct white hyaline AFW spots in median band, one square spot below cell, and smaller subapical bar; below gray-brown with deep lavender overscaling; BFW with hyaline spots and muted apical spots; BHW with darker inner margin, one postbasal spot, and two wavy bands.

Food Plants: Fabaceae - *Acacia angustissima*.

Life History: Multivoltine.

Range: Brazil to southwestern U.S.; Texas—Far West, Trans-Pecos, Big Bend; stray to Rio Grande Valley along Texas-Mexico border.

Comments: Usually in desert, evergreen woodland, or grassland; recorded (Apr–Sep).

296

OUTIS SKIPPER
Cogia outis

Description: 1¼–1½ in (32–38 mm); similar to Acacia Skipper (*C. hippalus*) but smaller with smaller hyaline AFW spots, both wing margins checkered, and BHW with three dark bands.

Food Plants: Fabaceae - *Acacia angutissima*.

Life History: Bivoltine (Apr–May; Jul–Aug).

Range: South-central U.S.; Texas—North Central, Central; strays into South.

Comments: Closely related to Acacia Skipper (*C. hippalus*).

297

ARTEUROTIA SKIPPER
Arteurotia tractipennis

Description: 1–1¼ in (25–32 mm); slightly extended forewing and hindwing outer angle; above pale brown; AFW with diagnostic dark brown costal margin patch with three distinct white hyaline apical spots; below more gold-brown; BHW with vague white postmedian patch.

Food Plants: Unknown; Euphorbiaceae - *Croton niveus, C. reflexifolius* in Mexico.

Life History: Unknown; multivoltine in Mexico.

Range: Bolivia to extreme southern U.S.; Texas—rare stray to Rio Grande Valley.

Comments: Suitable food plants available, could establish resident population; Texas subspecies *-tractipennis.*

298

PURPLISH-BLACK SKIPPER
Nisoniades rubescens

Description: 1¼–1½ in (32–38 mm); extended forewing with pointed apex; above dark purple-brown with black bands; AFW with small subapical hyaline dots on costal margin; below similar.

Food Plants: Unknown; Convolvulaceae - *Ipomoea batatas* in Mexico.

Life History: Unknown.

Range: Bolivia to Mexico; Texas—rare stray to Rio Grande Valley.

Comments: One record, Hidalgo Co. (Nov).

299

CONFUSED PELLICIA
Pellicia angra

Description: 1¼–1½ in (32–38 mm); very similar to Purplish-Black
Skipper (*Nisoniades rubescens*) but without subapical hyaline
dots and more purple highlights; female more brown; nearly
identical to Glazed Pellica (*P. arina*), positive identification by
dissection of genitalia.

Food Plants: Unknown.

Life History: Unknown.

Range: Paraguay to extreme southern U.S.; Texas—periodic stray to
Rio Grande Valley.

Comments: Previously considered subspecies of *P. costimacula*,
found in South America; recorded (Mar–Dec).

300

GLAZED PELLICIA
Pellicia arina

Description: 1¼–1½ in (33–38 mm); very similar to Confused Pellicia
(*P. angra*) above dark brown with purple overscaling, darker
brown mottling; positive species separation by dissection of genitalia.

Food Plants: Unknown.

Life History: Unknown.

Range: Paraguay to extreme southern U.S.; Texas—rare stray to Rio
Grande Valley.

Comments: Previously considered subspecies of *P. costimacula*,
found in South America; Texas subspecies -*georgina*.

301

MORNING GLORY PELLICIA
Pellicia dimidiata

> **Description:** 1¼–1½ in (32–38 mm); very similar to Glazed Pellicia (*P. arina*) but without violet; BHW with swollen base of radial vein.
> **Food Plants:** Unknown; Convolvulaceae - *Ipomaea* in Brazil.
> **Life History:** Unknown.
> **Range:** Venezuela to extreme southern U.S.; Texas—very rare stray to Rio Grande Valley.
> **Comments:** Recorded (Oct); Texas subspecies *-dimidiata*.

302

MOTTLED BOLLA
Bolla clytius

> **Description:** 1–1¼ in (25–32 mm); similar to *Pellicia* spp. but smaller and hindwing more rounded; above dark brown with darker mottling; AFW with small white apical hyaline dots; below similar.
> **Food Plants:** Unknown.
> **Life History:** Unknown; multivoltine in Mexico.
> **Range:** Honduras to Mexico; Texas—periodic stray to Rio Grande Valley.
> **Comments:** Recorded (Jun–Nov).

303

OBSCURE BOLLA
Bolla brennus

Description: 1–1¼ in (25–32 mm); similar to Mottled Bolla (*B. clytius*) but smaller with scattered orange scales on BHW; female only with small white hyaline AFW dots; positive identification by dissection of genitalia.

Food Plants: Unknown; Solanaceae - *Lycopersicon esculentum* in El Salvador.

Life History: Unknown.

Range: Colombia to extreme southern U.S.; Texas–rare stray to Rio Grande Valley.

Comments: Recorded (Oct); older records need more recent verification.

304

CEOS SKIPPER
Staphylus ceos

Description: 1–1¼ in (25–32 mm); orange head and palps; above mottled dark brown with a few tiny white subapical AFW dots; female paler brown.

Food Plants: Unknown; Chenopodiaceae - *Chenopodum fremontii* in Arizona.

Life History: Multivoltine (Apr–Sep in northwest, Apr–Dec in south).

Range: Mexico to southwestern U.S.; Texas–Far West, Trans-Pecos, Big Bend, Southwest, Rio Grande Valley, and southern half of South.

Comments: Prefers gulches and narrow canyons.

305   A

SOUTHERN SCALLOPED SOOTY WING
Staphylus mazans

> **Description:** 1–1¼ in (25–32 mm); wide scallops on hindwing; above black-brown with obscure darker bands and uncheckered dark fringes; AFW with one tiny white dot below cell and two tiny subapical dots; below similar.
>
> **Food Plants:** Chenopodiaceae - *Chenopodium album, C. ambrosioides*; Amaranthaceae - *Amaranthus retroflexus*; also *Achyranthes aspera* in Mexico.
>
> **Life History:** Multivoltine (Mar–Nov).
>
> **Range:** Bolivia to extreme southern U.S.; Texas–Rio Grande Valley, Southwest, South, southern two-thirds of Coastal Margin, and into Central.
>
> **Comments:** Closely related to Scalloped Sooty Wing (*S. hayhurstii*) with which it shares a narrow overlap zone in the San Antonio to Austin area.

306

SCALLOPED SOOTY WING
Staphylus hayhurstii

> **Description:** 1–1¼ in (25–32 mm); similar to Southern Scalloped Sooty Wing (*S. mazans*) but paler brown, making bands more distinct, and black and tan checkered fringes.
>
> **Food Plants:** Chenopodiaceae - *Chenopodium album*; Amaranthaceae - *Alternanthera*.
>
> **Life History:** Multivoltine (Mar–Nov); deep green larvae with purple-black heads, body covered with short white hairs.
>
> **Range:** Southeastern, south central U.S.; Texas–East; eastern halves of North Central and Central.

Comments: Often considered a subspecies of Southern Scalloped Sooty Wing (*S. mazans*) with which it shares a narrow overlap zone in the San Antonio to Austin area.

307

AZTEC SOOTY WING
Staphylus azteca

Description: 1–1¼ in (25–32 mm); similar to Southern Scalloped Sooty Wing (*S. mazans*) but more brown with smaller spots,and margins less scalloped.

Food Plants: Unknown; Amaranthaceae - *Achyranthes aspera, Celosia nitida* in Mexico.

Life History: Unknown; multivoltine in Mexico.

Range: Honduras to extreme southern U.S.; Texas—rare in Trans-Pecos, north of Alpine in Brewster Co.

Comments: Single record (Jun, 1940).

308

VARIEGATED SKIPPER
Gorgythion vox

Description: ¾–1¼ in (19–32 mm); above brown with almost concentric darker brown bands with violet overscaling; AFW with two tiny subapical hyaline dots; below similar but without violet; white outer angle BHW patch on some individuals.

Food Plants: Unknown.

Life History: Unknown.

Range: Argentina to extreme southern U.S.; Texas—very rare stray to Rio Grande Valley.

Comments: Single record (Mar); previously identified as *G. begga pyralina*.

309

BLUE-STUDDED SKIPPER
Sostrata bifasciata

Description: 1–1⅛ in (25–28 mm); similar to Variegated Skipper (*G. vox*) but darker with some blue overscaling on above (male) and four pale subapical forewing hyaline dots; female brown with larger forewing spots.

Food Plants: Unknown.

Life History: Unknown.

Range: Argentina to extreme southern U.S.; Texas—very rare stray to Rio Grande Valley.

Comments: Single record (Oct); Texas subspecies *-nordica*.

310

HOARY SKIPPER
Carrhenes canescens

Description: 1–1½ in (25–38 mm); above dusty brown turning gray-brown near outer margins, vague wavy bands; AFW with three groups of hyaline spots in median, postmedian, and submarginal; below gray-white and pale brown five wavy narrow dark lines.

Food Plants: Unknown; Malvaceae - *Hibiscus* in El Salvador.

Life History: Unknown.

Range: Argentina to extreme southern U.S.; Texas—very rare stray to Rio Grande Valley.

Comments: Recorded (Feb–May; Oct–Dec).

311

GLASSY-WINGED SKIPPER
Xenophanes trixus

> **Description:** 1¼–1½ in (32–38 mm); slightly scalloped wings; above gray-brown with large white hyaline AFW spots forming median band and subapical bar on costal margin; below mostly white; pale brown BFW postmedian through outer margin; pale brown BHW outer margin.
> **Food Plants:** Malvaceae - *Malvaviscus arboreus* var. *drummondii*.
> **Life History:** Multivoltine (Jul–Nov).
> **Range:** Argentina to extreme southern U.S.; Texas–Rio Grande Valley.
> **Comments:** Species name has been incorrectly spelled *tryxus* in past; occasionally common.

312   A

TEXAS POWDERED SKIPPER
Systasea pulverulenta

> **Description:** 1–1¼ in (25–32 mm); hindwing with two small lobes; above gray-brown mottled with dark brown, white hyaline AFW median line from costal margin across AHW submargin, and checkered fringes; AFW with dark tear-shaped postmedian mark and submarginal band; AHW orange-brown past white line; below similar but lighter with cream, pale brown, and yellow.
> **Food Plants:** Malvaceae - *Abutilon abutiloides, A. fruticosum, A. wrightii, Allowissadula holosericea, A. lozanii, Sphaeralcea angustifolia, Wissadula amplissima.*
> **Life History:** Multivoltine (Feb–Dec in south, Apr–Sep in west).
> **Range:** Guatemala to southern U.S.; Texas–Rio Grande Valley; South; Southwest; Big Bend; southern areas of Trans-Pecos, Central, and Coastal Margin.

313

ARIZONA POWDERED SKIPPER
Systasea zampa

> **Description:** 1–1½ in (25–38 mm); similar to Texas Powdered Skipper (*S. pulverulenta*) but slightly larger, more deeply scalloped hindwing, paler, and white line broken on forewing; above gray-olive mottled with brown and white lines; AFW with pale orange-brown spot at end of cell; below similar but paler without orange on BFW.
> **Food Plants:** Malvaceae - *Abutilon, Herissantia* in Arizona.
> **Life History:** Multivoltine.
> **Range:** Northwestern Mexico and southwestern U.S.; Texas–Far West, Big Bend, and Trans-Pecos.
> **Comments:** Prefers arid desert canyons and arroyos.

314   A

SICKLE-WINGED SKIPPER
Achlyodes mithridates

> **Description:** 1½–2 in (38–51 mm); forewing with pointed apex and indented outer margin below point; sexually dimorphic; above (male) black-brown with pale brown blotches and spots, heavier on forewing, and iridescent purple overscaling; or above (female) pale brown with darker blotches without purple; below similar but paler without purple.
> **Food Plants:** Rutaceae - *Zanthoxylum fagara; Poncirus* in Latin America.
> **Life History:** Multivoltine; green larvae with green-brown head, yellow collar, yellow dashes, and tiny dark dots.
> **Range:** Argentina to West Indies and southern U.S.; Texas–Rio Grande Valley, southern areas of South and Coastal Margin; migrates northward to North Central.
> **Comments:** Rare migrants reach Kansas; Texas subspecies *-tamenund.*

315

HERMIT
Grais stigmatica

Description: 1¾–2¼ in (44–57 mm); sexually dimorphic with palps orange below; above deep brown with two darker brown median and postmedian broken spot bands, narrow dark brown outer margins; (female) with three tiny white hyaline subapical AFW dots; below similar but pale yellow-brown, dark lines more narrow.
Food Plants: Unknown.
Life History: Unknown.
Range: Argentina to West Indies and south central U.S.; Texas—Rio Grande Valley, Southwest, South, and southern half of Coastal Margin.
Comments: Rare migrant to Kansas; named for this species' habit of hiding with spread wings under large leaves; recorded (Apr, Jul–Oct).

316   A

BROWN-BANDED SKIPPER
Timochares ruptifasciatus

Description: 1½–1¾ in (38–44 mm); above pale brown AFW and orange-brown AHW with concentric bands of dark brown spots; below similar but more orange with more narrow dark brown bands.
Food Plants: Malphigiaceae - *Malphigia glabra.*
Life History: Multivoltine; blue-green larvae speckled with yellow, side stripes of yellow with light orange dots, white and yellow heads.
Range: West Indies and Mexico to extreme southern U.S.; Texas—Rio Grande Valley.
Comments: Rare migrants to New Mexico and Illinois.

317   A

ASYCHIS SKIPPER
Chiomara asychis

Description: 1¼–1½ in (32–38 mm); highly variable; above gray-brown with large white patches and spots from submedian to outer margins; generally BHW with more white; below white with brown BFW costal margin and brown spotted outer margins; BHW often lightly overscaled with long pale gray.

Food Plants: Malphigiaceae - *Malphigia glabra*.

Life History: Multivoltine (Mar–Jun; Aug–Dec).

Range: Argentina to West Indies and extreme southern U.S.; Texas–Rio Grande Valley; strays northward.

Comments: Rare migrants to Kansas and Nevada; Texas subspecies -*georgina*.

318

COMMON DUSKY WING
Gesta gesta

Description: 1¼–1½ in (32–38 mm); above brown with dark brown concentric bands; AFW with submarginal blue-gray band; AHW with white fringe; below similar but slightly paler.

Food Plants: Fabaceae - *Indigofera lindheimeriana, I. suffruticosa*; also *Senna* in Mexico.

Life History: Multivoltine (Apr–Nov).

Range: Argentina to West Indies and extreme southern U.S.; Texas–Rio Grande Valley; strays northward.

Comments: Only dusky wing with blue; Texas subspecies -*invisus* (Gesta Dusky Wing).

319

SLEEPY DUSKY WING
Erynnis brizo

Description: 1¼–1½ in (32–38 mm); female paler making markings more distinct; AFW gray-brown with median lines like open chain, gray overscaling past postmedian; AHW with vague buff submarginal spots; both wings with narrow dark brown outer margins and brown fringes; below similar but paler with less distinct markings.

Food Plants: Fagaceae - *Quercus gambelii, Q. macrocarpa, Q. pauciloba, Q. turbinella*; also *Castanea dentata* in eastern U.S.

Life History: Univoltine (Apr); possibly bivoltine in southernmost range.

Range: Mexico to southwestern and eastern U.S.; Texas—entire except northern Panhandle, Rio Grande Valley, and Coastal Margin south of Houston.

Comments: Roosting adults fold wings downward around twig like tent; Texas subspecies *-brizo* (Sleepy Dusky Wing) in east and south Texas with brown AFW and scalloped black median line; *-burgessi* (Burgess's Dusky Wing) in west Texas with gray-brown AFW and straight black median line.

320   A

JUVENAL'S DUSKY WING
Erynnis juvenalis

Description: 1¼–1¾ in (32–44 mm); sexually dimorphic; AFW (male) deep brown or pale brown (female) with white postmedian spots in open band (also within cell on male), vague black marks, and submarginal line; AHW (male) brown with vague tan submarginal spots or paler (female) with brown spots in broad yellow-brown submargin; below similar but lighter.

Food Plants: Fagaceae - *Quercus alba, Q. fusiformis, Q. marilandica, Q. nigra, Q. stellata, Q. velutina.*

Life History: Univoltine (Apr–Jun).

Range: Western Mexico, southwestern and eastern U.S.; Texas–East; eastern areas of North Central, Central, and Coastal Margin; isolated populations in High Plains and Trans-Pecos.

Comments: Eggs laid only on young leaves; West Texas populations may be subspecies *-clitus* with white hindwing fringe; Texas subspecies *-juvenalis.*

321

ROCKY MOUNTAIN DUSKY WING
Erynnis telemachus

Description: 1½–1¾ in (38–44 mm); very similar to Juvenal's Dusky Wing (*E. juvenalis*) but AFW paler with fewer reduced white spots; positive species separation by examination of genitalia; normally can be separated by geographic location.

Food Plants: Fagaceae - *Quercus gambelii.*

Life History: Univoltine (Apr–Jul).

Range: Southwestern U.S.; Texas–Guadalupe Mountains in Trans-Pecos.

Comments: Prefers oak woodland in mountains.

322

MERIDIAN DUSKY WING
Erynnis meridianus

Description: 1½–1¾ in (38–44 mm); similar to Rocky Mountain Dusky Wing (*E. telemachus*) but darker, AFW with less gray, reduced or lacking white spots; above (male) dark brown with three tiny white AFW subapical dots on costal margin, darker brown bands on outer half of both wings; or above (female) dark brown; AFW with scattered white dots, including one on cell and subapical bar on costal margin, gray overscaling on outer half; AHW more yellow-brown; below (both sexes) similar but paler.

Food Plants: Fagaceae - *Quercus* .

Life History: Multivoltine (Jun–Sep).

Range: Mexico to southwestern U.S.; Texas–Far West, Trans-Pecos, Southwest, into Central and South.

Comments: Some workers consider *E. meridianus* to be a subspecies of Propertius Dusky Wing (*E. propertius*) of the western U.S.

323   A

HORACE'S DUSKY WING
Erynnis horatius

Description: 1¼–1¾ in (32–44 mm); similar to Juvenal's Dusky Wing (*E. juvenalis*) but darker (especially female, which resembles male Juvenal), AFW with reduced white spots and prominent black median markings.

Food Plants: Fagaceae - *Quercus buckleyi, Q. fusiformis, Q. gambelii, Q. laurifolia, Q. marilandica, Q. nigra, Q. phellos, Q. shumardii, Q. stellata, Q. virginiana.*

Life History: Multivoltine (Jan–Oct); light green larvae speckled with short hairs and red or orange heads.

Range: Eastern and southwestern U.S.; Texas–East; eastern areas of North Central, Central, Coastal Margin; and isolated population in High Plains.

Comments: Prefers warm, sunny clearings beside oak woodlands.

324

MOURNFUL DUSKY WING
Erynnis tristis

Description: 1¼–1¾ in (30–45 mm); similar to Juvenal's Dusky Wing (*E. juvenalis clitus*) with distinctive white hindwing fringe but AFW darker with reduced mottling (essentially solid deep brown on male).

Food Plants: Fagaceae - *Quercus emoryi, Q. grisea.*

Life History: Multivoltine (Mar–Nov).

Range: Mexico to southwestern U.S.; Texas–Far West, Trans-Pecos, Big Bend; stray into Southwest, South, and Rio Grande Valley.

Comments: Texas subspecies *-tatius* (Tatius Dusky Wing).

325

MOTTLED DUSKY WING
Erynnis martialis

Description: 1–1½ in (25–38 mm); similar to Horace's Dusky Wing (*E. horatius*) but with fewer reduced white AFW spots, violet overscaling, and larger, more distinct, black AHW outer margin spots; above gray-brown with hazy dotted outer margins and brown fringes; AFW with tiny white subapical hyaline dots near costal margin, large irregular black patches, and violet overscaling; AHW dark yellow-brown with bands of hazy dark brown spots; below medium brown turning to cream past median with dark brown submarginal spots and narrow dark outer margins.

Food Plants: Rhamnaceae - *Ceanothus americanus.*

Life History: Bivoltine (Mar–Dec); larvae live in silken leaf nests.

Range: Eastern North America; Texas–entire except Panhandle, South, and Rio Grande Valley.

Comments: Seldom common; often flies with Southern Cloudy Wing (*Thorybes bathyllus*) and Northern Cloudy Wing (*T. pylades*).

326

SCUDDER'S DUSKY WING
Erynnis scudderi

Description: 1¼–1½ in (32–38 mm); similar to Mottled Dusky Wing (*E. martialis*) but with white hindwing fringe; similar to Juvenal's Dusky Wing (*E. juvenalis*) but paler brown, smaller, AFW with white spots and violet overscaling; above deep brown with dark brown mottling, several tiny white hyaline AFW sub-apical dots, and violet overscaling; below brown with yellow-brown mottling and small pale outer marginal spots; reliably separated from Juvenal's Dusky Wing (*E. juvenalis*) by examination of genitalia.

Food Plants: Unknown, possibly Fagaceae - *Quercus.*

Life History: Bivoltine (May–Aug).

Range: Mexico to southwestern U.S.; Texas–mountane areas of Big Bend and Trans-Pecos.

Comments: Uncommon in mountane woodlands.

327

ZARUCCO DUSKY WING
Erynnis zarucco

Description: 1–1¾ in (25–44 mm); forewing somewhat narrower than other *Erynnis;* above dark brown with vague darker mottling and brown fringes; several tiny white hyaline AFW subapical dots, and pale brown upper postmedian spot; male with pale brown AFW costal margin from base to edge of pale spot; AHW dark brown mottling more distinct on female.

Food Plants: Fabaceae - *Robinia pseudo-acacia, Lespedeza hirta, Clitoria mariana, Centrosema virginiana, Sesbania vesicaria, Wisteria frutesceus.*

Life History: Multivoltine (Mar–Oct); pale yellow-green larvae with dense white hairs, green and yellow stripes, orange dot on each segment, and yellow-spotted black heads.

Range: West Indies to southeastern U.S.; Texas–East, eastern area of Coastal Margin.

Comments: Strays northward to Indiana and Massachusetts.

328   A

FUNEREAL DUSKY WING
Erynnis funeralis

Description: 1–1¾ in (25–44 mm); very similar to Zarucco Dusky Wing (*E. zarucco*) but more gray-brown with white hindwing fringe, forewing even more narrow and pointed.

Food Plants: Fabaceae - *Indigofera, Lotus, Medicago, Robinia, Sesbania, Vicia.*

Life History: Multivoltine (Mar–Dec).

Range: Argentina to southwestern U.S.; Texas–entire.

Comments: Some workers consider *E. funeralis* to be a subspecies of Zarucco Dusky Wing (*E. zarucco*).

329

WILD INDIGO DUSKY WING
Erynnis baptisiae

Description: 1¼–1½ in (32–38 mm); similar to Zarucco Dusky Wing (*E. zarucco*) but male without pale brown AFW costal margin and outer half of AFW paler; above dark lavender-brown with pale brown AFW upper postmedian spot; AHW with submarginal and outer marginal band of small lavender-brown spots; below similar but markings more faint.

Food Plants: Fabaceae - *Baptisia laevicaulis, B. tinctoria; Astragalus, Lupinus,* possibly also *Coronilla varia.*

Life History: Bivoltine (Apr–Jun, Jul–Aug).

Range: Eastern U.S.; Texas–East; eastern halves of North Central, Central, and Coastal Margin.

Comments: If this butterfly will use crown vetch (*C. varia*), its range might increase because this plant is used for erosion prevention along roads.

330

SMALL CHECKERED SKIPPER
Pyrgus scriptura

Description: ½–1 in (13–25 mm); seasonal variations, dark summer adults with small white spots or spring and late fall adults with larger white spots; above dark gray-brown becoming paler toward outer margins, white spots (many on AFW, fewer on AHW), no spots on outer margins, and distinctive long white fringes with shorter black streaks; below olive-brown with white spotted BFW and distinct white bands on paler olive-brown BHW.

Food Plants: Malvaceae - *Sida hederacea, Sphaeralcea coccinea.*

Life History: Multivoltine (Mar–Nov).

Range: Northwestern Mexico, southwestern U.S.; Texas–Far West; Trans-Pecos, Big Bend.

Comments: Adults visit mud, dung, or flowers.

331   A

CHECKERED SKIPPER
Pyrgus communis

Description: ¾–1¼ in (19–32 mm); sexually dimorphic; above (male) dark gray with hairy blue overscaling on body and wings through submedian with scattered white spots, a broad white median band broken by dark vein lines, a submarginal band of smaller white spots, and white fringes (checkered on forewing); or above (female) darker gray-brown with reduced white spots and without blue; BFW similar to above but paler; BHW cream (male) or more yellow (female) with bands of olive brown spots (broken median band on male, solid median band on female), and dark outer angle spot on female.

Food Plants: Malvaceae - *Callirhoe leiocarpa, Sida abutifolia, S. lindheimeri, S. rhombifolia, Sphaeralcea angustifolia, lindheimeri, Alcea, Hibiscus, Malvastrum.*

Life History: Multivoltine; tan larvae with brown and white lines, black heads.

Range: Argentina to southern Canada; Texas—entire, except South, Southwest, Rio Grande Valley, southern part of Coastal Margin.

Comments: Closely related to Western Checkered Skipper (*P. albescens*), but habitat preferences aid in identification; *P. communis* prefers the cooler, moister, northern habitats while *P. albescens* prefers warmer, drier, southern habitats.

332 A

WESTERN CHECKERED SKIPPER
Pyrgus albescens

Description: ¾–1¼ in (19–32 mm); very similar to Checkered Skipper (*P. communis*) but slightly paler, more gray than brown, male with gray-blue hairy overscaling; below similar but paler yellow-cream with light olive-brown bands and outer angle spot reduced to smudge.

Food Plants: Malvaceae - *Alcea, Callirhoe, Hibiscus, Malvastrum, Sphaeralcea.*

Life History: Multivoltine.

Range: Southwestern U.S.; Texas—Rio Grande Valley, South, Southwest, Trans-Pecos, Big Bend, Far West, southern part of Coastal Margin.

Comments: Closely related to Checkered Skipper; see comment under *P. communis.*

333   A

TROPICAL CHECKERED SKIPPER
Pyrgus oileus

Description: 1–1¼ in (25–32 mm); similar to Checkered Skipper (*P. communis*) but male hair overscaling more gray, submarginal spots are larger; above dark gray with rows of white spots, almost checkerboard patterned from median to outer margins, and checkered fringes; below pale brown spotted BFW and tan or cream BHW with three dark spots on costal margin, two tan or pale gray bands outlined with black.

Food Plants: Malvaceae - *Malvastrum, Sida rhombifolia.*

Life History: Multivoltine; green larvae with black heads, faint line down back, and small white bumps.

Range: Argentina to West Indies and southern U.S.; Texas–Rio Grande Valley, Coastal Margin, strays to Central and East.

Comments: Geographic location is helpful for reliable identification.

334

PHILETAS SKIPPER
Pyrgus philetas

Description: ¾–1¼ in (19–32 mm); similar to Tropical Checkered Skipper (*P. oileus*) but smaller with smaller spots, especially on AHW, forewing fringes more checkered than hindwing; below much plainer, often with silver-gray BHW.

Food Plants: Unknown; Malvaceae - *Sida* in Arizona.

Life History: Multivoltine.

Range: Mexico to southwestern U.S.; Texas–Big Bend, Southwest, and western areas of Rio Grande Valley, South, and Central.

Comments: Prefers habitats even drier and warmer than Western Checkered Skipper (*P. albescens*).

335

ERICHSON'S SKIPPER
Heliopetes domicella

Description: 1–1½ in (25–38 mm); above dark gray-brown with broad white median band, white submarginal spot band, and checkered fringes; below similar but muted yellow-brown, white restricted to BFW; BHW with cream median band.

Food Plants: Unknown; Malvaceae - *Abutilon fruticosum, Herissantia crispa* in Arizona.

Life History: Bivoltine (Apr; Aug–Oct).

Range: Argentina to southwestern U.S.; Texas–Rio Grande Valley, Southwest, Big Bend, southwestern area of South, and southern areas of Coastal Margin and Trans-Pecos.

Comments: Found near water in arid environments.

336   A

LAVIANA SKIPPER
Heliopetes lavianus

Description: 1¼–1¾ in (32–44 mm); above white except small dark gray-brown spots on AFW outer margin and apex, pale brown fringes; male may appear shiny, female with heavier markings; BFW similar; BHW tan with large brown patches sharply restricted to upper two thirds, lower third white.

Food Plants: Malvaceae - *Abutilon abutiloides, Malvastrum americanum, Meximalva filipes.*

Life History: Multivoltine.

Range: Argentina to extreme southern U.S.; Texas–Rio Grande Valley.

Comments: Occasional stray to Central.

337

MACAIRA SKIPPER
Heliopetes macaira

Description: 1¼–1½ in (32–38 mm); similar to Laviana Skipper (*H. lavianus*) but with tan AFW costal margin line, dashes rather than spots on outer margin, gray smudges on middle of AHW outer margin; below more olive-brown without darker brown marks; more white on BHW with vague rose-brown (especially when newly emerged) postmedian area and olive-brown inner margin line.

Food Plants: Malvaceae - *Malvaviscus arboreous* var. *drummondii.*

Life History: Multivoltine (May–Nov).

Range: Paraguay to extreme southern U.S.; Texas–Rio Grande Valley.

Comments: Prefers brush or subtropical woodland.

338

COMMON WHITE SKIPPER
Heliopetes arsalte

Description: 1¼–1½ in (32–38 mm); above white with brown bases, AFW apex, outer margins, and AHW inner margin; below white with dark gray BHW veins, BFW veins dark gray past median; orange edge on BFW costal margin from base to post median.

Food Plants: Unknown, possibly Malvaceae.

Life History: Unknown.

Range: Argentina to West Indies and extreme southern U.S.; Texas–regular stray to Rio Grande Valley.

Comments: Recorded (Oct).

339   A

STREAKY SKIPPER
Celotes nessus

Description: ¾–1 in (19–25 mm); above brown to orange-brown with many dark brown streaks covering wings, tiny white hyaline median dots, and strongly checkered fringes; below similar but less streaks on BFW, dark brown V-shaped marks on BHW.

Food Plants: Malvaceae - *Abutilon fruticosum, Alcea rosea, Meximalva filipes, Sphaeralcea augustifolia* var. *lobata, Wissadula amplissima*

Life History: Multivoltine (Mar–Nov).

Range: Mexico to southwestern U.S.; Texas—entire except East, or eastern halves of North Central, Central, and Coastal Margin.

Comments: Rare stray to Oklahoma and Louisiana.

340

SCARCE STREAKY SKIPPER
Celotes limpia

Description: ¾–1 in (19–25 mm); very similar to Streaky Skipper (*C. nessus*) but slightly larger; reliable identification based on examination of genitalia.

Food Plants: Malvaceae - *Abutilon, Sphaeralcea, Wissadula.*

Life History: Multivoltine (Mar–Sep).

Range: Northern Mexico and adjacent U.S.; Texas—Far West, Trans-Pecos, Big Bend.

Comments: Restricted range of this species is helpful for separation from *C. nessus.*

341   A

COMMON SOOTY WING
Pholisora catullus

Description: ¾–1¼ in (19–32 mm); number of AFW spots vary; above very dark brown-black, often appearing glossy, two lines of small white hyaline postmedian and submarginal spots, and brown fringes; female with more spots and AHW submarginal line of spots; below sooty brown with vague pale submarginal spots.

Food Plants: Amaranthaceae - *Amaranthus albus, A. hypochondriacus, A. retroflexus, A. spinosus;* Chenopodiaceae - *Chenopodium album, C. ambrosioides, C. berlandieri.*

Life History: Multivoltine; light yellow-green larvae with black heads, black plates behind head, and lighter dots each with a short hair.

Range: Mexico to most of U.S.; Texas—entire.

Comments: Most common small black-brown skipper.

342

MEXICAN SOOTY WING
Pholisora mejicana

Description: ¾–1¼ in (19–32 mm); very similar to Common Sooty Wing (*P. catullus*) but slightly smaller; BHW with blue-gray highlights and black vein lines.

Food Plants: Amaranthaceae - *Amaranthus;* Chenopodicaeae-*Chenopodium.*

Life History: Multivoltine (May–Sep).

Range: Northern Mexico and southwestern U.S.; Texas–Trans-Pecos.

Comments: Females of both *P. catullus* and *P. mejicana* will oviposit on the same individual food plant.

343

SALTBUSH SOOTY WING
Hesperopsis alpheus

Description: ¾–1¼ in (19–32 mm); above dark brown with checkered fringes; AFW gray from median to outer margin with dark brown wedge-shaped spots, several small white subapical dots; below similar but BFW less patterned.

Food Plants: Chenopodiaceae - *Atriplex, Chenopodium.*

Life History: Multivoltine (Apr–Oct in west, Apr–Nov in south).

Range: Mexico and southwestern U.S.; Texas–Far West,Trans-Pecos, Big Bend, Southwest, Rio Grande Valley, and western areas of South and Panhandle.

Comments: Texas subspecies *-alpheus* (Saltbush Sooty Wing) in Panhandle has more distinct dashes; *-texanus* (Texas Sooty Wing) in south and west has less distinct dashes.

INTERMEDIATE SKIPPERS—SUBFAMILY HETEROPTERINAE

The few species in this subfamily have previously been placed in the subfamily Hesperiinae, but they differ from the branded skippers in several details of the antennal structure. Only five species are known from North America, two of which occur in Texas. Both species are known only from the southern borders of Texas. The broad wings with rounded outer margins are generally dark with hyaline spots; the forewings are held at a 45° angle over the horizontal hindwings when perching. Overall, the species are small, but the abdomen is long, extending beyond the wings.

344

SMALL-SPOTTED SKIPPERLING
Piruna microstictus

> **Description:** ¾–⅞ in (19–22 mm); above dark chestnut brown with
> scattered small white spots (heavier on AFW); below dark brown
> with ochre highlights and small white spots; BHW with submar-
> ginal white spots ringed with black.
> **Food Plants:** Unknown, possibly Poaceae.
> **Life History:** Unknown; multivoltine in Mexico; other spp. south-
> western U.S.; *Piruna* reported univoltine.
> **Range:** Mexico; Texas–rare stray to Rio Grande Valley.
> **Comments:** Recorded (Oct).

345

HAFERNIK'S SKIPPERLING
Piruna haferniki

> **Description:** ¾–⅞ in (19–22 mm); similar to Small-Spotted Skipper-
> ling (*P. microstictus*) but less spotted; darker BHW without spots.
> **Food Plants:** Unknown; possibly Poaceae.
> **Life History:** Multivoltine (Mar–Aug).
> **Range:** North central Mexico and adjacent U.S.; Texas–Green
> Gulch in Chisos Mountains in Big Bend.
> **Comments:** Prefers grassy banks of streams.

BRANDED SKIPPERS–SUBFAMILY HESPERIINAE

Male skippers in this subfamily have a stigma (or "brand"), which is
a patch of raised scent scales (often appearing felt-like), on the upper
surface of the forewing that contains specialized cells used for sexual
attraction. Therefore, males of this subfamily do not have these specialized cells in a costal fold. This subfamily is very large with 2,150
species occurring worldwide; 137 of these occur in North America,

and 92 of these are found in Texas. Larvae of most species feed on monocotyledons, mostly Poaceae (grasses) and Cyperaceae (sedges). The larvae of bivoltine species often have different body colors for each brood; spring broods are usually green and fall broods are tan or buff. This dimorphism could be linked to the seasonal changes in the food plant colors. Adults rest or perch with the forewings at about a 45° angle over the horizontal hindwings.

346

MALICIOUS SHADY SKIPPER
Synapte malitiosa

> **Description:** 1–1¼ in (25–32 mm); above brown with distinct yellow AFW streak below cell from base through submargin; below yellow-brown with darker BFW; BHW with narrow dark brown postmedian and submarginal leaf-like reticulations.
> **Food Plants:** Poaceae - *Paspalum*; also *Panicum maximum* in Mexico.
> **Life History:** Multivoltine (May–Nov).
> **Range:** Argentina to West Indies and extreme southern U.S.; Texas–Rio Grande Valley.
> **Comments:** Texas subspecies *-pecta*.

347

SALENUS SKIPPER
Synapte salenus

> **Description:** 1–1¼ in (25–32 mm); similar to Malicious Shady Skipper (*S. malitiosa*) but darker brown, yellow AFW band is pale (male) or absent (female); below both wings with dark blotches.
> **Food Plants:** Unknown.
> **Life History:** Unknown.
> **Range:** Bolivia to extreme southern U.S.; Texas–rare stray to Rio Grande Valley.
> **Comments:** First Texas record (Aug 1968) after Hurricane Beulah.

348

REDUNDANT SWARTHY SKIPPER
Corticea corticea

Description: 1 in (25 mm); similar to Malicious Shady Skipper (*S. malitiosa*); above with pale forewing band; below unmarked yellow-brown.
Food Plants: Unknown.
Life History: Unknown.
Range: Paraguay to extreme southern U.S.; Texas—rare stray to Rio Grande Valley.
Comments: Recorded (Sep–Dec).

349

SATURN SKIPPER
Callimormus saturnus

Description: ¾–1 in (19–25 mm); above olive-brown with two pale yellow hyaline AFW cell spots; below similar but more brown; BHW tan through postmedian to small brown dots, dark outer margin.
Food Plants: Unknown.
Life History: Unknown; multivoltine in Mexico.
Range: Argentina to extreme southern U.S.; Texas—very rare stray to Rio Grande Valley.
Comments: Found in woodlands.

350

PERIGENES SKIPPER
Vidius perigenes

Description: 1–1¼ in (25–32 mm); above medium brown; AFW with pale orange streak on costal margin from base through postmedian; below dark brown and rust-brown with pale vein lines; BHW rust-brown with distinct pale streak through cell with adjacent white vein.

Food Plants: Unknown; Poaceae - *Stenotaphrum secundatum* in lab.

Life History: Multivoltine (Mar–Oct).

Range: Colombia to extreme southern U.S.; Texas–Rio Grande Valley.

Comments: Occasionally common in Cameron Co.

351

VIOLET PATCH SKIPPER
Monca tyrtaeus

Description: ¾–1 in (19–25 mm); above black-brown with smudged fringes; AFW with few small pale yellow postmedian dots; below brown with distinct violet-gray patches (on BFW apex, from base through postmedian on BHW); BFW with rust-brown costal margin dash; BHW violet-gray patch divided by brown median band.

Food Plants: Poaceae - *Paspalum.*

Life History: Bivoltine (Jan–May, Oct–Dec).

Range: Central America to extreme southern U.S.; Texas–Rio Grande Valley.

Comments: Common in wet years, possibly producing third brood.

352   A

SWARTHY SKIPPER
Nastra lherminier

Description: ⅞–1 in (22–25 mm); less rounded forewing; above brown with slight olive tint, occasionally very vague pale brown scales near discal cell; below yellow-brown; sometimes BHW veins lighter.

Food Plants: Poaceae - *Schizachyrium scoparium.*

Life History: Bivoltine (May–Sep); white larvae with pale brown heads.

Range: Eastern U.S.; Texas–East, eastern third of Coastal Margin.

Comments: Prefers moist areas with grass.

353   A

JULIA'S SKIPPER
Nastra julia

Description: 1–1⅛ in (25–28 mm); similar to Swarthy Skipper (*N. lherminier*) but with vague white AFW spots; below yellow-brown without paler veins.

Food Plants: Poaceae - *Cynodon dactylon.*

Life History: Multivoltine (Apr–Oct).

Range: Costa Rica to southern U.S.; Texas–Big Bend, Southwest, South, Rio Grande Valley, southern areas of Coastal Margin, Central, and Trans-Pecos.

Comments: Can often be found on or near grass covered irrigation levees.

354

NEAMATHLA SKIPPER
Nastra neamathla

Description: 1–1⅛ in (25–28 mm); similar to Swarthy Skipper (*N. lherminier*) but no hint of forewing spots; below more orange-brown.
Food Plants: Poaceae.
Life History: Multivoltine.
Range: Southeastern U.S.; Texas–eastern area of Coastal Margin.
Comments: Prefers open grassy areas adjacent to water.

355   A

FAWN-SPOTTED SKIPPER
Cymaenes odilia

Description: 1–1¼ in (25–32 mm); above brown, small white hyaline AFW spots at end of discal cell; below similar but BHW paler with two paler bands (inner band touches costal margin).
Food Plants: Poaceae - *Paspalum*; also *Panicum maximum* in Mexico.
Life History: Multivoltine (Apr–Dec).
Range: Argentina to extreme southern U.S.; Texas–Rio Grande Valley.
Comments: Prefers grassy areas in woodlands. Texas subspecies -*trebius*.

356 A

CLOUDED SKIPPER
Lerema accius

Description: 1–1½ in (25–38 mm); similar to Fawn-Spotted Skipper (*Cymaenes odilia*) but darker above and below; AFW with several small white hyaline dots on postmedian; variable BHW with violet-gray overscaling; sometimes with lighter outer margin patches on both wings.

Food Plants: Poaceae - *Stenotaphrum secundatum, Zea mays, Andropogon, Erianthus, Oryzopsis, Paspalum, Pennisetum.*

Life History: Multivoltine (Feb–Nov).

Range: Venezuela to southern U.S.; Texas–Rio Grande Valley, Southwest, South, Coastal Margin, and southern area of Central; strays northward.

Comments: Rare migrants to northern U.S., including records in Indiana and Massachusetts.

357

LIRIS SKIPPER
Lerema liris

Description: 1 in (25 mm); similar to Clouded Skipper (*L. accius*) but below uniformly yellow-brown.

Food Plants: Unknown; Poaceae - *Bambusa vulgaris, Saccharum officinarum* in Tamaulipas, Mexico.

Life History: Unknown.

Range: Brazil to extreme southern U.S.; Texas–rare stray to Rio Grande Valley.

Comments: Recorded (1944, 1948), after Hurricane Beulah (1967), (Sep 1968), (Oct 1973).

358

FANTASTIC SKIPPER
Vettius fantasos

Description: 1¼ in (32 mm); above brown with four white AFW median spots; BFW warm brown with white median oblong spot, distinct orange outer costal margin curving along outer margin; BHW white with orange-brown veins, white cell spot above dark brown blotch, and brown patch on outer angle.

Food Plants: Unknown; Poaceae - *Lasiacis, Panicum* in Latin America.

Life History: Unknown.

Range: Paraguay to West Indies and extreme southern U.S.; Texas—very rare stray to Rio Grande Valley, Hidalgo Co.

Comments: Single record (Oct 1975).

359

GREEN-BACKED SKIPPER
Perichares philetes

Description: 1¾–2¼ in (44–57 mm); green highlights on body and AHW; above purple-brown with large white AFW spots; below similar but more mottled without green; BHW with large dark brown patch on lower postmedian.

Food Plants: Unknown; Poaceae - *Bambusa vulgaris, Panicum maximum, Saccharum officinarum, Zea mays*; Arecaceae in Latin America.

Life History: Unknown; multivoltine in Mexico.

Range: Argentina to West Indies and extreme southern U.S.; Texas—rare stray to Rio Grande Valley.

Comments: Adults fly at dusk; Texas subspecies -*adela*.

360

OSCA SKIPPER
Rhinthon osca

Description: 2 in (51 mm); hindwing slightly lobed at outer angle; green highlights on body; above dark brown; AFW with large white hyaline median spots, tiny subapical dots; AHW paler with dark brown costal margin; below similar but paler.

Food Plants: Unknown, probably Poaceae.

Life History: Unknown.

Range: Ecuador to extreme southern U.S.; Texas—rare stray to Rio Grande Valley.

Comments: Found in wooded areas; formerly a subspecies of *R. cubana* from the Antilles.

361   A

PERCOSIUS SKIPPER
Decinea percosius

Description: ¾–1 in (19–25 mm); above brown; AFW with two angled white hyaline postmedian spots below cell, two very small subapical dots; AHW with single postmedian spot; below similar but more yellow-brown; BFW with yellow haze near tornus; BHW with three small pale spots (one on median, two submarginal).

Food Plants: Poaceae.

Life History: Unknown; multivoltine in Central America.

Range: Guyana to extreme southern U.S.; Texas—Rio Grande Valley.

Comments: Very common some years; recorded (Apr–Nov).

362

CHYDEA SKIPPER
Conga chydaea

Description: ¾ in (19 mm); similar to Percocius Skipper (*Decinea percosius*) but AFW spots smaller, subapical dots may be absent; below yellow-brown, spots very vague.
Food Plants: Unknown.
Life History: Unknown.
Range: Argentina to extreme southern U.S.; Texas—rare stray to Rio Grande Valley.
Comments: Recorded (Jul–Oct).

363   A

LEAST SKIPPER
Ancyloxypha numitor

Description: ¾–1 in (19–25 mm); above orange (lighter on hindwing) with broad black outer margins, more narrow costal margins and inner margins; BFW black with orange-brown costal margin and apex; BHW clear orange.
Food Plants: Poaceae - *Leersia oryzoides, Oryza sativa, Panicum, Poa, Setaria, Spartina, Zizaniopsis miliacea, Zea mays.*
Life History: Multivoltine; light green larvae with white-spotted dark brown head.
Range: Eastern North America; Texas—East, eastern areas of North Central, Central, South, and Coastal Margin.
Comments: Flies near ground with weak flight.

364

TROPICAL LEAST SKIPPER
Ancyloxypha arene

> **Description:** ¾–1 in (19–25 mm); above orange with narrow dark brown outer margins; BFW orange with yellow apex; bright yellow BHW.
>
> **Food Plants:** Unknown; Poaceae - *Echinochloa crusgalli* in Arizona.
>
> **Life History:** Unknown; possibly bivoltine.
>
> **Range:** Costa Rica to southwestern U.S.; Texas—Far West, Trans-Pecos, Big Bend, Southwest, Rio Grande Valley, western areas of Central and South, and southern Coastal Margin.
>
> **Comments:** Found in arid environments near water; recorded (May–Aug).

365

EDWARD'S SKIPPERLING
Oarisma edwardsi

> **Description:** 1 in (25 mm); above tawny orange to brown-orange with narrow brown outer wing edges and fringes; below similar but BFW with dark orange-brown area on inner margin; BHW gray-orange on upper half.
>
> **Food Plants:** Unknown, probably Poaceae.
>
> **Life History:** Univoltine (Apr–Jul).
>
> **Range:** Mexico and southwestern U.S.; Texas—Trans-Pecos.
>
> **Comments:** Found in arid montane woodland habitats.

366   A

ORANGE SKIPPERLING
Copaeodes aurantiacus

Description: ¾–1 in (19–25 mm); above tawny orange with brown bases, and very narrow vague dark outer margins (most distinct at AFW apex) (heavier on female); below similar but paler.

Food Plants: Poaceae - *Bouteloua curtipendula, Cynodon dactylon.*

Life History: Multivoltine; green larvae with pink and purple heads with two knobs, purple dorsal stripes.

Range: Panama to southwestern U.S.; Texas—entire; more common in southern half.

Comments: Found in arid open woodlands, grasslands, and lawns.

367   A

SOUTHERN SKIPPERLING
Copaeodes minimus

Description: ½–¾ in (13–19 mm); similar to Orange Skipperling (*C. aurantiacus*) but smaller; female with darker veins above; BHW divided by white streak from base to outer margin (more distinct on male).

Food Plants: Poaceae - *Cynodon dactylon.*

Life History: Multivoltine; (Mar–Nov); all year in Rio Grande Valley.

Range: Panama to southeastern U.S.; Texas—entire, except Panhandle, High Plains, Far West, Trans-Pecos, Big Bend, or most western area of Central.

Comments: Probably smallest skipper in North America.

368

SUNRISE SKIPPER
Adopaeoides prittwitzi

> **Description:** ⅞–1 in (22–25 mm); similar to Orange Skipperling (*Copaeodes aurantiacus*) but above with brown vein lines; above orange-brown with brown vein lines (male with unmarked veins through median, darker veins on female); below gold; BHW with pale yellow streak from base to outer margin.
> **Food Plants:** Unknown; Poaceae - *Paspalum distichum* in Arizona.
> **Life History:** Bivoltine (May–Jun, Sep).
> **Range:** Mexico and southwestern U.S.; Texas–Davis Mountains in Trans-Pecos.
> **Comments:** Common name refers to pale yellow streak on BHW.

369   A

FIERY SKIPPER
Hylephila phyleus

> **Description:** 1–1¼ in (25–32 mm); sexually dimorphic, very short antennae; above (male) yellow-orange with brown dentate outer margins, narrow dark brown stigma on AFW median; or above (female) mostly brown with jagged orange postmedian and sub-marginal bands; below (both sexes) yellow-orange mottled with yellow; dark BFW mark from base into median; BHW with brown streak from base to outer angle (narrow, distinct, dark on male; broad, hazy, pale on female).
> **Food Plants:** Poaceae - *Cynodon dactylon, Stenotaphrum secundatum, Eragrostis hypnoides, Poa pratensis.*
> **Life History:** Multivoltine.
> **Range:** Argentina to West Indies and southern U.S.; Texas–entire, less common Panhandle, High Plains.
> **Comments:** Commonly seen flying over lawns, occasionally a pest in Bermuda grass lawns; Texas subspecies *-phyleus.*

370 A

MORRISON'S SKIPPER
Stinga morrisoni

Description: 1–1¼ in (25–32 mm); hindwing with small bump above outer angle; all colors deeper and brighter on larger female; above orange with brown bases and broadly dentate outer margins; below brown and gold; BFW with narrow wavy white subapical line, lighter area near tornus; BHW with distinctive bright white arrow marking (disconnected arrow shaft from base to median, arrowhead shape on postmedian).
Food Plants: Unknown, probably Poaceae.
Life History: Bivoltine (May, Sep).
Range: Southwestern U.S.; Texas–Trans-Pecos.
Comments: Found in mountain meadows.

371

UNCAS SKIPPER
Hesperia uncas

Description: 1–1½ in (25–38 mm); above orange and gray-brown with off-white fringes; AFW with small white subapical spots, (male with curved dark stigma; female darker past cell with more white spots, including cell spot); below olive-gray (male) or olive-brown (female); BFW with dark base, white oblong spots, white subapical costal margin bar; BHW with curved bright white submarginal band (resembles a loop from base outward), small black spots along band, and white veins from band outward.
Food Plants: Poaceae - *Bouteloua gracilis, Erioneuron pilosum, Stipa.*
Life History: Multivoltine.
Range: Mexico to southern Canada; Texas–Panhandle, Trans-Pecos.
Comments: Found in prairie, sagebrush, open woodland habitats; Texas subspecies *-uncas.*

372   A

COMMON BRANDED SKIPPER
Hesperia comma

Description: 1¼–1½ in (32–38 mm) highly variable; above brown with orange bases and outer margins; male with long AFW stigma; BFW orange-yellow from base through postmedian, dark brown streak from base, olive-brown submargin to wing edge with small white subapical spots; BHW olive-brown with broad pale orange streak on lower third, bright white spots: one near base, crescent cell spot, and short jagged broken postmedian band.

Food Plants: Poaceae - *Andropogon, Bouteloua, Bromus, Muhlenbergia, Stipa.*

Life History: Univoltine (Jul–Sep).

Range: Southern Canada and western U.S.; Texas–Trans-Pecos.

Comments: The Common Branded Skipper is incredibly variable over North America with numerous subspecies described; Texas subspecies -*susanae* (Susan's Skipper).

373

APACHE SKIPPER
Hesperia woodgatei

Description: 1¼–1½ in (32–38 mm); sexually dimorphic; more intense colors on female; above (male) orange with hazy brown outer margins, stigma on AFW, and small bright orange subapical AFW spots; or above (female) brown with deep orange AFW median, pale yellow subapical AFW spots, and orange submarginal AHW spots; (both sexes) BFW orange and pale yellow with small white subapical dots, broad pale brown outer margin band; BHW light brown with broad orange inner margin wedge (narrow at base, broad at outer margin), white spots forming loop and open submargin band (reduced on female to scattered spots).

Food Plants: Cyperaceae - *Carex planostachys*; also Poaceae - *Bouteloua uniflora* in Mexico.

Life History: Univoltine (Sep–Oct).

Range: Northern Mexico and southwestern U.S.; Texas–Central, Trans-Pecos; disjunct populations.

Comments: Texas populations isolated from main range; prefers open, grassy areas in mountains.

374

OTTOE SKIPPER
Hesperia ottoe

Description: 1¼–1½ in (32–38 mm); above orange (male more orange, female more brown-orange) with hazy brown outer margins, narrow cream fringes; black stigma on male AFW; below unmarked light tawny orange, occasionally female with vague pale BFW spots.

Food Plants: Poaceae - *Andropogon, Bouteloua, Panicum, Sporobolus,* Cyperaceae - *Carex.*

Life History: Univoltine (Jun–Aug); green larvae with dark brown heads.

Range: North Central U.S.; Texas–Panhandle.

Comments: In mixed and tall grass prairies.

375

PAHASKA SKIPPER
Hesperia pahaska

Description: 1¼–1½ in (32–38 mm); above tawny orange (female deeper orange) with brown bases and hazy broad outer margins; white (male) or pale orange (female) subapical AFW dots; dark, narrow stigma with pale center on male AFW; BFW orange and pale yellow with dark base, olive-brown subapical through apex with small white subapical dots; BHW mostly pale olive-brown with yellow-orange inner margin wedge (narrow at base, broad at outer angle), white spots: one basal, two submedian, curved open submarginal row.

Food Plants: Poaceae - *Bouteloua, Erioneuron.*

Life History: Bivoltine (Apr–Oct).

Range: Northern Mexico to southwestern Canada; Texas–Far West, Trans-Pecos, Big Bend, western areas of Panhandle and High Plains.

Comments: Female Pahaska Skipper difficult to separate from female Green Skipper (*H. viridis*) without dissection of genitalia; Texas subspecies -*pahaska.*

376

COBWEB SKIPPER
Hesperia metea

Description: 1¼–1½ in (32–38 mm); rather dark for *Hesperia;* above dark dull olive-brown, vague orange through median (restricted to AHW on female), small pale subapical AFW dots; below similar but without orange (orange cell on male BFW); BHW with narrow white bent submarginal band (male) or mottled with black (female).

Food Plants: Poaceae - Andropogon, *Schizachyriumn scoparium.*

Life History: Univoltine (Mar–Apr).

Range: Eastern U.S.; Texas–East, eastern half of Coastal Margin.

Comments: Common name refers to white scaling often present on BHW veins outward from white band; Texas subspecies -*licinus* (Licinus Skipper).

377

GREEN SKIPPER
Hesperia viridis

Description: 1¼–1½ in (32–38 mm); very similar to Pahaska Skipper (*H. pahaska*) but female more orange above, BHW with two oblong white spots at base; above (male) tawny orange with hazy olive-brown outer margins, dark stigma with pale center on

AFW; or above (female) orange with more restricted darker outer margins; below olive-brown; BFW with dark base, yellow-orange on costal margin, light yellow near tornus, and pale submarginal dots; BHW with yellow (male) or orange (female) inner margin wedge (narrow at base, wide at outer margin), scattered white oblong spots.

Food Plants: Poaceae - *Bouteloua gracilis, Erioneuron pilosum, Buchloe, Tridens.*

Life History: Bivoltine (Apr–Jun, Aug–Oct).

Range: Mexico to south central U.S.; Texas–Panhandle, High Plains, western areas of North Central and Central, northeastern half of Trans-Pecos.

Comments: Common name refers to green tint on BHW of newly emerged adults; female difficult to separate from female Pahaska Skipper (*H. pahaska*) without dissection of genitalia.

378

DOTTED SKIPPER
Hesperia attalus

Description: 1–1½ in (25–32 mm); similar to Meske's Skipper (*H. meskei*) but lighter with more yellow below, without dark BFW inner margin on male; sexually dimorphic; pointed forewing, above (male) tawny orange with narrow dark stigma on AFW; or above (female) gray-brown with yellow smudged spots on AFW and AHW (darker yellow on AHW); below (male) dull yellow with narrow dark brown BFW streak; or below (female) brown-yellow with broader streak, scattered white spots.

Food Plants: Poaceae - *Aristida, Bouteloua, Leptoloma, Panicum.*

Life History: Bivoltine (May–Sep).

Range: Southeastern U.S.; Texas–North Central, northern Central.

Comments: Subspecies in Texas, Oklahoma, Kansas, and Missouri widely separated from eastern subspecies from Mississippi to New Jersey and Florida; geographic location helps to separate from Meske's Skipper; Texas subspecies -*attalus.*

379

MESKE'S SKIPPER
Hesperia meskei

Description: 1–1¼ in (25–32 mm); similar to Dotted Skipper (*H. attalus*) but forewing not as extended, more intensely colored, female below without spots; above dark tawny brown, distinct rich orange patches (more orange on male); long dark narrow stigma on male AFW; below bright orange; BFW with brown patches, brown inner margin and tornus (male) or with single large brown patch (female).

Food Plants: Poaceae - *Schizachyrium scoparius, Aristida purpurascens.*

Life History: Bivoltine (May–Jun, Sep–Oct).

Range: Southeastern U.S.; Texas–East; eastern areas of North Central, Central, and Coastal Margin.

Comments: Geographic location helps to separate from Dotted Skipper *(H. attalus)*; Texas subspecies *-meskei.*

380   A

PECK'S SKIPPER
Polites peckius

Description: ¾–1 in (19–25 mm); above olive-brown (female darker) with small orange spots, and tan fringes; male with orange AFW costal margin; orange AHW patch with brown veins; below orange and brown; BHW with distinctive yellow median patch bordered and broken by brown.

Food Plants: Poaceae - *Leersia oryzoides, Poa pratensis.*

Life History: Bivoltine (May–Jun, Aug–Sep).

Range: Southern Canada and northern U.S.; Texas–stray to Panhandle.

Comments: Found in open, grassy habitats.

381

RHESUS SKIPPER
Polites rhesus

Description: 1–1¼ in (25–32 mm); above pale brown with white fringes; AFW with few scattered white postmedian spots; below pale gray-brown with white spots (fewer on BFW); BHW with dark brown spots outside curving white postmedian band.

Food Plants: Poaceae - *Bouteloua gracilis.*

Life History: Univoltine (Jun).

Range: Northwestern Mexico, west central U.S., southern Canada; Texas–Trans-Pecos.

Comments: In arid short grass and mixed prairies; *P. rhesus* extends from Canada to southwest U.S. while similar species, *P. carus* and *P. subreticulata,* range from southwest U.S. to Panama; recently reclassified, this species was previously known as *Yvretta rhesus.*

382

CARUS SKIPPER
Polites carus

Description: ⅞–1¼ in (22–32 mm); above gray-yellow with dull cream spots forming almost complete postmedian AFW band and short postmedian AHW band; long narrow dark stigma on male AFW; below paler with dark BFW base (male) or paler (female) with complex of cream bands (postmedian BHW band most distinct).

Food Plants: Unknown, probably Poaceae - *Bouteloua gracilis.*

Life History: Multivoltine (Apr–Sep).

Range: Panama through western Mexico, southwestern U.S.; Texas–Big Bend, southern Trans-Pecos.

Comments: Found in desert grassland and oak-pinyon woodland; recently reclassified, this species was previously known as *Yvretta carus.*

383

SUBRETICULATE SKIPPER
Polites subreticulata

Description: ¾–1¼ in (19–32 mm); very similar to Carus Skipper (*P. carus*) but AFW spots orange; darker below with distinct dark brown blotches, brighter white bands.
Food Plants: Unknown, probably Poaceae.
Life History: Multivoltine (Apr–Sep).
Range: Northwestern Mexico and southwestern U.S.; Texas–Big Bend, southern Trans-Pecos.
Comments: In desert grassland and oak-pinyon woodland; recently reclassified, this species was previously known as *Yvretta carus subreticulata.*

384

TAWNY-EDGED SKIPPER
Polites themistocles

Description: ¾–1 in (19–25 mm); above olive-brown; AFW with orange costal margin, wavy dark stigma (male), pale orange spots (female), and buff fringes; below orange-brown; BHW bright orange (duller on female).
Food Plants: Poaceae - *Digitaria filiformi, Poa pratensis, Panicum.*
Life History: Multivoltine.
Range: Eastern and central North America; Texas–East.
Comments: May feed on lawn grasses.

385

CROSSLINE SKIPPER
Polites origenes

> **Description:** 1–1¼ in (25–32 mm); sexually dimorphic; above (male) dull olive-brown with broad pale orange AFW costal margin band and long dark stigma; or above (female) dark olive-brown with small cream subapical AFW spots; below dull yellow-brown with vague pale AFW marks; occasional individual with vague small submarginal BHW spots.
> **Food Plants:** Poaceae - *Schizachyrium scoparius, Tridens flavus.*
> **Life History:** Univoltine (Jun–Aug).
> **Range:** Eastern U.S.; Texas–northern area of East.
> **Comments:** Texas subspecies *-origenes.*

386   A

WHIRLABOUT
Polites vibex

> **Description:** 1–1¼ in (25–32 mm); sexually dimorphic, many geographic variations; above (male) orange-brown with brown outer margins, AFW stigma, and buff fringes; or above (female) sooty brown with submarginal AFW row of spots, buff fringes; below (male) orange-brown with dull brown spots; or below (female) gray-brown with small submarginal BFW spots, paler BHW with broad wavy pale gray band.
> **Food Plants:** Poaceae - *Cynodon dactylon, Paspalum setaceum, Stenotaphrum secundatum.*
> **Life History:** Bivoltine; may produce third brood in southern areas.
> **Range:** Argentina to West Indies and southern U.S.; Texas–East, Coastal Margin, Rio Grande Valley, South, eastern area of Central; strays northward.

Comments: Texas subspecies -*brettoides* in upper northwestern area of range with pale AFW, narrow dark outer margin on male; -*praeceps* in south Texas with female more gray, small BHW spots; -*vibex* in east Texas with female more yellow, larger BHW spots.

387   A

BROKEN DASH
Wallengrenia otho

Description: 1–1¼ in (25–32 mm); sexually dimorphic; above (male) deep brown with orange (heavier on AFW), broken AFW stigma; or above (female) deep brown with small orange submarginal AFW spots; below orange-brown.

Food Plants: Unknown; Poaceae - *Digitaria, Oryza, Saccharum* in Puerto Rico; *stenotaphron secundatum* in lab.

Life History: Multivoltine (Apr–Oct).

Range: Argentina to West Indies and southern U.S.; Texas—East, Coastal Margin, Rio Grande Valley, eastern area of South; strays west and northwest.

Comments: Common name probably refers to break in stigma on male AFW; Texas subspecies -*otho*.

388   A

NORTHERN BROKEN DASH
Wallengrenia egremet

Description: 1–1¼ in (25–32 mm); very similar to female Broken Dash (*W. otho*) but slightly paler brown; above sooty brown with few small yellow submarginal AFW spots (cream spots on female); below brown with vague pale postmedian BFW spots.

Food Plants: Poaceae - *Dichanthelium.*

Life History: Bivoltine (Apr–Sep).

Range: Eastern U.S.; Texas—East; eastern halves of North Central, Central, and Coastal Margin.

Comments: This species is less common than *W. otho.*

389 A

LITTLE GLASSYWING
Pompeius verna

> **Description:** 1–1¼ in (25–32 mm); above dark brown with glassy white hyaline AFW square spots (in band on male, fewer and separate on female) and buff fringes; below dark brown with vague pale brown submarginal bands; occasionally BHW with light overscaling (purple on male, yellow on female).
> **Food Plants:** Poaceae - *Tridens flavus* var. *flavus.*
> **Life History:** Bivoltine (Apr–May, Jul–Aug); green or tan larvae with dark rust heads, body with dark stripes and speckles with short pale hairs.
> **Range:** Eastern U.S.; Texas–East, extreme eastern area of Coastal Margin.
> **Comments:** Distinctive square glassy spot at end of cell helps to separate from *Wallengrenia* spp.

390 A

SACHEM
Atalopedes campestris

> **Description:** 1–1½ in (25–38 mm); larger female with more brown; above orange with brown outer margins, gold fringes; AFW (male) with large square black spot below stigma or AFW (female) with small orange spots, hazy orange inner margin, and square white hyaline spot at end of cell; below yellow-orange with faint mottling.
> **Food Plants:** Poaceae -*Cynodon dactylon, Digitaria, Eleusine, Festuca, Stenotaphrum secundatum.*
> **Life History:** Multivoltine; olive-green larvae with dark tubercles and short black hairs.

Range: Brazil to southern U.S.; Texas—entire, less common in northwestern half.

Comments: This species is one of few skippers that wander and colonize areas in which they cannot overwinter; Texas subspecies -*huron*.

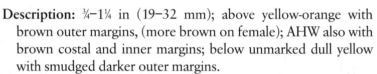

391

AROGOS SKIPPER
Atrytone arogos

Description: ¾–1¼ in (19–32 mm); above yellow-orange with brown outer margins, (more brown on female); AHW also with brown costal and inner margins; below unmarked dull yellow with smudged darker outer margins.

Food Plants: Poaceae - *Andropogon gerardii; Schizachyrium scoparium.*

Life History: Bivoltine (Mar–May, Aug–Sep); light green larvae with rust spots and stripes.

Range: Southeastern and Great Plains U.S., gap between populations: Texas—North Central, middle of Central.

Comments: Texas subspecies -*arogos*.

392   A

DELAWARE SKIPPER
Atrytone logan

Description: 1–1½ in (25–38 mm); above tawny yellow with narrow dark brown outer margins (more extensive on female), dark brown veins past cell; AHW with dark brown costal and inner margins; below brighter yellow with brown restricted to BFW inner margin.

Food Plants: Poaceae - *Andropogon gerardii, Panicum virgatum.*

Life History: Unknown; flies in early summer.

Range: Eastern U.S.; Texas—entire except Far West, Trans-Pecos, Big Bend, or western areas of Central or Southwest.

Comments: This species was formerly called *Atrytone delaware*; closely related to Mazai Skipper (*A. mazai*); Texas subspecies *-lagus* (Lagus Skipper) in north, central, and west Texas with narrow dark margins above; *-logan* (Delaware Skipper) in East Texas with moderate dark margins above.

393

MAZAI SKIPPER
Atrytone mazai

Description: 1–1½ in (25–38 mm); very similar to Delaware Skipper (*A. logan*) but below veins darker orange.

Food Plants: Unknown, probably Poaceae.

Life History: Unknown.

Range: El Salvador to extreme southern U.S.; Texas—Laredo in Webb Co. in South.

Comments: Single specimen; closely related to and previously considered a subspecies of *A. logon*.

394

BYSSUS SKIPPER
Problema byssus

Description: 1¼–1½ in (32–38 mm); sexually dimorphic; above (male) orange with dark brown outer margins (narrow on AFW, broader on AHW), black streak in AFW cell, and buff fringes; or above (female) dark olive-brown, orange crescent at end of AFW cell, wavy postmedian orange band with brown veins, below (male) dull yellow-orange with brown BFW inner margin, paler BHW; or below (female) orange with brown BFW inner margin or similar to above but rich rust-brown.

Food Plants: Poaceae - *Andropogon gerardii, Tripsacum dactyloides.*

Life History: Univoltine (Jun–Jul); dull blue-green larvae with pale rust heads that are spotted and streaked with cream; body covered with fine short white hairs.

Range: Midwest and southeastern U.S.; Texas–extreme eastern Coastal Margin, extreme southern area of East.

Comments: Although occurring over a wide range, this species tends to have localized populations; Texas subspecies -*byssus*.

395

HOBOMOK SKIPPER
Poanes hobomok

Description: 1–1½ in (25–38 mm); sexually dimorphic; above orange with broad irregular dark brown margins (brown veins on male); below paler orange with dark margins (outer margins often with violet overscaling); female has at least three color forms: a form similar to male has broader dark margins; the form *pocohontas* has brown wings with small hazy white subapical and submarginal AFW spots; the subspecies -*P. h. wetona* in Colorado and New Mexico paler with narrow diffuse borders.

Food Plants: Poaceae - *Panicum, Poa.*

Life History: Univoltine (May–Sep).

Range: Southern Canada, midwest and northeastern U.S.; Texas–extreme northeastern area of East.

Comments: Found in a variety of habitats from deciduous woods to open meadows.

396   A

ZABULON SKIPPER
Poanes zabulon

Description: 1–1½ in (25–38 mm); sexually dimorphic; similar to Hobomok Skipper (*P. hobomok*) but more orange relative to reduced brown margins on male; dark brown female with larger

AFW cream spots; below with distinctive broad blue-gray over-scaling on BHW basal area and outer margins of both wings.

Food Plants: Poaceae - *Eragrostis, Tridens.*

Life History: Bivoltine (Apr–Sep).

Range: Eastern and southeastern U.S.; Texas–East.

Comments: Several sources place this species in eastern Mexico and Panama, which is puzzling because Texas records are restricted to the most eastern region of Texas.

397

TAXILES SKIPPER
Poanes taxiles

Description: 1¼–1½ in (32–38 mm); sexually dimorphic; above (male) similar to Zabulon Skipper (*P. zabulon*) but brighter orange, very reduced brown margins; or above (female) brown with large irregular orange median, two groups of small pale orange submarginal spots; below orange with pale brown bases and outer margins, gray-violet overscaling (restricted to BFW apex on male, more extensive on female); male BHW with yellow postmedian band.

Food Plants: Poaceae - *Agropyron, Agrostis, Bromus, Dactylus, Elymus, Poa.*

Life History: Univoltine (Jun–Aug).

Range: Northern Mexico, southwestern U.S.; Texas–Far West, Big Bend, southwestern half of Trans-Pecos.

Comments: Prefers clearings near water.

398   A

YEHL SKIPPER
Poanes yehl

Description: 1–1½ in (25–38 mm); sexually dimorphic; above (male) deep orange with brown margins; AFW with broad stigma; AHW with brown veins; or above (female) warm brown with few small cream and one larger orange AFW spots; AHW with large orange median triangle; below (male) orange; BFW with large brown basal patch and inner margin, hazy brown spots at tornus; bright orange BHW; or below (female) brown, BFW with orange costal margin patch, cream inner margin patch, and small cream subapical dots; (both sexes) BHW with postmedian band of 4 to 5 pale spots.

Food Plants: Poaceae - *Arundinaria gigantea.*

Life History: Bivoltine (May–Jun, Aug–Oct).

Range: Southeastern U.S.; Texas–East, eastern area of Coastal Margin.

Comments: Unusually distinct male stigma for *Poanes* spp.; found near wooded swamps.

399

BROAD-WINGED SKIPPER
Poanes viator

Description: 1¼–1¾ in (32–44 mm); more distinct, brighter colors on female; above similar to female Taxiles Skipper (*P. taxiles*) but margins slightly darker, with only one group of AFW subapical spots; AFW brown with orange markings on median (female with additional square white hyaline spots) ; AHW mostly orange with brown margins; below (male) dull orange with pale orange median bands; or BFW (female) brown with yellow-orange inner margin streak, square white BFW spots; BHW (female) dull orange with brown costal margin and outer margin.

Food Plants: Cyperaceae - *Carex,* Poaceae - *Panicum, Phragmites, Zizania, Zizaniopsis miliacea.*

Life History: Bivoltine (May–Aug).

Range: Eastern U.S., northern U.S.; Texas–East, southern area of Central, eastern Coastal Margin.

Comments: Despite broad range, populations are widely separated; Texas subspecies *-zizaniae.*

400

UMBER SKIPPER
Poanes melane

Description: 1–1½ in (25–38 mm); female larger; above brown with pale orange postmedian hyaline AFW spots (spots larger, paler on female) and diffuse orange median AHW band; below similar but paler, with lavender-gray overscaling on BFW outer margin and most of BHW.

Food Plants: Poaceae - *Bromus, Cynodon dactylon, Stenotaphrum secundatum.*

Life History: Bivoltine (May–Sep); dull yellow larvae with black dorsal stripes, light yellow side stripes, short white hairs, and tan heads.

Range: Northern Mexico and southwestern U.S.; Texas–Big Bend.

Comments: Recently reclassified, formerly placed in genus *Paratrytone;* common in lawns in California; Texas subspecies *-vitellina* (Vitelline Skipper).

401

EULOGIUS SKIPPER
Mellana eulogius

Description: 1–1¼ in (25–32 mm); above tawny orange with broad brown outer margins (less orange on female); below yellow-orange; BFW with limited brown in discal cell and on inner margin.

Food Plants: Unknown.

Life History: Unknown; multivoltine in Mexico.

Range: Paraguay to Mexico; Texas–stray to Rio Grande Valley.

Comments: Recorded (May, Nov).

402

ALABAMA SKIPPER
Euphyes alabamae

> **Description:** 1¼–1½ in (32–38 mm); above brown with orange median spots (male may have more orange); below orange-brown with brown inner margins (more extensive on BFW); pale orange BFW spots.
> **Food Plants:** Cyperaceae - *Carex, Scirpus.*
> **Life History:** Bivoltine (May–Sep).
> **Range:** Southeastern U.S.; Texas–Northeastern area of East.
> **Comments:** Found in marshy areas, including roadside sedge stands in drainage areas; may be a dark form of Dion Skipper (*E. dion*).

403

DUKE'S SKIPPER
Euphyes dukesi

> **Description:** 1¼–1½ in (30–35 mm); short, rounded wings; above (male) dark brown with darker brown AFW stigma; or above (female) brown with pale orange postmedian hyaline AFW spots; AHW with diffuse orange wedge (narrow at base, wide on postmedian); below similar but with pale tan BHW.
> **Food Plants:** Cyperaceae - *Carex.*
> **Life History:** Bivoltine (Jun–Sep), possible third brood in South.
> **Range:** Southeastern U.S.; Texas–eastern half of East, not common on coast.
> **Comments:** Despite wide range, populations are restricted and widely separated; found in marshes and swamps.

404

DUN SKIPPER
Euphyes vestris

Description: 1–1¼ in (25–32 mm); above dark brown; AFW with darker stigma (male), or with two groups of small white hyaline spots (female); below tawny brown; BHW (female) may have row of small vague spots.

Food Plants: Cyperaceae - *Carex* .

Life History: Bivoltine (May–Sep), may fly later in southern areas of range.

Range: Southern Canada to most of U.S.; Texas–East; eastern areas of North Central, Central, and Coastal Margin; Trans-Pecos.

Comments: Texas subspecies *-metacomet* (Eastern Dun Skipper).

405

DUSTED SKIPPER
Atrytonopsis hianna

Description: 1¼–1½ in (32–38 mm); pointed forewing on male; above gray-brown with brown fringes; AFW with small white hyaline subapical spots (usually one group on male, two on female); below dark brown with dense pale gray overscaling on outer half of wings (lavender cast to overscaling on newly emerged adults); BHW with one white spot at base, limited vague paler brown mottling.

Food Plants: Poaceae - *Andropogon, Schizachyrium.*

Life History: Univoltine (May–Jun).

Range: Eastern North America; Texas–Panhandle, northeastern half of North Central, northern half of East.

Comments: Texas subspecies *-turneri* (Turner's Skipper).

406

VIERECK'S SKIPPER
Atrytonopsis vierecki

> **Description:** 1¼–1½ in (35–40 mm); above pale brown with buff fringes; AFW with white hyaline spots (distinct hourglass-shaped cell spot), long narrow stigma on male; below similar but paler brown with light lavender-gray overscaling (restricted to BFW inner margin, entire BHW); BHW with small basal spot, two vague narrow dark lines.
>
> **Food Plants:** Unknown, probably Poaceae.
>
> **Life History:** Unknown.
>
> **Range:** Southwestern U.S.; Texas–Trans-Pecos.
>
> **Comments:** Found in arid grassland and open woodland; recorded (Apr–May).

407

PITTACUS SKIPPER
Atrytonopsis pittacus

> **Description:** 1¼–1½ in (32–38 mm); above gray-brown with white fringes; AFW with white hyaline spots (distinct hourglass-shaped cell spot), narrow stigma on male; AHW with white hyaline post-median band; below similar but paler; BHW with pale gray overscaling.
>
> **Food Plants:** Unknown, probably Poaceae.
>
> **Life History:** Bivoltine (Mar–May).
>
> **Range:** Northern Mexico and southwestern U.S.; Texas–Big Bend, extreme southern Trans-Pecos.
>
> **Comments:** Found on rocky slopes and dry stream beds.

408

PYTHON SKIPPER
Atrytonopsis python

Description: 1¼–1½ in (32–38 mm); above light brown with check-
ered fringes; white hyaline spots on both wings (more on AFW
with distinct hourglass-shaped cell spot, spots on AHW in short
band); AFW with vague narrow stigma on male; below similar;
BHW with dense lavender-gray overscaling, vague mottling.
Food Plants: Unknown, probably Poaceae.
Life History: Univoltine (Jun–Jul).
Range: Northern Mexico and southwestern U.S.; Texas–Trans-
Pecos.
Comments: Mottling on BHW is distinctive.

409

SHEEP SKIPPER
Atrytonopsis edwardsi

Description: 1¼–1⅝ in (35–41 mm); similar to Pittacus Skipper (*A.
pittacus*) but with separated white spots on hindwing, with
checkered fringes; below similar but with lavender-gray overscal-
ing (restricted to outer margin on BFW, entire BHW).
Food Plants: Unknown, probably Poaceae - *Bouteloua curtipendula*.
Life History: Univoltine (Apr–Jun).
Range: Northwestern Mexico and southwestern U.S.; Texas–
Trans-Pecos.
Comments: Formerly classified as *A. ovinia edwardsi*; found in
shrubby thorn forests, open woodlands with grassy areas.

410

SIMIUS ROADSIDE SKIPPER
Amblyscirtes simius

Description: ⅞–1 in (22–25 mm); above with extensive orange-brown bases turning pale orange or orange-tan postmedian to edges; AFW with one round pale cell spot, few pale subapical hyaline spots, stigma on male; below gray with narrow white postmedian line; BFW with brown-orange wedge (narrow at base, widest on postmedian).

Food Plants: Poaceae - *Bouteloua gracilis.*

Range: Northern Mexico and west central U.S.; Texas–Trans-Pecos, Panhandle; separate populations.

Life History: Bivoltine (Apr–Aug).

Comments: Not a true member of *Amblyscirtes* but proper generic placement unsettled at this writing; adults often visit cactus flowers.

411

CASSUS ROADSIDE SKIPPER
Amblyscirtes cassus

Description: 1–1¼ in (25–32 mm); similar to Simius Roadside Skipper (*A. simius*) but darker with checkered fringes; above orange-brown with narrow checkered fringes; AFW with pale orange cell bar, wavy postmedian band; below similar but gray with large BFW wedge (narrow at base, widest on postmedian with dark brown inner margin).

Food Plants: Unknown; Poaceae - *Panicum bulbosum* in Arizona.

Life History: Univoltine (Jun–Jul).

Range: Northwestern Mexico and southwestern U.S.; Texas–Davis Mountains in Trans-Pecos.

412 A

BRONZE ROADSIDE SKIPPER
Amblyscirtes aenus

Description: 1–1¼ in (25–32 mm); above brown with narrow checkered fringes; AFW with few pale brown spots (most distinct on subapical costal margin); below gray-brown with dull orange-brown BFW wedge (narrow at base, widest on postmedian) bordered by band of separate pale spots; BHW with paler gray spots; form *erna* identified by lack of spotting below.

Food Plants: Poaceae - *Bouteloua curtipendula, Chasmanthium latifolia.*

Life History: Bivoltine (May–Aug in north, May–Sep in west); pale blue-white larvae with white hairs, pale blue dorsal stripe and black and white heads.

Range: Northwestern Mexico through southwestern U.S. to Missouri; Texas–Big Bend, Trans-Pecos, Panhandle, areas of North Central.

413

OSLAR'S ROADSIDE SKIPPER
Amblyscirtes oslari

Description: 1–1⅜ in (25–35 mm); pointed forewings; above gray-brown with vague orange overscaling; AFW with stigma on male; below gray with narrow pale postmedian band; BFW with muted brown-orange wedge (narrow at base, widest on postmedian).

Food Plants: Unknown; Poaceae - *Cynodon dactylon* in lab.

Life History: Univoltine (Apr–Jul).

Range: Central U.S.; Texas–Big Bend; Trans-Pecos; Panhandle; areas of North Central, Central, and High Plains.

Comments: Found in canyons or prairie ravines.

414

PEPPER AND SALT SKIPPER
Amblyscirtes hegon

Description: 1–1⅜ in (25–35 mm); above brown-black with paler bases, narrow checkered fringes; AFW with small white spots; below gray-brown with blurred pale spots in vague curved postmedian band.
Food Plants: Poaceae - *Chasmanthium, Poa, Sorghastrum.*
Life History: Univoltine (Apr–Jul); pale green larvae with dark brown heads with pale marks and black collar.
Range: Eastern U.S.; Texas—extreme eastern half of East.
Comments: Formerly classified as *A. samoset.*

415

TEXAS ROADSIDE SKIPPER
Amblyscirtes texanae

Description: 1–1¼ in (25–32 mm); similar to Pepper and Salt Skipper (*A. hegon*) but more yellow-brown; AFW (male) with cream spot band; below with more spots; BFW yellow-brown; BHW pale gray.
Food Plants: Unknown; Poaceae - *Panicum bulbosum* in Arizona.
Life History: Bivoltine (Apr–Sep).
Range: Northwestern Mexico and southwestern U.S.; Texas—Big Bend, areas of Trans-Pecos, Panhandle.
Comments: Found in dry, rocky ravines.

416   A

LACE-WINGED ROADSIDE SKIPPER
Amblyscirtes aesculapius

Description: 1–1¼ in (25–32 mm); sexually dimorphic; above (male) dark gray-brown with brightly checkered fringes; AFW with small white subapical spots and buff median band extending across AHW; or above (female) brown with brightly checkered fringes; AFW with white cell spots, curved postmedian spot band; AHW with pale brown postmedian band; below dark gray-brown with distinctive white bands, white vein lines.
Food Plants: Poaceae - *Arundinaria.*
Life History: Multivoltine (Feb–Sep).
Range: Southeastern U.S.; Texas–extreme eastern margin of East.
Comments: Found in open areas in or adjacent to moist woods.

417

SLATY ROADSIDE SKIPPER
Amblyscirtes nereus

Description: ⅞–1 in (22–25 mm); above brown-black with brassy sheen, narrow pale fringes, and irregular white postmedian spot band (less spots on AHW); below light gray with pale brown BFW wedge (narrow at base, widest on postmedian) bordered by small cream spots; BHW with indistinct small white postmedian spots.
Food Plants: Unknown, probably Poaceae.
Life History: Multivoltine (Mar–Sep).
Range: Northern Mexico and southwestern U.S.; Texas–Big Bend, area of Trans-Pecos.
Comments: Uncommon.

418   A

NYSA ROADSIDE SKIPPER
Amblyscirtes nysa

Description: ⅞–1 in (22–25 mm); above dark black-brown with narrow checkered fringes; AFW with three small white subapical spots; below with gray-brown mottling, pale purple overscaling.

Food Plants: Poaceae - *Digitaria, Echinochloa, Paspalum, Setaria, Stenotaphrum secundatum.*

Life History: Multivoltine (Mar–Oct above South, all year in Rio Grande Valley).

Range: Mexico to southwestern U.S.; Texas—entire, except for East, eastern areas of North Central, Central or Coastal Margin.

Comments: Most common in late summer.

419   A

EOS ROADSIDE SKIPPER
Amblyscirtes eos

Description: ¾–1 in (19–25 mm); above brown-black with slight sheen, narrow checkered fringes; AFW with several small white subapical spots; below similar but paler; BHW with small white spots, sparse gray overscaling.

Food Plants: Unknown, probably Poaceae - *Panicum obtusum* in Arizona.

Life History: Unknown.

Range: Northern Mexico and southwestern U.S.; Texas—Far West, Trans-Pecos, Big Bend, Panhandle, High Plains, western areas of North Central and Central; disjunct records in eastern Coastal Margin and Rio Grande Valley.

Comments: Recorded (Apr–Sep).

420

ROADSIDE SKIPPER
Amblyscirtes vialis

Description: ⅞–1 in (22–25 mm); above brown-black (without sheen) with narrow checkered fringes; AFW with very small pale subapical dots; below similar but with violet overscaling.

Food Plants: Poaceae - *Agrostis, Chasmanthium latifolium, Poa.*

Life History: Univoltine (Mar–Jul), may produce partial second brood in most southern areas of range.

Range: Southern Canada, eastern U.S., also montane areas in west; Texas–North Central, northern area of East.

Comments: One of the more common small dark roadside skippers.

421

CELIA'S ROADSIDE SKIPPER
Amblyscirtes celia

Description: 1–1¼ in (25–32 mm); similar to Roadside Skipper (*A. vialis*) but AFW with two additional spots, below with spotting; above dark gray-brown with narrow checkered fringes; AFW with small white subapical and (two) postmedian spots; below paler gray-brown with small white spots (more on BHW).

Food Plants: Poaceae - *Paspalum, Stenotaphrum secundatum.*

Life History: Multivoltine (all year in Rio Grande Valley), (May–Sep north of Rio Grande Valley).

Range: Mexico to southern U.S.; Texas–Rio Grande Valley, South, Southwest, southern half of Coastal Margin.

Comments: This species can stray to Trans-Pecos.

422

BELL'S ROADSIDE SKIPPER
Amblyscirtes belli

> **Description:** 1–1¼ in (25–32 mm); similar to Celia's Roadside Skipper (*A. celia*) but darker; larger AFW spots form postmedian band; below similar but with pale gray-blue overscaling.
>
> **Food Plants:** Poaceae - *Chasmanthium latifolium.*
>
> **Life History:** Bivoltine (Mar–Oct); light chalk green larvae with darker green dorsal stripe, light green side stripes, black collar behind cream head with dull orange bands.
>
> **Range:** Southeastern U.S.; Texas–northern area of East, eastern area of North Central.
>
> **Comments:** Previously considered an eastern ranging subspecies of *A. celia;* prefers woodlands near water.

423   A

LEAST FLORIDA SKIPPER
Amblyscirtes alternata

> **Description:** ¾–1 in (19–25 mm); similar to Roadside Skipper (*A. vialis*) but forewings more pointed, above with darker bases; AFW with small white subapical dots extended onto postmedian; below similar but overscaling more gray-blue than lavender.
>
> **Food Plants:** Unknown, probably Poaceae.
>
> **Life History:** Bivoltine (Mar–Nov).
>
> **Range:** Southeastern U.S.; Texas–East, eastern areas of North Central and Central.
>
> **Comments:** Flies close to ground in open pine woods.

424

PHYLACE ROADSIDE SKIPPER
Amblyscirtes phylace

Description: 1–1¼ in (25–32 mm); orange head and palps, forewing with squared outer margin; above unmarked black-brown with buff fringes; AFW with vague stigma on male; below similar.
Food Plants: Unknown, probably Poaceae.
Life History: Univoltine (Jun–Aug).
Range: Southwestern U.S.; Texas–Trans-Pecos.
Comments: Sometimes refered to as the Red-Headed Roadside Skipper for the distinctive color on the head.

425

ORANGE-EDGED ROADSIDE SKIPPER
Amblyscirtes fimbriata

Description: 1–1¼ in (25–32 mm); very similar to Phylace Roadside Skipper (*A. phylace*) but darker with orange fringes.
Food Plants: Unknown; Poaceae - *Bromus anomalus; Elymus arizonicus* in Arizona.
Life History: Unknown; univoltine in Arizona; multivoltine in Mexico; immature larvae bright green with black heads.
Range: Mexico to southwestern U.S.; Texas–Big Bend, southern Trans-Pecos.
Comments: Recorded (Jun–Jul); previously known as *Amblyscirtes bellus.*

426 A

EUFALA SKIPPER
Lerodea eufala

Description: ¾–1¼ in (19–32 mm); female larger, lighter colored; above gray-brown; AFW with three to five small white hyaline postmedian dots, female may have small vague cell spot; below similar but BHW paler.

Food Plants: Poaceae - *Cenchrus ciliaris, Cynodon dactylon, Echinochloa crusgalli, Oryza sativa, Saccharum officinarum, Setaria verticillata, Sorghum halepense, Sorghum vulgare, Zea mays.*

Life History: Bivoltine (Feb–Oct, all year in south Texas).

Range: Argentina to West Indies and southern U.S.; Texas–entire, more common in south and southwestern Texas.

Comments: Widely distributed; prefers open, sunny areas and agricultural fields.

427

OLIVE-CLOUDED SKIPPER
Lerodea dysaules

Description: ¾–1¼ in (19–32 mm); very similar to Eufala Skipper (*L. eufala*) but more olive-brown with additional AFW hyaline spot (square spot below cell on female); below similar but BHW with darker basal patch edged with bent pale postmedian band.

Food Plants: Unknown; Poaceae - *Cynodon dactylon* in lab.

Life History: Multivoltine (Jun–Nov).

Range: El Salvador to extreme southern U.S.; Texas–Rio Grande Valley.

Comments: Previously considered to be a subspecies of the Violet-Clouded Skipper (*L. arabus*) which is found in Arizona and Mexico.

428 A

TWIN-SPOT SKIPPER
Oligoria maculata

> **Description:** 1¼–1½ in (32–38 mm); broad wings; above dark brown with brown fringes; AFW with four white hyaline spots (two small subapical, two larger below cell), below similar but BHW with three diagnostic white median spots (one separate above a pair of spots).
>
> **Food Plants:** Poaceae.
>
> **Life History:** Bivoltine (Apr–May, Aug–Sep).
>
> **Range:** Southeastern U.S., near coast; Texas—extreme eastern area of Coastal Margin.
>
> **Comments:** Rare migrant up Atlantic Coast as far north as New York and Massachusetts.

429 A

BRAZILIAN SKIPPER
Calpodes ethlius

> **Description:** 1¾–2¼ in (44–57 mm); pointed forewing, smaller hindwing; above dark brown with orange-buff fringe; AFW with band of angulated white hyaline postmedian spots; AHW with three white hyaline spots; below similar but red-brown.
>
> **Food Plants:** Cannaceae.
>
> **Life History:** Multivoltine; after cutting slit in leaf, larva folds leaf over to form retreat in which pupation occurs.
>
> **Range:** Argentina to West Indies and southern U.S.; Texas—entire; most common in Rio Grande Valley and Coastal Margin (food plant is more common and winters less severe).
>
> **Comments:** A tropical species that has extended its natural range northward along with the planting of ornamental food plant.

430 A

SALT MARSH SKIPPER
Panoquina panoquin

Description: 1¼ in (32 mm); above pale yellow-brown with paler bases; AFW with several small pale submarginal spots; below similar but with yellow veins; BHW with diagnostic white dash projecting from cell.

Food Plants: Poaceae, probably *Distichlis* or *Spartina*.

Life History: Multivoltine (Apr–Oct).

Range: Gulf Coast and Atlantic Coast to New York; Texas–extreme Coastal Margin, restricted to coastal area northeast of Corpus Christi in Nueces Co.

Comments: Found in coastal salt marshes at low tide.

431 A

OBSCURE SKIPPER
Panoquina panoquinoides

Description: 1–1¼ in (25–32 mm); similar to Salt Marsh Skipper (*P. panoquin*) but smaller with smaller spots; BHW without white dash.

Food Plants: Poaceae - *Cynodon dactylon*; also *Saccharum officinarum* in the Antilles.

Life History: Bivoltine (Feb–Dec).

Range: South America to West Indies and southern U.S.; Texas–Coastal Margin.

Comments: Uncommon; found in coastal marshes and dunes.

432

OCOLA SKIPPER
Panoquina ocola

Description: 1¼–1½ in (32–38 mm); similar to Salt Marsh Skipper (*P. panoquin*) but with extended forewing; larger; above darker brown; AFW with small cream triangular spots; below similar; BHW unmarked (female BHW may have faint purple sheen).

Food Plants: Poaceae, probably *Oryza sativa, Saccharum officinarum.*

Life History: Multivoltine.

Range: Argentina to West Indies and southern U.S.; Texas–Rio Grande Valley, Coastal Margin, southeastern areas of South and Central, southern area of East; strays northwest.

Comments: Known to emigrate in large masses.

433

HECEBOLUS SKIPPER
Panoquina hecebola

Description: 1¼–1½ in (32–38 mm); similar to Ocola Skipper (*P. ocola*) but larger, more red-brown; AFW with pale cream spots (one in discal cell, two on postmedian); below similar but more yellow-brown with paler vein lines.

Food Plants: Unknown, possibly Poaceae - *Saccharum officinarum.*

Life History: Unknown; multivoltine in Mexico.

Range: Paraguay to extreme southern U.S.; Texas–Rio Grande Valley.

Comments: Occasionally common; recorded (Jul–Dec).

434

SYLVICOLA SKIPPER
Panoquina sylvicola

Description: 1¼–1½ in (32–38 mm); similar to Ocola Skipper (*P. ocola*) but slightly larger; AFW with additional small cream discal cell spot above postmedian spots; below similar but BHW with short straight row of small white postmedian spots (female BHW with blue haze).

Food Plants: Poaceae - *Saccharum officinarum*; also *Axonopus compressus*; *Eriochloa polystachya, Oryza sativa, Saccharum officinarum, Sorghum halepense* in the Antilles.

Life History: Multivoltine (Aug–Dec).

Range: Argentina to West Indies and extreme southern U.S.; Texas–Rio Grande Valley, strays northward.

Comments: Often found near fields of sugar cane.

435

EVAN'S SKIPPER
Panoquina evansi

Description: 1½–1¾ in (38–44 mm); similar to Sylvicola Skipper (*P. sylvicola*) but definitely larger; larger AFW spots more amber and more elongated; below similar; BHW with blue haze (male BHW with vague pale band).

Food Plants: Unknown, probably Poaceae - *Saccharum officinarum*.

Life History: Unknown; multivoltine in Mexico.

Range: Guatemala to extreme southern U.S.; Texas–stray to Rio Grande Valley.

Comments: Recorded Oct–Nov; considered by some workers to be subspecies of *P. fusina*.

436

NYCTELIUS SKIPPER
Nyctelius nyctelius

Description: 1⅜–1½ in (35–38 mm); above brown with pale brown fringes; AFW with white hyaline spots (one square spot below cell); AHW with short band of vague pale yellow postmedian spots; below similar but more white on BFW; BHW with dark brown and violet-brown blotch and band.

Food Plants: Unknown; Poaceae - *Oryza sativa, Saccharum officinarum, Zea mays* in West Indies.

Life History: Unknown.

Range: Argentina to West Indies and extreme southern U.S.; Texas–strays to Rio Grande Valley and extreme southern area of South.

Comments: Occasionally a pest on rice and sugar cane in Latin America.

437

VARIEGATED SKIPPER
Thespieus macareus

Description: 1½ in (38 mm); body and wing bases with hairy blue-gray overscaling; above dark brown with large square white hyaline postmedian spots; below mottled gray, brown, blue, red, white (distinct BFW red apical dash).

Food Plants: Unknown.

Life History: Unknown.

Range: Venezuela to extreme southern U.S.; Texas–stray to Rio Grande Valley.

Comments: Recorded (Jul–Nov).

GIANT SKIPPERS—SUBFAMILY MEGATHYMINAE

The large skippers of this subfamily are found mostly in the deserts of the southern United States and northern Mexico. A single species occurs as far south as Panama. Twenty species occur worldwide; nine of the 13 occurring in the United States are known from Texas. Several of these species have been divided into numerous subspecies. The larvae of this group typically burrow into the leaf, trunk, and roots of plants of the Liliaceae (lily family) or the Amaryllidaceae (amaryllis family), although the food plants are neither lillies or amaryllis. The larvae have small heads and lack the "ring neck" that is typical of most skippers. Adults bask with the forewings spread partially open and the hindwings fully spread. Giant skippers are able to fly extremely fast due to their heavy, muscular bodies and large wing spans. Despite their flying strength, they do not migrate. The adults are frequently observed sipping water at mud puddles. The two tribes of Megathyminae are the Aegialini (agave borers) and the Megathymini (yucca borers). Generally speaking, *Agathymus* and *Megathymus* are univoltine, characteristically flying in the autumn and spring, respectively. *Stallingsia* is bivoltine with a spring generation and a fall generation.

438

NEUMOEGEN'S GIANT SKIPPER
Agathymus neumoegeni

> **Description:** 2–3 in (51–76 mm); above varying between bright orange to orange-brown with black-brown median blotch, costal margin bar (blurred, lighter on AHW), outer margins, and checkered fringes; below generally gray-brown; BFW with orange median band, white costal margin bar; BHW with white cell spot, white (or gray) postmedian band.
> **Food Plants:** Amaryllidaceae - *Agave neomexicana*; *A. lechuguilla*.
> **Life History:** Univoltine; eggs dropped, on or near food plant.
> **Range:** Northern Mexico and southwestern U.S.; Texas—Far West, Trans-Pecos; montane areas.

Comments: Recorded (Sep–Oct); Texas subspecies -*carlsbadensis* (Calsbad Agave Borer) in Guadalupe Mountains; -*diabloensis* (Diablo Mountains Agave Borer) in Sierra Diablo, Sierra Blanca Mountains; -*florenceae* (Florence's Agave Borer) in Davis Mountains; *judithae* (Judith's Agave Borer) in Hueco Mountains; -*mcalpinei* (McAlpine's Agave Borer) in Glass Mountains.

439

TAWNY GIANT SKIPPER
Agathymus chisosensis

Description: 2–3 in (51–76 mm); similar to Neumoegen's Giant Skipper (*A. neumoegeni*) but with darker wing bases; above orange with dark brown median patch, costal margin patch, broad outer margins, and checkered fringes; below similar but with lavender-gray overscaling (restricted to BFW outer margin, entire BHW); BHW with pale gray postmedian band bordered by smudged black spots.

Food Plants: Amaryllidaceae - *Agave scabra*.

Life History: Univoltine.

Range: Texas–Big Bend, known only from Chisos Mountains, Brewster Co.

Comments: Previously considered a subspecies of *A. neumoegeni*; geographic location helps to identify.

440

MARY'S GIANT SKIPPER
Agathymus mariae

Description: 1¾–2 in (44–51 mm); above varying between gray-black to dark brown or yellow-brown with yellow cell spot and submarginal band; AFW with pale yellow subapical costal margin bar; below similar but paler with gray overscaling (restricted to outer third on BFW, entire BHW); BHW without yellow.

Food Plants: Amaryllidaceae - *Agave gracilipes, A. lechuguilla, A. neomexicana, A. scabra.*

Life History: Univoltine (Oct–Nov).

Range: Northern Mexico and southwestern U.S.; Texas–Far West, Trans-Pecos, Big Bend.

Comments: Texas subspecies *-chinatiensis* (Chinati Mountains Agave Borer) in Chinati Mountains; *-lajitaensis* (Lajitas Agave Borer) in southern Presidio County; *-mariae* (Mary's Giant Skipper) in all Trans-Pecos counties; rindgei (Rindge's Agave Borer) in Kinney Co., Val Verde Co.; some workers do not divide *A. mariae* into this many subspecies as they contend it is normal variation within a species and occasional hybridization producing variance.

441   L,A

WEST TEXAS GIANT SKIPPER
Agathymus gilberti

Description: 2 in (51 mm); similar to two species of Mary's Giant Skipper (*A. m. mariae and A.m. rindgei*) but smaller, without AFW costal margin spots, more distinctly checkered fringes; above brown with orange-brown bases and distinct checkered fringes; AFW with yellow postmedian spots; AHW with pale orange submedian and postmedian spots; below similar but with gray overscaling (past yellow spots on BFW, entire BHW).

Food Plants: Amaryllidaceae - *Agave lecheguilla.*

Life History: Univoltine (Sep–Nov).

Range: Texas–areas of Trans-Pecos and Southwest: Kinney Co., Terrell Co., and Val Verde Co.

Comments: Very closely related to Mary's Giant Skipper (occurs together with *A. mariae rindgei*).

442

BROWN BULLET
Agathymus estellae

Description: 2–2¼ in (51–57 mm); very similar to West Texas Giant
Skipper (*A. gilberti*) but slightly larger, darker, with more spots
on AFW; above dark brown with pale yellow submarginal spots
(more on AFW) and checkered fringes (more distinct on hind-
wing); below similar but with gray overscaling (restricted on
BFW to apex); BHW with white spots.
Food Plants: Amaryllidaceae - *Agave lecheguilla.*
Life History: Univoltine (Sep–Oct).
Range: Mexico to southern U.S.; Texas–Southwest: Edwards Co.,
Kinney Co., Terrell Co., and Val Verde Co.
Comments: Closely related to Mary's Giant Skipper (*A. mariae*);
Texas subspecies -*valverdiensis.*

443

COLORADO GIANT SKIPPER
Megathymus coloradensis

Description: 2½–2¾ in (64–70 mm); extended forewing; above
gray-black with hazy yellow bases; AFW with two costal margin
bars (one pale yellow postmedian, one white subapical) pale yellow submarginal band, and checkered fringe; AHW with pale
yellow outer margin, and fringe (female with short yellow submarginal band); below similar but more gray; BHW with white
triangular submedian spot.
Food Plants: Liliaceae - *Yucca.*
Life History: Univoltine (Mar–Apr); white larvae with black heads,
black plates behind the head.
Range: Northern Mexico and southern U.S.; Texas–entire except
Coastal Margin; local in distribution.

Comments: Some workers combine these populations west of Mississippi River with those east of the river under Yucca Skipper (*Megathymus yuccae*); Texas subspecies *-coloradensis* (Colorado Giant Skipper) in Panhandle; *-kendalli* in Central; *-louiseae* (Louise's Yucca Borer) in Southwest; *-reinthali* in East; *-reubeni* (Reuben's Yucca Borer) in Hueco Mountains; *-stallingsi* in North; *-wilsonorum* in western part of Rio Grande Valley; *-winkensis* (Wink Yucca Borer) in West.

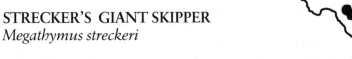

444 A

STRECKER'S GIANT SKIPPER
Megathymus streckeri

Description: 2¼–3 in (55–75 mm); sexually dimorphic; above (male) gray-black with white and cream oblong spots (cell spot half white and half cream), AHW with scalloped pale yellow outer margin band; or above (female) orange-brown, AFW with square pale yellow cell spot, jagged band of submarginal spots, AHW with orange crescent cell spot, postmedian band, scalloped outer margin band; both sexes with pale fringes (lightly streaked on AFW) below similar with gray overscaling (restricted to outer margin on BFW); BHW with scattered small white spots.

Food Plants: Lilliaceae - *Yucca constricta, Y. glauca.*

Life History: Univoltine (Apr–Jul).

Range: West central U.S.; Texas–Panhandle; areas in Central and South; disjunct populations.

Comments: Texas subspecies *-texanus* (Giant Texas Skipper).

445

URSINE GIANT SKIPPER
Megathymus ursus

Description: 3–3¼ in (76–82 mm); white antennae, pale gray head and thorax; above dark gray-brown with smudged checkered fringes; AFW with broad orange patch, white subapical bar on costal margin; below similar but paler with gray overscaling (more extensive on BHW); BHW with vague small pale spots.

Food Plants: Liliaceae - *Yucca torreyi, Y. treculeana* var. *canaliculata.*

Life History: Univoltine (Apr–Jun).

Range: Northern Mexico, southwestern U.S.; Texas–Far West, Big Bend, areas of Southwest and Trans-Pecos.

Comments: Texas subspecies -*violae* (Viola's Yucca Borer).

446

MANFREDA GIANT SKIPPER
Stallingsia maculosa

Description: 1¾–2 in (44–51 mm); above dark yellow-brown, one light orange cell spot, row of pale orange submarginal spots,and checkered fringes; below similar but with gray overscaling between spots and fringes; BFW with white subapical spots; BHW with row of dark submarginal spots with pale rings.

Food Plants: Amaryllidaceae - *Manfreda maculosa.*

Life History: Bivoltine (Apr–May, Sep–Oct).

Range: Northern Mexico and adjacent U.S.; Texas—Rio Grande Valley, southern area of South.

Comments: Adults have not been observed feeding; due to habitat destruction, this species is uncommon.

BUTTERFLIES—TO COLLECT OR TO WATCH ?

Classically, butterflies have been studied as pinned specimens after they have been collected, killed, and mounted on a spreading board. In the past decade, butterfly watching has become very popular, but collecting specimens has been frowned upon or even condemned by certain environmental or animal rights groups. At the present time, a person interested in the study of butterflies is left with the following question: Is it okay to collect butterflies? The answer to this question is: Certainly, it is okay, although certain rules of propriety and self-control are appropriate today.

A few legal restrictions apply to collecting butterflies. Certain species may not be legally collected without a permit. A number of butterflies are listed as threatened or endangered by the U. S. Fish and Wildlife Service. No butterflies occurring in Texas were listed at the time of writing of this book. Many areas of public land owned by the state or federal government and set aside for natural resource conservation or public visitation are closed to collecting without a permit. Some agencies may grant permits only to people meeting certain requirements, e. g., affiliation with a recognized institution of learning or research. If you wish to collect in a state or national park or some of the other public lands open to the public, plan your activities in advance and have a specific reason to collect there. Restricting of collecting activities in these areas protects the resources present in these lands and also allows the natural resource managers to track the resources that exist in these areas.

Habitat destruction is usually much more damaging to butterfly populations than collecting. The reproductive potential of butterflies is usually so great that normal collecting activities pose little threat to the survival of butterfly populations; however, a few species may be so restricted in occurrence that collecting may have an impact during years of low population levels. These population levels might be low due to normal fluctuations, unfavorable weather conditions, or the loss of significant amounts of suitable habitat for a particular species. Nevertheless, collecting activities should be limited to a reasonable number of specimens of any species present in the area.

Very little specialized equipment is required to collect butterflies. The basic piece of equipment is a net. This net may be homemade or could be one of any of a large number of models available from biological supply houses. Once you have collected your specimens, place carefully into glassine envelopes and then place the envelopes into a metal or cardboard box to prevent crushing of the specimens. Write the date and place of collection on each envelope as you place the specimens in them. At home, you can spread the specimen using a mounting board (smaller specimens can be mounted using a piece of styrofoam with a channel pressed into it for the butterfly's body) and thin insect pins. Then, when dry, pin in a case with a tag identifying the species, sex, date, and location.

The alternative outdoor activity is to watch butterflies as they fly and feed. Butterfly watching can be very relaxing and incredibly interesting and stimulating to the mind—all at the same time. Try it! You will probably like it!

However, those persons who wish to collect—whether for educational or recreational purposes—should be allowed to do so. Recreational collecting allows people to understand the community of species at a particular site and to enjoy close-up the intricate details of the beautiful patterns on the wings of butterflies. Oftentimes, people release these specimens after examining them. Collecting in a prudent manner can increase our general knowledge of butterflies as well as ensure that the next generation will include sufficient lepidopterists to study butterflies, teach the general public about butterflies, and manage lands so that butterflies will have sufficient food plants to exist in an ever-increasing artificial world.

Texas Butterflies

CATTLE HEART — *Parides eurimedes*
PIPEVINE SWALLOWTAIL — *Battus philenor*
POLYDAMAS SWALLOWTAIL — *Battus polydamas*
ZEBRA SWALLOWTAIL — *Eurytides marcellus*
DARK ZEBRA SWALLOWTAIL — *Eurytides philolaus*
BLACK SWALLOWTAIL — *Papilio polyxenes*
THOAS SWALLOWTAIL — *Heraclides thoas*
GIANT SWALLOWTAIL — *Heraclides cresphontes*
ORNYTHION SWALLOWTAIL — *Heraclides ornythion*
LYCOPHRON SWALLOWTAIL — *Heraclides astyalus*
ANCHISIADES SWALLOWTAIL — *Heraclides anchisiades*
PHARNACES SWALLOWTAIL — *Heraclides pharnaces*
TIGER SWALLOWTAIL — *Pterourus glaucus*
TWO-TAILED SWALLOWTAIL — *Pterourus multicaudatus*
THREE-TAILED SWALLOWTAIL — *Pterourus pilumnus*
SPICEBUSH SWALLOWTAIL — *Pterourus troilus*
PALAMEDES SWALLOWTAIL — *Pterourus palamedes*
VICTORINE SWALLOWTAIL — *Pterourus victorinus*

MISTLETOE WHITE — *Catasticta nimbice*
TROPICAL WHITE — *Appias drusilla*
CALIFORNIA WHITE — *ontia sisymbrii*
CHECKERED WHITE — *Pontia protodice*
MUSTARD WHITE — *Pieris napi*
CABBAGE BUTTERFLY — *Pieris rapae*
GREAT SOUTHERN WHITE — *Ascia monuste*
GIANT WHITE — *Ganyra josephina*
PEARLY MARBLE — *Euchloe hyantis*

OLYMPIA MARBLE – *Euchloe olympia*
PIMA ORANGE TIP – *Anthocharis pima*
SARA ORANGE TIP – *Anthocharis sara*
FALCATE ORANGE TIP – *Paramidea midea*
CLOUDED SULPHUR – *Colias philodice*
ALFALFA BUTTERFLY – *Colias eurytheme*
DOG FACE – *Zerene cesonia*
WHITE ANGLED SULPHUR – *Anteos chlorinde*
YELLOW BRIMSTONE – *Anteos maerula*
CLOUDLESS SULPHUR – *Phoebis sennae*
ORANGE-BARRED SULPHUR – *Phoebis philea*
ARGANTE GIANT SULPHUR – *Phoebis argante*
LARGE ORANGE SULPHUR – *Phoebis agarithe*
YELLOW LONG-TAILED SULPHUR – *Phoebis neocypris*
STATIRA – *Aphrissa statira*
LYSIDE – *Kricogonia lyside*
BARRED YELLOW – *Eurema daira*
BOISDUVAL'S YELLOW – *Eurema boisduvalianum*
MEXICAN YELLOW – *Eurema mexicanum*
SALOME YELLOW – *Eurema salome*
TAILED ORANGE – *Eurema proterpia*
LITTLE YELLOW – *Eurema lisa*
JAMAICAN SULPHUR – *Eurema nise*
DINA YELLOW – *Eurema dina*
SLEEPY ORANGE – *Eurema nicippe*
DAINTY SULPHUR – *Nathalis iole*
TROPICAL MIMIC WHITE – *Enantia albania*

HARVESTER – *Feniseca tarquinius*
GREAT COPPER – *Gaeides xanthoides*
CYCAD BUTTERFLY – *Eumaeus toxea*
GREAT BLUE HAIRSTREAK – *Atlides halesus*
TELEA HAIRSTREAK – *Chlorostrymon telea*
SIMAETHIS HAIRSTREAK – *Chlorostrymon simaethis*
SOAPBERRY HAIRSTREAK – *Phaeostrymon alcestis*
CORAL HAIRSTREAK – *Harkenclenus titus*
BEHR'S HAIRSTREAK – *Satyrium behrii*
EDWARDS' HAIRSTREAK – *Satyrium edwardsii*

BANDED HAIRSTREAK – *Satyrium calanus*
KING'S HAIRSTREAK – *Satyrium kingi*
STRIPED HAIRSTREAK – *Satyrium liparops*
BLACK HAIRSTREAK – *Ocaria ocrisia*
CLYTIE HAIRSTREAK – *Ministrymon clytie*
LEDA HAIRSTREAK – *Ministrymon leda*
AZIA HAIRSTREAK – *Tmolus azia*
ECHION HAIRSTREAK – *Tmolus echion*
TEPHRAEUS HAIRSTREAK – *Siderus tephraeus*
AQUAMARINE HAIRSTREAK – *Oenomaus ortygnus*
MARIUS HAIRSTREAK – *Rekoa marius*
PALEGON HAIRSTREAK – *Rekoa palegon*
BLUE-METAL HAIRSTREAK – *Allosmaitia pion*
RED-BANDED HAIRSTREAK – *Calycopis cecrops*
DUSKY-BLUE HAIRSTREAK – *Calycopis isobeon*
MISERABILIS HAIRSTREAK – *Cyanophrys miserabilis*
GOODSON'S HAIRSTREAK – *Cyanophrys goodsoni*
TROPICAL GREEN HAIRSTREAK – *Cyanophrys herodotus*
JUNIPER HAIRSTREAK – *Mitoura siva*
OLIVE HAIRSTREAK – *Mitoura grynea*
XAMI HAIRSTREAK – *Xamia xami*
SANDIA HAIRSTREAK – *Sandia mcfarlandi*
FROSTED ELFIN – *Incisalia irus*
HENRY'S ELFIN – *Incisalia henrici*
EASTERN PINE ELFIN – *Incisalia niphon*
JADA HAIRSTREAK – *Arawacus jada*
NORTHERN HAIRSTREAK – *Fixsenia ontario*
POLING'S HAIRSTREAK – *Fixsenia polingi*
WHITE-M HAIRSTREAK – *Parrhasius m-album*
GRAY HAIRSTREAK – *Strymon melinus*
REDDISH HAIRSTREAK – *Strymon rufofuscus*
MEXICAN GRAY HAIRSTREAK – *Strymon bebrycia*
YOJOA HAIRSTREAK – *Strymon yojoa*
WHITE HAIRSTREAK – *Strymon albatus*
LACEY'S HAIRSTREAK – *Strymon alea*
COLUMELLA HAIRSTREAK – *Strymon columella*
CESTRI HAIRSTREAK – *Strymon cestri*
BAZOCHII HAIRSTREAK – *Strymon bazochii*

SERAPIO HAIRSTREAK – *Strymon serapio*
ARIZONA HAIRSTREAK – *Erora quaderna*
ENDYMION HAIRSTREAK – *Electrostrymon endymion*
MUTED HAIRSTREAK – *Electrostrymon canus*
PYGMY BLUE – *Brephidium exile*
EASTERN PYGMY BLUE – *Brephidium isophthalma*
CASSIUS BLUE – *Leptotes cassius*
MARINE BLUE – *Leptotes marina*
CYNA BLUE – *Zizula cyna*
CERAUNUS BLUE – *Hemiargus ceraunus*
REAKIRT'S BLUE – *Hemiargus isola*
EASTERN TAILED BLUE – *Everes comyntas*
SPRING AZURE – *Celastrina argiolus*
RITA BLUE – *Euphilotes rita*
SILVERY BLUE – *Glaucopsyche lygdamus*
MELISSA BLUE – *Lycaeides melissa*
ACMON BLUE – *Icaricia acmon*

LITTLE METALMARK – *Calephelis virginiensis*
FATAL METALMARK – *Calephelis nemesis*
LOST METALMARK – *Calephelis perditalis*
RAWSON'S METALMARK – *Calephelis rawsoni*
FREEMAN'S METALMARK – *Calephelis freemani*
RED-BORDERED METALMARK – *Caria ino*
BLUE METALMARK – *Lasaia sula*
PIXIE – *Melanis pixe*
EMESIA METALMARK – *Emesis emesia*
FALCATE EMESIA – *Emesis tenedia*
MORMON METALMARK – *Apodemia mormo*
NARROW-WINGED METALMARK – *Apodemia multiplaga*
HEPBURN'S METALMARK – *Apodemia hepburni*
PALMER'S METALMARK – *Apodemia palmerii*
WALKER'S METALMARK – *Apodemia walkeri*
CHISOS METALMARK – *Apodemia chisosensis*

SNOUT BUTTERFLY – *Libytheana bachmanii*
TROPICAL SNOUT – *Libytheana carinenta*
CUBAN SNOUT BUTTERFLY – *Libytheana motya*

GULF FRITILLARY – *Agraulis vanillae*
MEXICAN SILVERSPOT – *Dione moneta*
BANDED ORANGE – *Dryadula phaetusa*
JULIA – *Dryas iulia*
ISABELLA TIGER – *Eueides isabella*
ZEBRA – *Heliconius charitonius*
CRIMSON-PATCHED LONGWING – *Heliconius erato*

VARIEGATED FRITILLARY – *Euptoieta claudia*
MEXICAN FRITILLARY – *Euptoieta hegesia*
GREAT SPANGLED FRITILLARY – *Speyeria cybele*
DOTTED CHECKERSPOT – *Poladryas minuta*
THEONA CHECKERSPOT – *Thessalia theona*
CHINATI CHECKERSPOT – *Thessalia chinatiensis*
FULVIA CHECKERSPOT – *Thessalia fulvia*
BORDERED PATCH – *Chlosyne lacinia*
DEFINITE PATCH – *Chlosyne definita*
ENDEIS PATCH – *Chlosyne endeis*
ERODYLE PATCH – *Chlosyne erodyle*
JANAIS PATCH – *Chlosyne janais*
ROSITA PATCH – *Chlosyne rosita*
STRIPED PATCH – *Chlosyne ehrenbergi*
YELLOW PATCH – *Chlosyne melitaeoides*
GORGONE CHECKERSPOT – *Charidryas gorgone*
SILVERY CHECKERSPOT – *Charidryas nycteis*
ELF – *Microtia elva*
DYMAS CHECKERSPOT – *Dymasia dymas*
ELADA CHECKERSPOT – *Texola elada*
TEXAN CRESCENT – *Anthanassa texana*
SEMINOLE CRESCENT – *Anthanassa seminole*
FALSE BLACK CRESCENT – *Anthanassa ptolyca*
TULCIS CRESCENT – *Anthanassa tulcis*
VESTA CRESCENT – *Phyciodes vesta*
PHAON CRESCENT – *Phyciodes phaon*
PEARL CRESCENT – *Phyciodes tharos*
PAINTED CRESCENT – *Phyciodes pictus*
ANIETA – *Tegosa anieta*
CHALCEDON CHECKERSPOT – *Euphydryas chalcedona*

BALTIMORE – *Euphydryas phaeton*
QUESTION MARK – *Polygonia interrogationis*
HOP MERCHANT – *Polygonia comma*
MOURNING CLOAK – *Nymphalis antiopa*
AMERICAN PAINTED LADY – *Vanessa virginiensis*
PAINTED LADY – *Vanessa cardui*
WEST COAST LADY – *Vanessa annabella*
RED ADMIRAL – *Vanessa atalanta*
ORANGE MAP WING – *Hypanartia lethe*
BUCKEYE – *Junonia coenia*
GENOVEVA – *Junonia genoveva*
WEST INDIAN BUCKEYE – *Junonia evarete*
WHITE PEACOCK – *Anartia jatrophae*
FATIMA – *Anartia fatima*
MALACHITE – *Siproeta stelenes*
RED-SPOTTED PURPLE – *Basilarchia arthemis*
VICEROY – *Basilarchia archippus*
MEXICAN SISTER – *Adelpha fessonia*
TROPICAL SISTER – *Adelpha basiloides*
CALIFORNIA SISTER – *Adelpha bredowii*
DIMORPHIC BARK WING – *Epiphile adrasta*
BLUE WING – *Myscelia ethusa*
CYANANTHE BLUE WING – *Myscelia cyananthe*
DINGY PURPLE WING – *Eunica monima*
FLORIDA PURPLE WING – *Eunica tatila*
BLUE-EYED GREEN WING – *Dynamine dyonis*
SPOTTED GREEN WING – *Dynamine tithia*
MEXICAN EIGHTY-EIGHT BUTTERFLY – *Diaethria asteria*
EIGHTY-EIGHT BUTTERFLY – *Diaethria anna*
AMYMONE – *Mestra amymone*
RED RIM – *Biblis hyperia*
GRAY CRACKER – *Hamadryas februa*
BLUE CRACKER – *Hamadryas feronia*
CENTRAL AMERICAN CRACKER – *Hamadryas guatamalena*
RINGLESS BLUE CRACKER – *Hamadryas iphthime*
RED CRACKER – *Hamadryas amphinome*
STINKY LEAF WING – *Historis odius*
DASH-WING – *Historis acheronta*

KARWINSKI'S BEAUTY – *Smyrna karwinskii*
BLOMFILD'S BEAUTY – *Smyrna blomfildia*
WAITER – *Marpesia zerynthia*
MANY-BANDED DAGGER WING – *Marpesia chiron*
RUDDY DAGGER WING – *Marpesia petreus*

TROPICAL LEAF WING – *Anaea aidea*
GOATWEED BUTTERFLY – *Anaea andria*
ANGLED LEAF WING – *Memphis glycerium*
BLUE LEAF WING – *Memphis pithyusa*
CHESTNUT LEAF BUTTERFLY – *Memphis echemus*

HACKBERRY BUTTERFLY – *Asterocampa celtis*
EMPRESS LEILIA – *Asterocampa leilia*
TAWNY EMPEROR – *Asterocampa clyton*
PAVON – *Doxocopa pavon*
LAURE – *Doxocopa laure*

COMMON MORPHO – *Morpho peleides*

PEARLY EYE – *Enodia portlandia*
CREOLE PEARLY EYE – *Enodia creola*
WARM BROWN – *Cyllopsis pertepida*
GEMMED SATYR – *Cyllopsis gemma*
HERMES SATYR – *Hermeuptychia hermes*
GEORGIA SATYR – *Neonympha areolata*
LITTLE WOOD SATYR – *Megisto cymela*
RED SATYR – *Megisto rubricata*
COMMON WOOD NYMPH – *Cercyonis pegala*
MEAD'S WOOD NYMPH – *Cercyonis meadii*

MONARCH – *Danaus plexippus*
QUEEN – *Danaus gilippus*
SOLDIER – *Danaus eresimus*
LARGE TIGER – *Lycorea cleobaea*

KLUG'S DIRCENNA – *Dircenna klugii*
POLIS TRANSPARENT – *Greta polissena*

ARAXES SKIPPER – *Pyrrhopyge araxes*
GUAVA SKIPPER – *Phocides polybius*
URANIA SKIPPER – *Phocides urania*
MERCURIAL SKIPPER – *Proteides mercurius*
SILVER-SPOTTED SKIPPER – *Epargyreus clarus*
EXADEUS SKIPPER – *Epargyreus exadeus*
HAMMOCK SKIPPER – *Polygonus leo*
MANUEL'S SKIPPER – *Polygonus manueli*
WHITE-STRIPED LONGTAIL – *Chioides catillus*
ZILPA LONGTAIL – *Chioides zilpa*
GOLD-SPOT AGUNA – *Aguna asander*
EMERALD GREEN AGUNA – *Aguna claxon*
TAILED AGUNA – *Aguna metophis*
MOTTLED LONGTAIL – *Typhedanus undulatus*
MEXICAN POLYTHRIX – *Polythrix mexicana*
EIGHT-SPOTTED POLYTHRIX – *Polythrix octomaculata*
SHORT-TAILED ARIZONA SKIPPER – *Zestusa dorus*
ALCAEUS SKIPPER – *Codatractus alcaeus*
ARIZONA SKIPPER – *Codatractus arizonensis*
LONG-TAILED SKIPPER – *Urbanus proteus*
SHORT-TAILED GREEN LONGTAIL – *Urbanus pronus*
ESMERALDA LONGTAIL – *Urbanus esmeraldus*
DORANTES SKIPPER – *Urbanus dorantes*
TELEUS LONGTAIL – *Urbanus teleus*
TANNA LONGTAIL – *Urbanus tanna*
PLAIN LONGTAIL – *Urbanus simplicius*
BROWN LONGTAIL – *Urbanus procne*
WHITE-TAILED SKIPPER – *Urbanus doryssus*
FLASHING ASTRAPTES – *Astraptes fulgerator*
GREEN FLASHER – *Astraptes egregius*
WHITE FLASHER – *Astraptes alardus*
GILBERT'S FLASHER – *Astraptes gilberti*
YELLOW FLASHER – *Astraptes anaphus*
GOLDEN-BANDED SKIPPER – *Autochton cellus*
WHITE-BANDED SKIPPER – *Autochton cinctus*
HOARY EDGE – *Achalarus lyciades*
DESERT HOARY EDGE – *Achalarus casica*

COYOTE SKIPPER – *Achalarus toxeus*
JALAPUS SKIPPER – *Achalarus jalapus*
SOUTHERN CLOUDY WING – *Thorybes bathyllus*
NORTHERN CLOUDY WING – *Thorybes pylades*
CONFUSED CLOUDY WING – *Thorybes confusis*
DRUSIUS CLOUDY WING – *Thorybes drusius*
POTRILLO SKIPPER – *Cabares potrillo*
FRITZ SKIPPER – *Celaenorrhinus fritzgaertneri*
STALLING'S SKIPPER – *Celaenorrhinus stallingsi*
EURIBATES SKIPPER – *Dyscophellus euribates*
FALCATE SKIPPER – *Spathilepia clonius*
CALCHAS SKIPPER – *Cogia calchas*
ACACIA SKIPPER – *Cogia hippalus*
OUTIS SKIPPER – *Cogia outis*
ARTEUROTIA SKIPPER – *Arteurotia tractipennis*
PURPLISH-BLACK SKIPPER – *Nisoniades rubescens*
CONFUSED PELLICIA – *Pellicia angra*
GLAZED PELLICIA – *Pellicia arina*
MORNING GLORY PELLICIA – *Pellicia dimidiata*
MOTTLED BOLLA – *Bolla clytius*
OBSCURE BOLLA – *Bolla brennus*
CEOS SKIPPER – *Staphylus ceos*
SOUTHERN SCALLOPED SOOTY WING – *Staphylus mazans*
SCALLOPED SOOTY WING – *Staphylus hayhurstii*
AZTEC SOOTY WING – *Staphylus azteca*
VARIEGATED SKIPPER – *Gorgythion begga*
BLUE-STUDDED SKIPPER – *Sostrata bifasciata*
HOARY SKIPPER – *Carrhenes canescens*
GLASSY-WINGED SKIPPER – *Xenophanes trixus*
TEXAS POWDERED SKIPPER – *Systasea pulverulenta*
ARIZONA POWDERED SKIPPER – *Systasea zampa*
SICKLE-WINGED SKIPPER – *Achlyodes mithridates*
HERMIT – *Grais stigmatica*
BROWN-BANDED SKIPPER – *Timochares ruptifasciatus*
ASYCHIS SKIPPER – *Chiomara asychis*
COMMON DUSKY WING – *Gesta gesta*
SLEEPY DUSKY WING – *Erynnis brizo*
JUVENAL'S DUSKY WING – *Erynnis juvenalis*

ROCKY MOUNTAIN DUSKY WING — *Erynnis telemachus*
MERIDIAN DUSKY WING — *Erynnis meridianus*
HORACE'S DUSKY WING — *Erynnis horatius*
MOURNFUL DUSKY WING — *Erynnis tristis*
MOTTLED DUSKY WING — *Erynnis martialis*
SCUDDER'S DUSKY WING — *Erynnis scudderi*
ZARUCCO DUSKY WING — *Erynnis zarucco*
FUNEREAL DUSKY WING — *Erynnis funeralis*
WILD INDIGO DUSKY WING — *Erynnis baptisiae*
SMALL CHECKERED SKIPPER — *Pyrgus scriptura*
CHECKERED SKIPPER — *Pyrgus communis*
WESTERN CHECKERED SKIPPER — *Pyrgus albescens*
TROPICAL CHECKERED SKIPPER — *Pyrgus oileus*
PHILETAS SKIPPER — *Pyrgus philetas*
ERICHSON'S SKIPPER — *Heliopetes domicella*
LAVIANA SKIPPER — *Heliopetes lavianus*
MACAIRA SKIPPER — *Heliopetes macaira*
COMMON WHITE SKIPPER — *Heliopetes arsalte*
STREAKY SKIPPER — *Celotes nessus*
SCARCE STREAKY SKIPPER — *Celotes limpia*
COMMON SOOTY WING — *Pholisora catullus*
MEXICAN SOOTY WING — *Pholisora mejicana*
SALTBUSH SOOTY WING — *Hesperopsis alpheus*
SMALL-SPOTTED SKIPPERLING — *Piruna microstictus*
HAFERNIK'S SKIPPERLING — *Piruna haferniki*
MALICIOUS SHADY SKIPPER — *Synapte malitiosa*
SALENUS SKIPPER — *Synapte salenus*
REDUNDANT SWARTHY SKIPPER — *Corticea corticea*

SATURN SKIPPER — *Callimormus saturnus*
PERIGENES SKIPPER — *Vidius perigenes*
VIOLET PATCH SKIPPER — *Monca tyrtaeus*
SWARTHY SKIPPER — *Nastra lherminier*
JULIA'S SKIPPER — *Nastra julia*
NEAMATHLA SKIPPER — *Nastra neamathla*
FAWN-SPOTTED SKIPPER — *Cymaenes odilia*
CLOUDED SKIPPER — *Lerema accius*
LIRIS SKIPPER — *Lerema liris*

FANTASTIC SKIPPER – *Vettius fantasos*
GREEN-BACKED SKIPPER – *Perichares philetes*
OSCA SKIPPER – *Rinthon osca*
PERCOSIUS SKIPPER – *Decinea percosius*
CHYDEA SKIPPER – *Conga chydaea*
LEAST SKIPPER – *Ancyloxypha numitor*
TROPICAL LEAST SKIPPER – *Ancyloxypha arene*
EDWARD'S SKIPPERLING – *Oarisma edwardsi*
ORANGE SKIPPERLING – *Copaeodes aurantiacus*
SOUTHERN SKIPPERLING – *Copaeodes minimus*
SUNRISE SKIPPER – *Adopaeoides prittwitzi*
FIERY SKIPPER – *Hylephila phyleus*
MORRISON'S SKIPPER – *Stinga morrisoni*
UNCAS SKIPPER – *Hesperia uncas*
COMMON BRANDED SKIPPER – *Hesperia comma*
APACHE SKIPPER – *Hesperia woodgatei*
OTTOE SKIPPER – *Hesperia ottoe*
PAHASKA SKIPPER – *Hesperia pahaska*
COBWEB SKIPPER – *Hesperia metea*
GREEN SKIPPER – *Hesperia viridis*
DOTTED SKIPPER – *Hesperia attalus*
MESKE'S SKIPPER – *Hesperia meskei*
PECK'S SKIPPER – *Polites peckius*
RHESUS SKIPPER – *Polites rhesus*
CARUS SKIPPER – *Polites carus*
SUBRETICULATE SKIPPER – *Polites subreticulata*
TAWNY-EDGED SKIPPER – *Polites themistocles*
CROSSLINE SKIPPER – *Polites origenes*
WHIRLABOUT – *Polites vibex*
BROKEN DASH – *Wallengrenia otho*
NORTHERN BROKEN DASH – *Wallengrenia egremet*
LITTLE GLASSYWING – *Pompeius verna*
SACHEM – *Atalopedes campestris*
AROGOS SKIPPER – *Atrytone arogos*
DELAWARE SKIPPER – *Atrytone logan*
MAZAI SKIPPER – *Atrytone mazai*
BYSSUS SKIPPER – *Problema byssus*
HOBOMOK SKIPPER – *Poanes hobomok*

ZABULON SKIPPER – *Poanes zabulon*
TAXILES SKIPPER – *Poanes taxiles*
YEHL SKIPPER – *Poanes yehl*
BROAD-WINGED SKIPPER – *Poanes viator*
UMBER SKIPPER – *Poanes melane*
EULOGIUS SKIPPER – *Mellana eulogius*
ALABAMA SKIPPER – *Euphyes alabamae*
DUKE'S SKIPPER – *Euphyes dukesi*
DUN SKIPPER – *Euphyes vestris*
DUSTED SKIPPER – *Atrytonopsis hianna*
VIERECK'S SKIPPER – *Atrytonopsis vierecki*
PITTACUS SKIPPER – *Atrytonopsis pittacus*
PYTHON SKIPPER – *Atrytonopsis python*
SHEEP SKIPPER – *Atrytonopsis edwardsi*
SIMIUS ROADSIDE SKIPPER – *Amblyscirtes simius*
CASSUS ROADSIDE SKIPPER – *Amblyscirtes cassus*
BRONZE ROADSIDE SKIPPER – *Amblyscirtes aenus*
OSLAR'S ROADSIDE SKIPPER – *Amblyscirtes oslari*
PEPPER AND SALT SKIPPER – *Amblyscirtes hegon*
TEXAS ROADSIDE SKIPPER – *Amblyscirtes texanae*
LACE-WINGED ROADSIDE SKIPPER – *Amblyscirtes aesculapius*
SLATY ROADSIDE SKIPPER – *Amblyscirtes nereus*
NYSA ROADSIDE SKIPPER – *Amblyscirtes nysa*
EOS ROADSIDE SKIPPER – *Amblyscirtes eos*
ROADSIDE SKIPPER – *Amblyscirtes vialis*
CELIA'S ROADSIDE SKIPPER – *Amblyscirtes celia*
BELL'S ROADSIDE SKIPPER – *Amblyscirtes belli*
LEAST FLORIDA SKIPPER – *Amblyscirtes alternata*
PHYLACE ROADSIDE SKIPPER – *Amblyscirtes phylace*
ORANGE-EDGED ROADSIDE SKIPPER – *Amblyscirtes fimbriata*
EUFALA SKIPPER – *Lerodea eufala*
OLIVE-CLOUDED SKIPPER – *Lerodea dysaules*
TWIN-SPOT SKIPPER – *Oligoria maculata*
BRAZILIAN SKIPPER – *Calpodes ethlius*
SALT MARSH SKIPPER – *Panoquina panoquin*
OBSCURE SKIPPER – *Panoquina panoquinoides*
OCOLA SKIPPER – *Panoquina ocola*
HECEBOLUS SKIPPER – *Panoquina hecebola*

SYLVICOLA SKIPPER — *Panoquina sylvicola*
EVAN'S SKIPPER — *Panoquina evansi*
NYCTELIUS SKIPPER — *Nyctelius nyctelius*
VARIEGATED SKIPPER — *Thespieus macareus*
NEUMOEGEN'S GIANT SKIPPER — *Agathymus neumoegeni*
TAWNY GIANT SKIPPER — *Agathymus chisosensis*
MARY'S GIANT SKIPPER — *Agathymus mariae*
WEST TEXAS GIANT SKIPPER — *Agathymus gilberti*
BROWN BULLET — *Agathymus estellae*
COLORADO GIANT SKIPPER — *Megathymus coloradensis*
STRECKER'S GIANT SKIPPER — *Megathymus streckeri*
URSINE GIANT SKIPPER — *Megathymus ursus*
MANFREDA GIANT SKIPPER — *Stallingsia maculosa*

Glossary

abdomen—posterior section of insects composed of the terminal ten segments of the typical insect body. Located immediately behind the thorax.

AFW—above forewing.

AHW—above hindwing.

allopatric—two or more species or subspecies whose geographical ranges do not overlap. Opposite of parapatric and sympatric.

androconial patch—area of wing of butterfly that contains specialized scent scales with the exposed edge made up of many fine tips, like a brush, that aid in dispersion of pheromone compounds.

antenna—(*pl.* **antennae**) one of a pair of slender clubbed sensory appendages on either side of the head of insects and other arthropods. Sensory organ that detects chemicals in the air.

anterior—forward, referring to the front portion of the body or other object. Opposite of posterior.

apiculus—a narrow extension on the antenna past the antennal club in skippers.

basal—the area on the wing closest to the thorax, referring to either forewing or hindwing.

basking—when a butterfly aligns the wings to the sun to absorb heat; wings may be together and tilted, spread open, or forewings partially open with hindwings spread.

Batesian mimicry—mimicry of a distasteful or poisonous species by a tasteful or non-poisonous species for protection from predators.

BFW—below forewing.

BHW—below hindwing.

bivoltine—producing two generations in one year.

brood—a butterfly generation. Generally, the adults from eggs laid in the same general time.

cell—the interior area of a wing encircled by veins, occasionally refered to as a discal cell.

club—the thickened end of an antenna.

chrysalis—(*pl.* chrysalids) pupal stage of butterflies during which the larva enclosed in a hard or at least firm case transforms itself into an adult. Third stage of complete metamorphosis.

cocoon—silken structure produced by most moth larvae prior to pupation. Butterflies do not produce a cocoon, but many skippers and a few true butterflies form a thin silken sheath in which they pupate.

costa—the upper edge of a wing, referring to either forewing or hindwing.

costal fold—a narrow flap along the costal margin of the forewing containing scent scales used for sexual attraction. Present on males of many species and females of some species.

cremaster—a short, hardened appendage at the posterior end of some pupae that contains small hooks that attach to the silk button spun by the last instar larva prior to pupation.

crucifer—plants of the family Brassicaceae (formerly called Cruciferae). Contains cultivated human foods, e.g., cabbage, broccoli, cauliflower, kale, brussel sprouts, as well as other species.

cucurbitacin—phytochemical in plants of the gourd family, Cucurbitaceae. Evolved to deter feeding by insects but used by some butterflies to locate suitable food plants.

dentate—having a toothed margin or edge.

dicotyledon—a plant of the group Dicotyledoneae containing flowering plants with two broad seed leaves that are usually broad with a network of non-parallel veins. Often shortened to "dicot."

dimorphic—having two forms. Usually refers to colors or patterns.

discal cell—large cell area encircled by veins located in the basal to center area of an insect wing.

dorsal—referring to the top or upper portion of a body.

disjunct—widely spaced or separated. Usually refers to populations.

ecdysis—the act of shedding an exoskeleton.

eclosion—the act of an adult insect emerging from a pupa.

exoskeleton—external skeleton of arthropods consisting of chitin and organic chemicals.

eyespots—spots of pigment, usually dark on a light background. Function in some species is to deter or deflect predatory attacks.

falcate—curved and hooked; sickle-shaped.

food plant—the plant required by a specific species as food for its larvae.

forewing—front wing of an insect that emerges from the second, or middle, thoracic segment.

form—an individual or subgroup of adult butterflies which differs from others of the same species in color, pattern, shape, or size. May be connected to seasonal changes or geographic location.

genus—(*pl.* **genera**) a group of closely related species. Genus name is italicized and capitalized .

hatch—act of an insect emerging from an egg.

head—anterior section of an insect body that contains mouthparts, eyes, antennae, and spinneretts of silk-producing glands.

hindwing—rear wing of an insect that is attached to the last, or third, thoracic segment.

hyaline spot—an area of the wing that is transparent or almost so, and often appears like glass.

imago—adult form of an insect.

inner margin—the lower, or trailing, edge of the wing. Refers to either the forewing or hindwing.

instar—stage between successive molts of an arthropod.

larva—(*pl.* **larvae**) immature, actively feeding stage of insects with complete metamorphosis; i.e., the caterpillar.

Lepidoptera—order of insects containing the butterflies and moths.

life history—summary of the form and behavior of a species from birth or hatching to death.

margin—the edge of the wing.

metamorphosis—process in which an individual is transformed from one life stage to another.

mimicry—act of resembling another species or object in order to escape differentiation, usually to avoid predation.

monocotyledonous—plants of the group Monocotyledoneae, containing flowering plants with a single seed leaf, frequently with narrow leaves with parallel veins. Often shortened to "monocot."

montane—areas or habitats associated with mountains.

moult—act of ecdysis, or shedding of skin.

Müllerian mimicry—mimicry of a distasteful or poisonous species by another distasteful or poisonous species for increased protection from predators.

multivoltine—producing three or more generations in one year.

nectar—sugary liquid in flowers. A source of energy for most adult butterflies.

New World—western hemisphere, specifically the Americas and adjacent islands.

Old World—eastern hemisphere, specifically Eurasia, Africa, Australia, and adjacent islands.

osmaterium—an eversible organ in larvae of swallowtail butterflies that releases powerful, foul-smelling chemicals that deter predation.

overscaling—a loose layer of scales, often hair-like, over a layer of generally shorter, more dense scales.

ovum—(*pl.* **ova**) egg.

oviposition—act of laying an egg.

palus—(*pl.* **palpi**) paired appendages on the head of insects used in olfaction ("smell") and cleaning of the proboscis in adult butterflies. Usually inconspicuous or small, but occasionally enlarged as in snout butterflies. Commonly referred to as "palps".

parapatric—two or more species having geographical ranges that meet along a narrow zone with no significant area of overlap. Opposite of allopatric and sympatric.

parasite—an organism that lives on or within a larger host organism. A parasite derives nutrition from the host but does not usually cause its death.

parasitoid—an organism that lives on or within a larger host organism and eventually causes the death of the host after the parasitoid attains a suitable stage of maturity.

pheromone—sex-attractant chemical scent released to affect behavior of other members of the same species that is used in mate attraction and courtship.

phytochemicals—chemicals manufactured by plants.

phytophagous—plant-eating organism.

polymorphism—having three or more forms. Usually refers to colors or patterns.

posterior—toward the back, referring to the rear portion of the body or other object. Opposite of anterior.

proboscis—a hollow coiled tube on the adult butterfly's head between and below the eyes used to siphon or suck liquid foods. It is composed of two interlocking halves that are fitted together immediately following emergence from the chrysalis.

prolegs—paired extensions of the larva's body wall. Found beneath the abdomen in five pairs, each proleg has a ring of hooks, or crochets, that aid in locomotion. Not segmented, or true legs.

pupa—third stage of insects with complete metamorphosis, usually inactive. A stage characterized by reorganization of all body systems between larval and adult stages.

range—the geographical area in which the species occurs.

ray—narrow band or line of color that contrasts with background. Usually present in a group that appear to originate from a single spot or from a line such as a wing edge.

scale—small shingle-like structure attached to wings of Lepidoptera that provide color and pheromone production.

seasonal dimorphism—variation in body or wing color, shape, or pattern within a species that is related to the season of the year that the butterfly lives. Usually referred to as dry, wet, winter, spring, or summer forms.

sexual dimorphism—variation in body or wing color, shape, or pattern that differs between male and female individuals of the same species.

stigma—(*pl.* **stigmata**) group of specialized scales that produce a scent. Commonly found in an elongated patch on the forewing of many male skippers and some hairstreaks.

species—a kind; a group of individuals that usually appear similar and are able to interbreed.

spiracle—an opening on the side of the body of the larva or adult butterfly through which air enters.

subspecies—a group of individuals within a species that are geographically separable and distinguishable by some characteristics of structure; related subspecies may interbreed.

sympatric—two or more species with geographical ranges that at least partially overlap. Opposite of allopatric and parapatric.

tarsus—the foot section of a butterfly leg that possesses a hook, or small claw, at the end for clinging.

thorax—middle section of an insect body that contains three segments and supports wings and true legs.

tibia—a section of the leg of an insect, usually the second long segment, although it is actually the fourth segment of the leg. Often contains long spines that are useful in identification of species and connects the femur to the tarsus (or foot).

trapline—constant flight lane used by certain adult butterflies to search for nectar sources, larval food plants, and mates.

tribe—a group of closely related genera.

tubercle—a small wart-like bump, or projection. Usually on the body of the larva.

univoltine—producing a single generation in one year.

vein—narrow tube that supports structural integrity of an insect wing. Often visible as raised lines on butterfly wings.

ventral—the bottom or lower surface of a body.

BIBLIOGRAPHY

An incredible number of books have been published on the butterflies of North America. Listed below are books most pertinent to the
Texas butterfly fauna or which provide general biological information
on butterflies, and would, therefore, be of the most interest to the
readers of this book.

Ajilvsgi, Geyata. *Butterfly Gardening for the South.* Dallas: Taylor Publishing
Company, 1991.

Bailowitz, Richard A. and James P. Brock. *The Butterflies of Southeastern
Arizona.* Tucson: Sonoran Arthropods, Inc., 1991.

Brewer, Jo and Dave Winter. *Butterflies and Moths.* New York: Prentice Hall
Press, 1991.

Burns, John M. "Split Skippers: Mexican Genus *Poanopsis* goes in the *Origenes* Group-and *Yvretta* Forms the *Rhesus* Group of Polites (Hesperiidae)." *J. Lepid. Soc.*, 48: 1994, 24–45.

Correll, Donovan S. and Marshall C. Johnston. *Manual of the Vascular
Plants of Texas.* Renner, TX: Texas Research Foundation, 1970.

Douglas, Matthew M. *The Lives of Butterflies.* Ann Arbor: The University of
Michigan Press, 1986.

Ehrlich, Paul R. and Anne H. Ehrlich. *How to Know the Butterflies.*
Dubuque: William C. Brown Co., 1961.

Ferris, Clifford D., Editor. *Supplement: A Catalogue/Checklist of the Butterflies of America.* The Lepidopterists' Society, Memoir No. 3, 1989.

Holland, W. J. *The Butterfly Book.* New York: Doubleday & Co., Inc., 1931.

Howe, William H. (coordinating editor and illustrator). *The Butterflies of
North America.* New York: Doubleday & Co., Inc., 1975.

Klots, Alexander B. *A Field Guide to the Butterflies of North America, East
of the Great Plains.* Boston: Houghton Mifflin Co., 1951.

Miller, Jacqueline Y. *The Common Names of North American Butterflies.*
Washington, D.C.: Smithsonian Institution Press, 1992.

Miller, Lee D. and F. Martin Brown. *A Catalogue/Checklist of the Butterflies
of America.* The Lepidopterists' Society, Memoir No. 2, 1982.

Mitchell, Robert T. and Herbert S. Zim. *Butterflies and Moths.* New York:
Golden Press, 1962.

Opler, Paul A. (Illustrated by Vichai Malikul). *A Field Guide to the Eastern Butterflies*. Boston: Houghton Mifflin, Co., 1992.

Pyle, Robert Michael. *The Audubon Society Field Guide to North American Butterflies*. New York: Alfred A. Knopf, 1981.

Pyle, Robert Michael. *Handbook for Butterfly Watchers*. Boston: Houghton Mifflin, Co., 1984.

Scott, James A. *The Butterflies of North America*. Stanford: Stanford University Press, 1986.

Tilden, James W. and Arthur Clayton Smith. *A Field Guide to Western Butterflies*. Boston: Houghton Mifflin Co., 1986.

PLANT INDEX

Plants are listed by family and by genus. (Specific genera found in each family are listed in parentheses.)

Texas Butterflies

Butterflies are listed by scientific and common names for families, genera, and individual species. Numbers in bold refer to plate numbers in the photo section.